IMAGES
of America

Carlton and Point Breeze

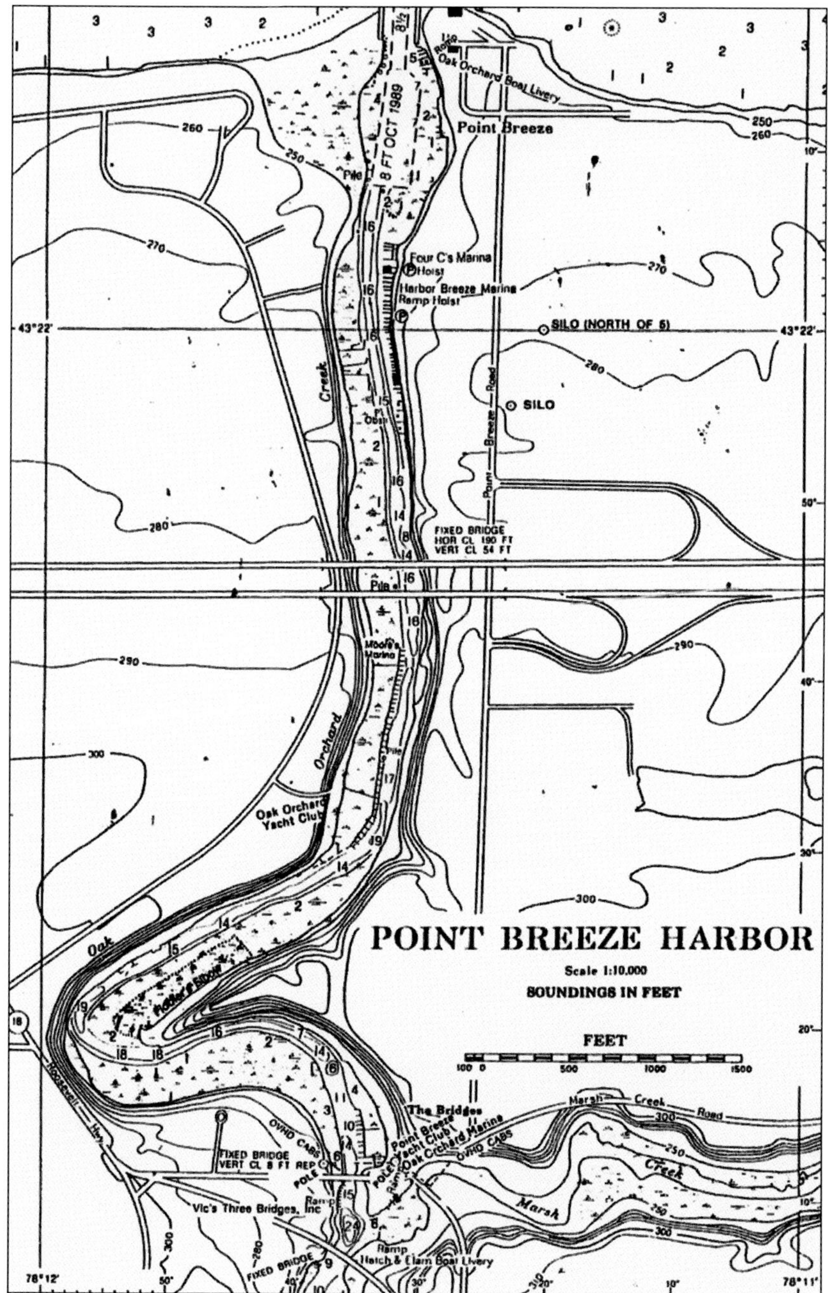

Map of Point Breeze. This map shows the Point Breeze Harbor, where Marsh Creek meets Oak Orchard Harbor by the Bridges. The actual hamlet called Point Breeze is a mile or so north, the final land area before the piers act as break walls, allowing boats to exit into Lake Ontario. Fiddler's Elbow is shown at the lower left. There is a photograph of that on page 107.

On the cover: Please see page 61. (Courtesy of Jessica Matson.)

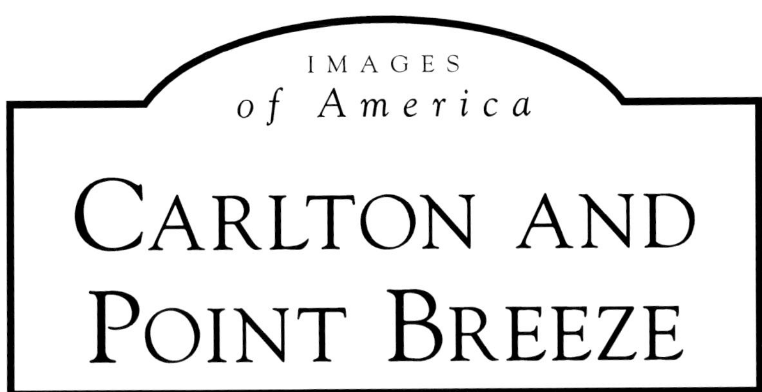

Hollis Ricci-Canham and Avis A. Townsend

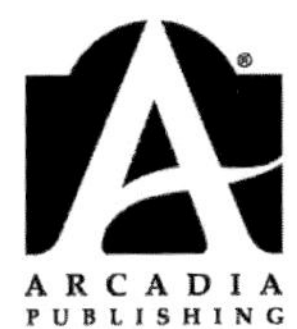

ISBN 978-0-7385-4550-9

Published by Arcadia Publishing
Charleston, South Carolina

Printed in the United States of America

Library of Congress Catalog Card Number: 2006924318

For all general information contact Arcadia Publishing at:
Telephone 843-853-2070
Fax 843-853-0044
E-mail sales@arcadiapublishing.com
For customer service and orders:
Toll-Free 1-888-313-2665

Visit us on the Internet at www.arcadiapublishing.com

Turn the pages of yesterday. View pictures that speak of another time and way of life. Our forefathers were drawn to the water. Many were fishermen. Some became shipbuilders. Others became farmers, dependent upon local help to harvest crops of grain, vegetables, or fruit. Hamlets like Point Breeze drew settlers who traveled Lake Ontario to make a home. The railroad brought visitors to Carlton Station who also opted to stay. Pioneer picnics at Lakeside Park drew people together on hot summer days. After the automobile, people visited others whenever they chose. It is astonishing how pictures can tell a story.

—Amelia Hoot Lovewell

* * *

Inside the pages of this book is a trip into the past, with many stops along the way. Our destination is the town of Carlton, with its several hamlets. Over land and water, down roads and lanes, and across bridges we travel—back to an earlier time. As we go, we learn about the interesting points along the way—a covered bridge, a dam, a lake, a lighthouse, a fishing village, and a recreation spot, to name a few. Our tour guides have done their homework, so please take a seat, relax, and enjoy the ride into the world of yesterday.

—Marie Mattern Carlston

Contents

ACKNOWLEDGMENTS

The people of Carlton are proud of their community, and when we asked for help in compiling this book, they came out in droves to offer assistance—from a public scanning session at the Carlton Town Hall, to meetings at various peoples' homes, to long drives seeking the information from those who moved away.

Contributors are listed in alphabetical order, whether they offered photographs, advice, or a tidbit of information. They are Matthew Ballard, Julia Bale, Bob Barrus, Joann Baxter, Shirley Bennett Belson, Douglas Bennett, Janice Yungfleisch Bennett, Homer Bergeman, David Bertsch, Dwight Bliss, Pauline Kast Broadwell, Pauline Holly Brown, Gordon Canham, Earl Canham, Majorie Axtell Canham, Marie Mattern Carlston, Gene Christopher, Fay Kubica Ciarico, Bill Consadine, Susan Dowe, Mike and Chris Elam, Betty Fetter, Sandy Tombari Freeman, Larry Grimes, David Kelsey, Jack Kemp, Harold Kenyon, C. W. "Bill" Lattin, Jack Lee, Amelia Hoot Lovewell, Jessica Matson, Douglas and Sherilyn Miller, Garland Miller, Winifred Miles Miller, Sandra Weaver Mitchell, Judy Mollica, Richard Palmer, Bobby Postel, Clark and Ellen Rath, Merle Kubica Ricci, Mark Rustay, Mary Sage-Eisvang, John Sawyer, Jeff and Judy Schwartz, Carlton assessor Leo Spohr, Joan Thomason, Norma Smith Vick, Ashley Ward, Jesse Weaver, Joann Weaver, Raymond Weaver, and Beatrice Axtell Young. Organizations that helped were the Charlotte-Genesee Lighthouse Museum, Orleans County Department of History, and National Grid via Robert Dischner.

Special thanks go out to Holly Canham's husband, Bud, for letting her use him as a perpetual "go-for" and her mother, "Mike" Ricci, for the numerous invasions of her kitchen, the homemade chicken soup, pizzas, cakes, and pies, and the never-ending cups of coffee.

This book was reviewed by C. W. Lattin, Orleans County historian.

INTRODUCTION

The Orleans County town of Carlton is situated on the south shore of Lake Ontario at the mouth of the Oak Orchard Harbor, bordered on the east by Kendall and the west by Yates. The southern border of the town meets Gaines. Carlton is centered between Niagara Falls and Rochester.

Original inhabitants were Native Americans who enjoyed the fertile lands and waterways along the trail that is now Oak Orchard Road. They continually traveled this trail, storing their cached tools in mounds along the high banks of the Oak Orchard River and fishing and hunting on the west side at Oak Orchard River at Lake Ontario. Over time, professional digs have recovered many Native American artifacts.

The first white men to settle and reside in Orleans County arrived by boat from Canada. Brothers William and James Walsworth built cabins at the mouths of Oak Orchard River and Johnson's Creek, respectively. They hunted and fished for a living. William arrived first with his family, having crossed the lake in an open boat in May 1803. The nearest neighbors were at Braddocks Bay on the east and Fort Niagara on the west. James followed soon after.

In 1805, Elijah and Bathshua Brown brought their family to the Oak Orchard River from Sodus via a large boat. Elijah died en route, and the family buried him in what became the first marked grave of Orleans County.

Matthew Dunham and sons arrived from New England and settled in nearby Kuckville in 1804. They built a dam across Johnson's Creek and erected a building for turning wood. The Holland Land Company provided them with iron and supplies to build grist and sawmills to promote development of the area.

By 1890, Waterport was the largest business place in Carlton, situated at the junction of Otter and Oak Orchard Creeks. It contained a post office, two general stores, a hardware store, drugstore, notion store, hotel and livery, jewelry store, two blacksmith shops, a meat market, harness shop, cooperage, and foundry. It also had a coal yard, gristmill, sawmill, church, school, and doctor.

The Bridges, located at the junction of Marsh Creek and Oak Orchard Creek, a mile south of Lake Ontario, also included similar businesses and additionally a dry house, public hall, and two churches. Elijah Brown's wife and children laid out the first apple orchard in 1810. Brown's farm flourishes to this day, once famous for having the world's largest quince orchard, and the seventh generation continues setting a high standard for agri-tourism in New York State.

Point Breeze is on Lake Ontario at the mouth of Oak Orchard Creek. From the mid-1800s, shipbuilding was carried on by the Murray family, and import and export businesses were carried out in the harbor. Lumber came in from Canada, and fruit and farm crops went out via the lake schooners. The river was busy with commerce, not only used for recreation and fishing. In 1867, the federal government appointed $87,000 for harbor improvements. Two wooden piers, each 1,600 feet long, a lighthouse, and a lighthouse keeper's home were built. The piers suffered terrible destruction from a storm in 1914, and another storm in 1916 took the lighthouse to its watery grave. On the west side of Oak Orchard River, a resort community originally called Lakeview, eventually dubbed "Oak Orchard on the Lake," developed. In the late 1800s, the area contained an upscale hotel and racetrack. The west side of the Oak Orchard is currently considered residential, and the east side business area bustles with marinas, restaurants, and agricultural enterprises.

Smaller hamlets of Kuckville, Kenyonville, and Kent each had a post office, store, and country school and a few small businesses. Kenyonville holds claim to the first church in the town of Carlton. Kenyonville also claimed a covered bridge over the Oak Orchard Creek. Essentially these areas are residential only now, although Kuckville does have a country store. Kent and Waterport still have their own post office.

Lakeside, at Johnson's Creek and Lake Ontario, once an active summer resort of the early 1900s, is now an area of a few year-round homes and several seasonal cottages. Just east of this area, however, is the 644-acre Lakeside Beach State Park, which draws many visitors and campers to the lakeshore each summer. The Lake Ontario State Parkway, the first dual-lane highway in Orleans County, brings tourists to this park from east and west.

The tiny area of Ashwood and Sawyers Corners, later called Curtis Corners, exists in name only now.

The Rome, Watertown and Ogdensburg Railroad (Hojack Line) changed Carlton when it opened in 1876. The remarks made by lifelong resident Robert Kelsey (1924–2004) in an oral history explain it best.

> At the time of my birth [1924] Carlton was a railroad town. There were six passenger trains a day when I was growing up, three each way. Several freights went through, and then there were two locals that come in, one from each way, morning and night. All the groceries that were sold at the grocery store come in on the train.
>
> On Saturday night they sent ice cream packed in dry ice, in a huge tub. People could go to the store with their container and get their ice cream. Bread also came in on the trains. Boxcars shipped out milk, cream, wool, apples, cattle, and quite a few other items. September was real busy with cucumber packin'. There was three packin' houses, and several carloads of pickles would go out each day to New York City. There was a butcher and he would bring lambs at Easter time to be shipped on the railroad to New York City. The lambs were all dressed and wrapped in burlap bags. I used to go over to the station and help the ticket agent load 'em 'cause she was a woman. There were cattle chutes just east of the depot where they could load and unload cattle. Henry Thomas, that lived in Carlton, was a cattle buyer and he would go to Kansas City and buy cattle by the carload, and bring 'em back. And he had sheep, too. They would unload them there in Carlton and drive them down the road to his farm where the golf course is today—Harbor Point. Then they would drive them back when they were ready to be sold back again and load 'em on the cars and out they would go again.
>
> Olin DeMay told me that in 1928 he shipped 500 carloads of apples out of the Carlton Cold Storage. That was a record!
>
> The mail came in on the train, too. I can see the train going through yet, with the man standing on the doorway of the mail car with a pistol on his hip. He guarded the mail. If you put letter on in Carlton, it was delivered in Kent when the train made its next stop because they sorted it right on the train.

The Hojack ceased to run in 1978. Carlton Station is quieter now, but the Carlton Grill, Catlin Tire, Orleans Outdoor, and Sweet Apple Guest Home are still conducting business. Some farms are still in operation, but the two United States Golf Association 18-hole golf courses, Harbor Point and Ricci Meadows, offer relaxation where farming was once carried out.

One

Early Lakeside Years

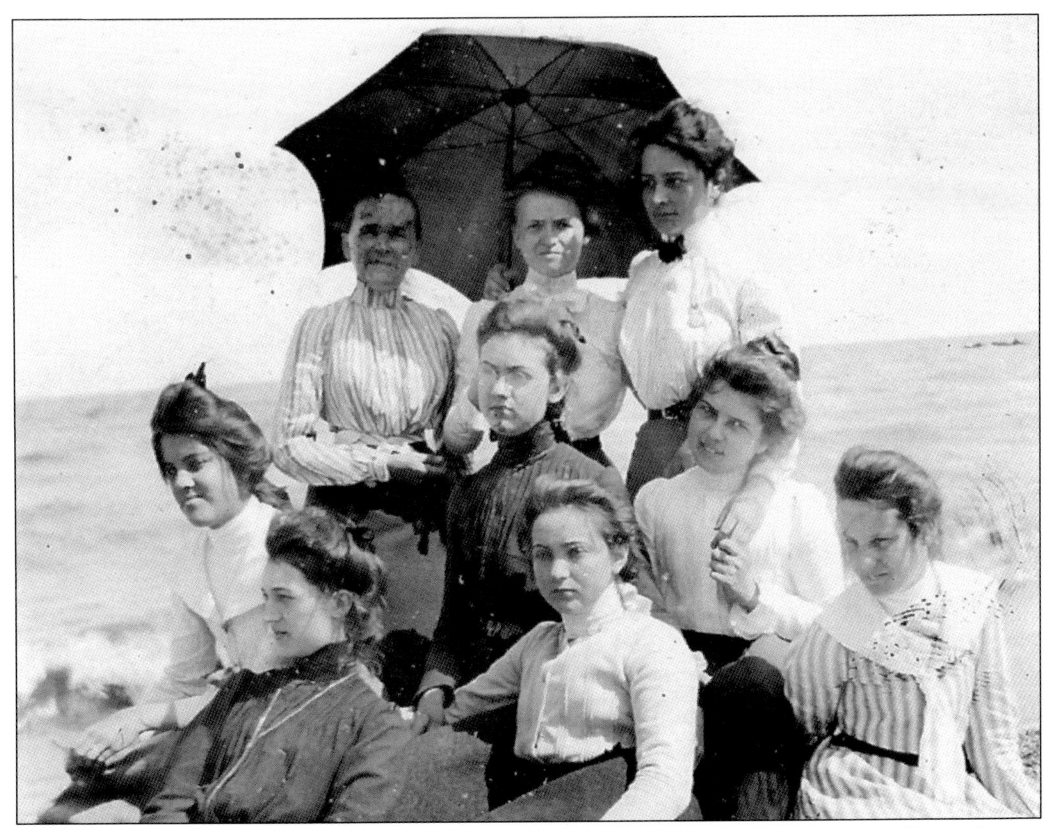

Seeking Shade. These unidentified women enjoy a day at Lake Ontario near Point Breeze around 1900. Their parasol is not very helpful in shading their faces from the sun, but they seem happy anyway. (Courtesy of Orleans County Department of History.)

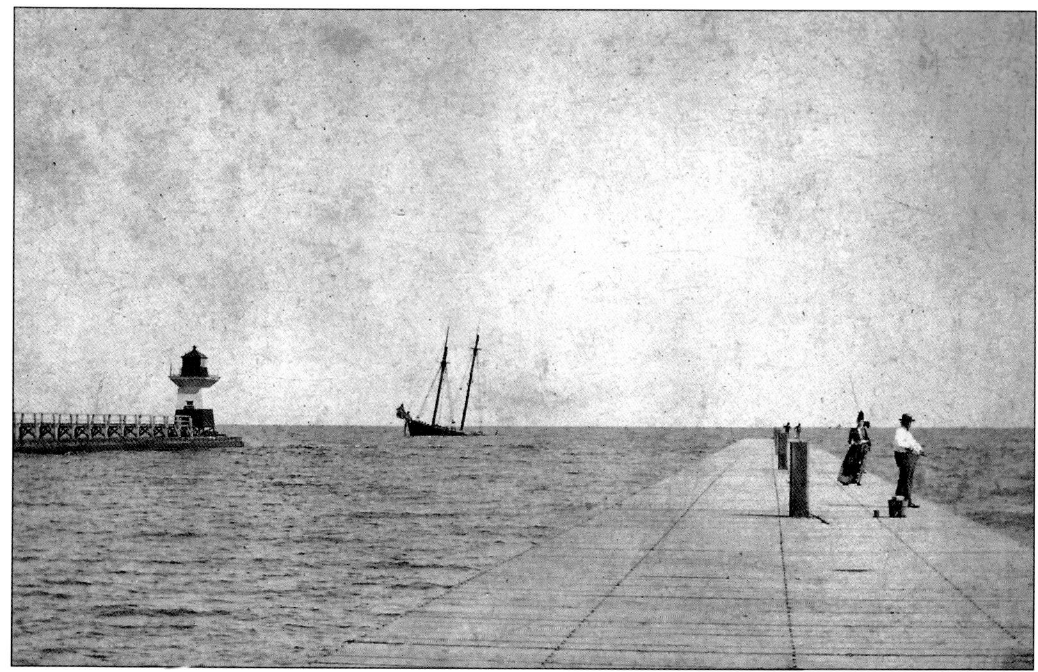

SUNKEN VESSEL. People on the pier seem oblivious to the ship that is partially submerged in the photograph above. Legend has it that divers removed the cargo of rum and let the lake claim the ship. (Courtesy of Shirley Bennett Belson.)

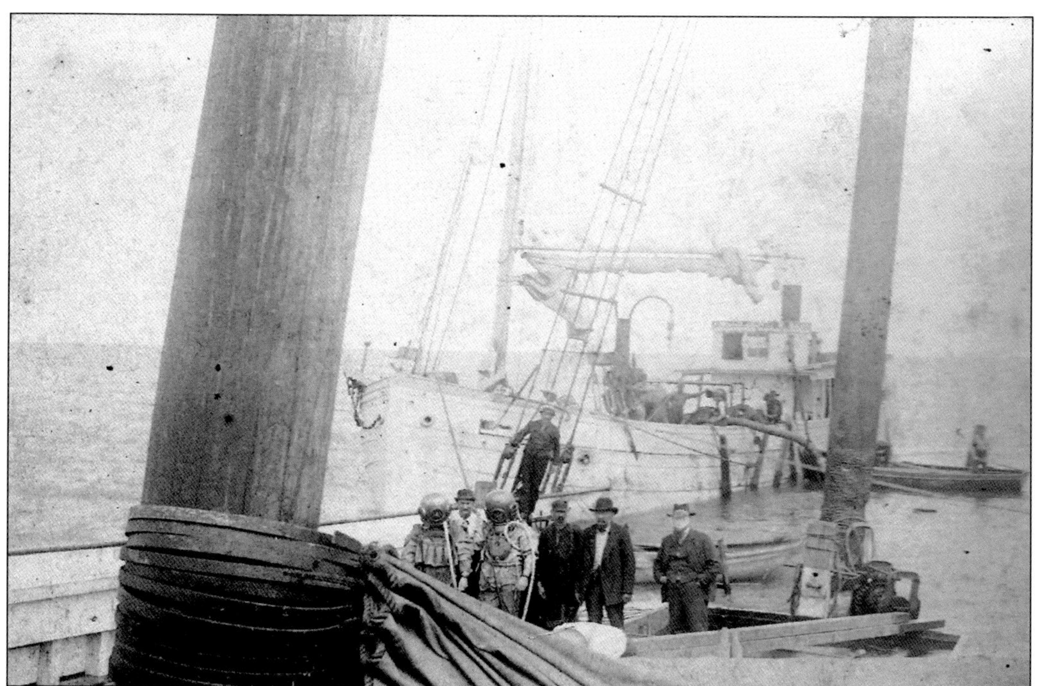

EARLY DIVERS. A ship docks next to the sunken ship off the harbor at Point Breeze. Note the diving suits on some of the men and the large mast of the ship, which appears to be the one submerged in the previous photograph. (Courtesy of Shirley Bennett Belson.)

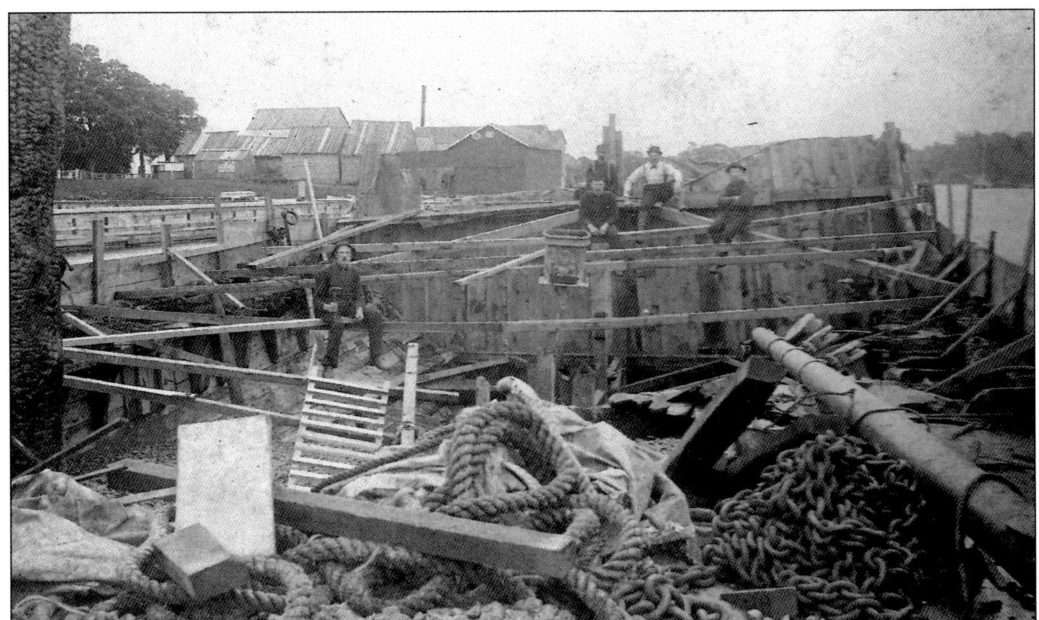

AFTER THE FIRE, C. 1890. Then and now a harbor of refuge, this ship was brought into the harbor to be repaired after it was nearly destroyed by fire. At left, the charred pieces of wood can be seen. (Courtesy of Orleans County Department of History.)

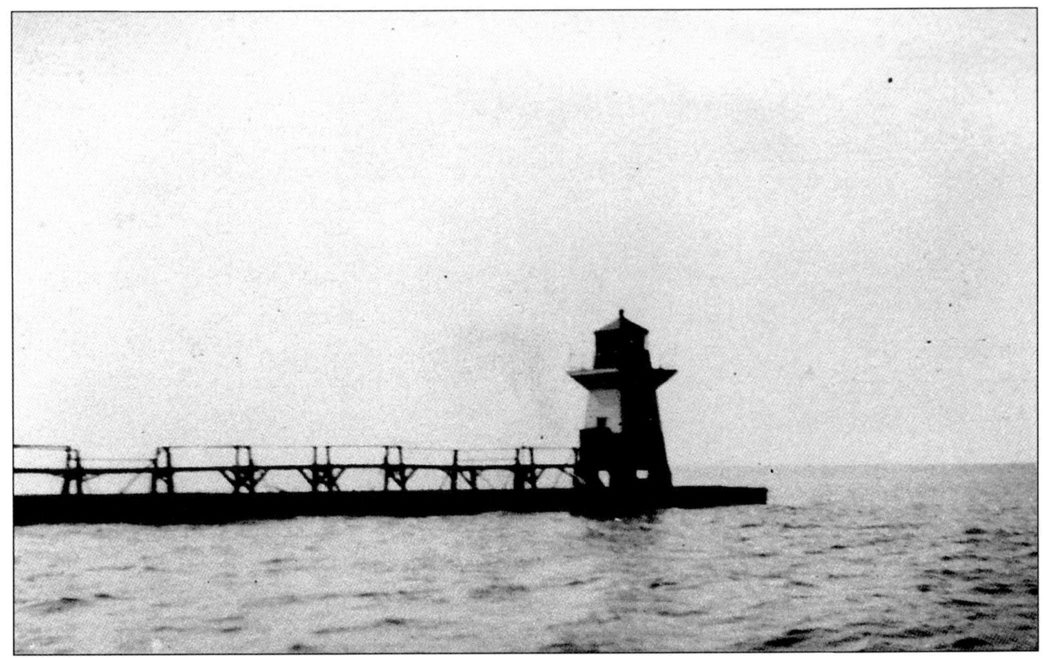

LIGHTHOUSE AT OAK ORCHARD HARBOR. In 1867, the federal government appropriated $87,000 for improvements to Oak Orchard Harbor. Two long wooden piers were built out into the lake in the approximate location of the present jetties. At the end of the west pier this lighthouse was completed in 1871. (Courtesy of Garland Miller.)

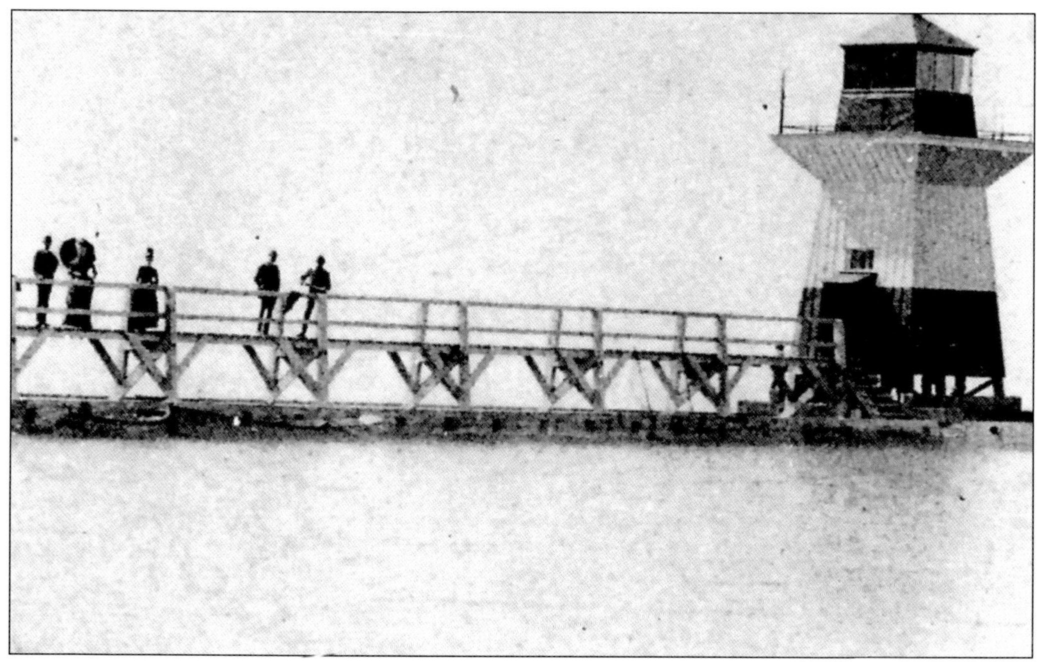

ON THE PIER. In 1905, due to the River and Harbor Act, maintenance was denied to the harbor facilities, and the lighthouse and piers were abandoned. After several years of neglect, waves tore apart the piers, and the lighthouse was blown over into the lake during a severe storm on December 28, 1916. (Courtesy of Orleans County Department of History.)

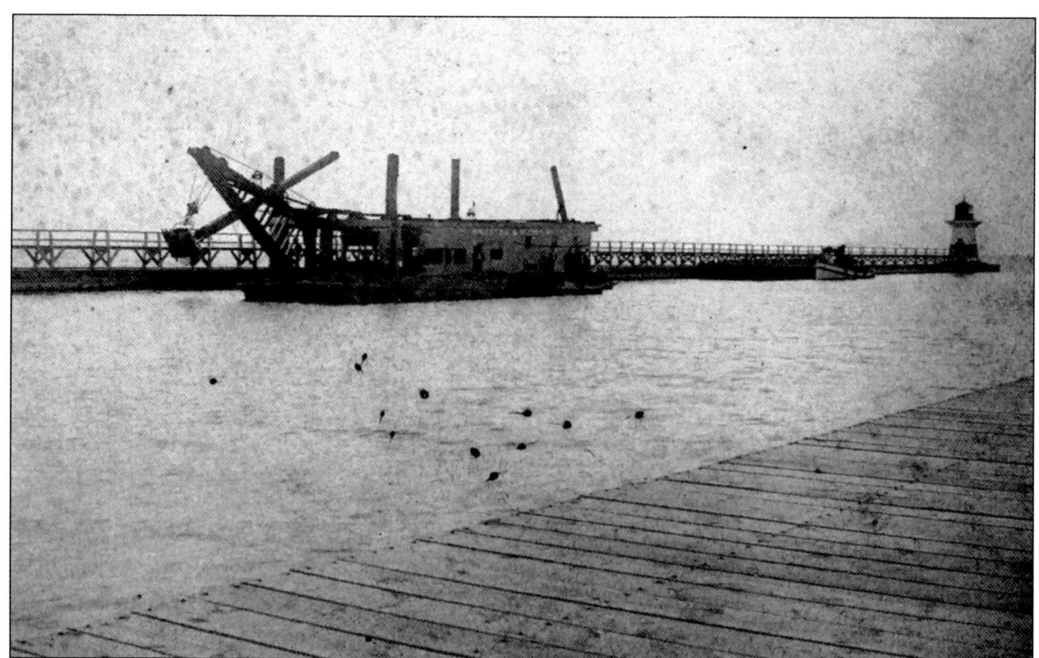

KINGSTON AND BLOGSON DREDGE. This dredge was docked by the piers at Oak Orchard Harbor prior to 1910. Dredges helped keep the harbor passable for low-hulled boats. (Courtesy of Shirley Bennett Belson.)

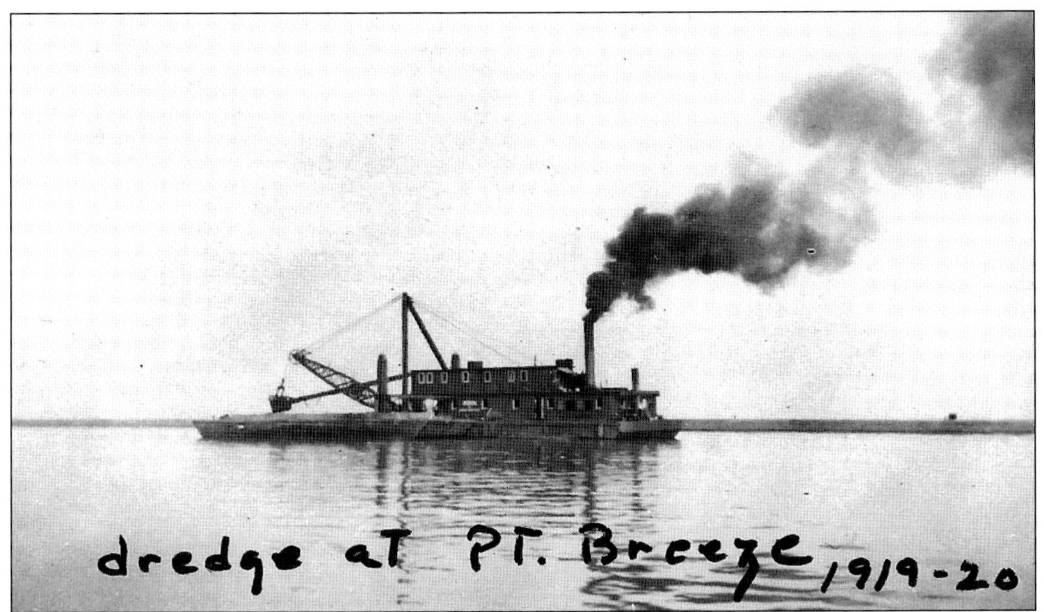

A Newer Dredge. A different dredge is moored in the harbor around 1920. Note the new break wall. (Courtesy of Garland Miller.)

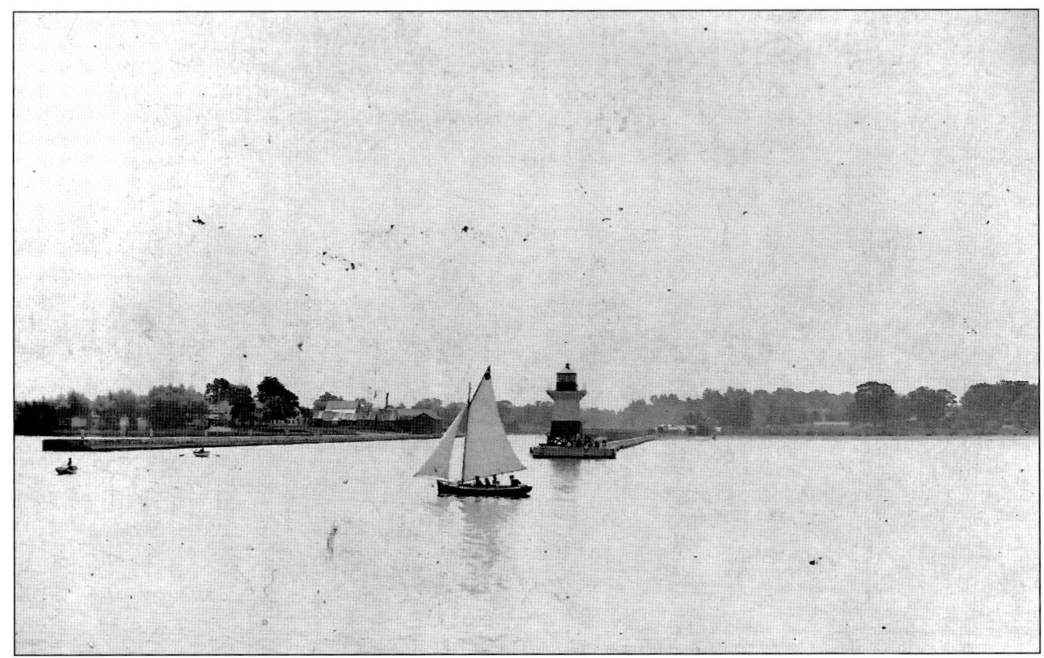

Two Piers. A solitary boat sails into Oak Orchard Harbor around 1900. Rowboats on the east side seem dwarfed by the larger boat. It was a lovely view before the piers and lighthouse deteriorated and were washed away by several storms between 1912 and 1916. (Courtesy of Orleans County Department of History.)

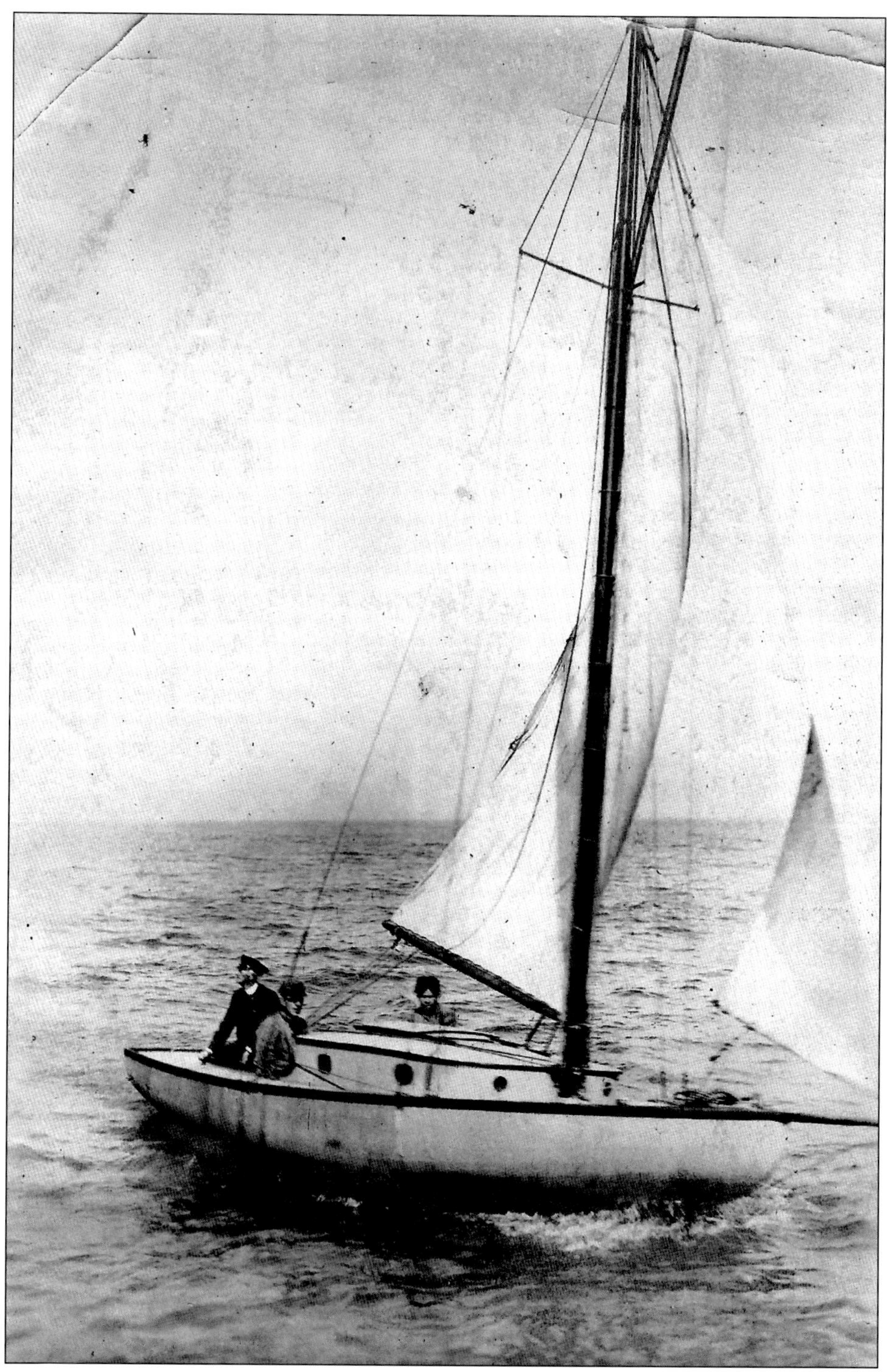

OUT ON THE LAKE. Sails are not completely unfurled as this crew sails the open waters of Lake Ontario near Oak Orchard Harbor. Sailing was very popular around 1900. Although the lake could be treacherous during winter months, sailors and fishermen took advantage of the calm seas between April and December. (Courtesy of Orleans County Department of History.)

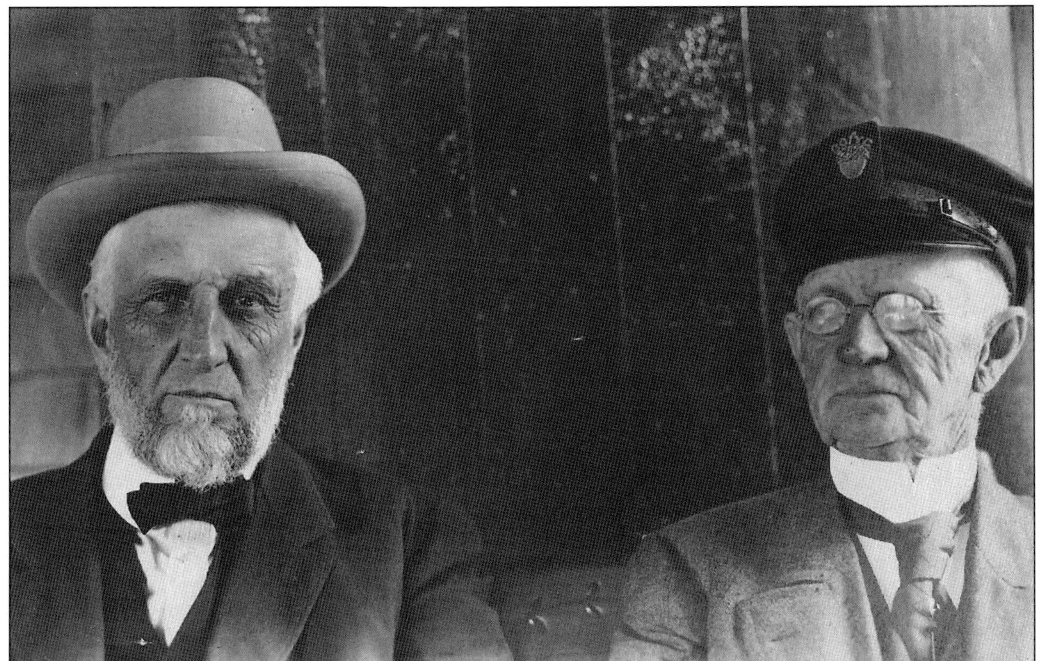

SALTY SEAMEN. The identity of these sailors is unknown, but they appear to be two of the men on the sailboat on the preceding page. It is possible the logo on the cap of the gentleman on the right is a yacht club symbol. The lines in their faces suggest that they spent most of their lives outdoors or on the water. (Courtesy of Orleans County Department of History.)

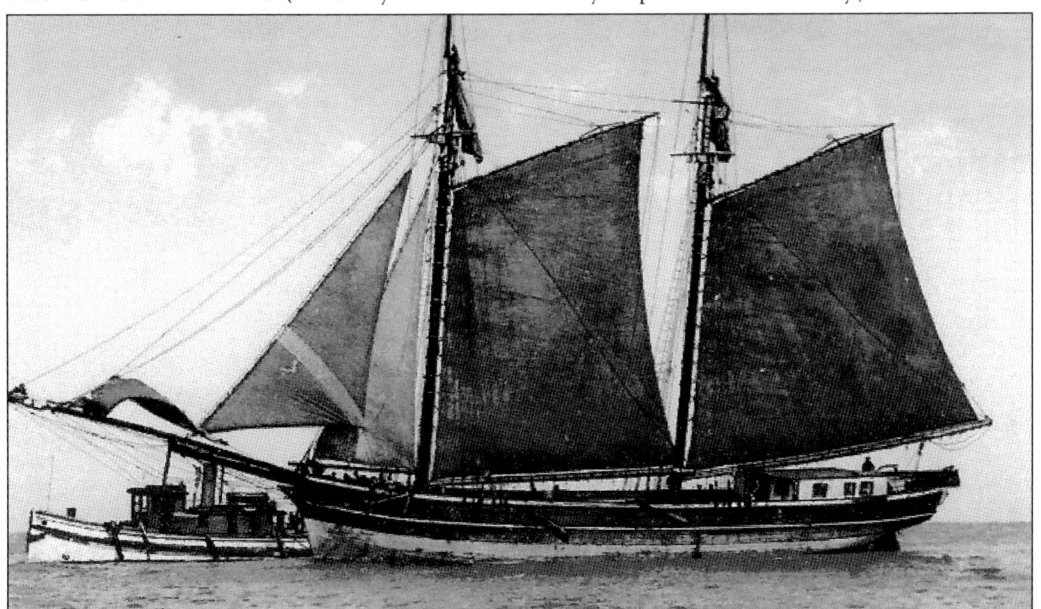

THE *BALLOU*. Built by the Murray family in 1865, the two-masted schooner *H. M. Ballou* was named after Hosea M. Ballou of Carlton, the collector of customs for the port of Oak Orchard. Its dimensions were 80 feet 9 inches by 17 feet 7 inches, and it weighed 77 tons. Years later, Capt. George Ruggles cut it in half, adding 16 feet to the midsection, increasing the tonnage to 108 and the length to 96 feet. (Courtesy of Charlotte-Genesee Lighthouse Museum.)

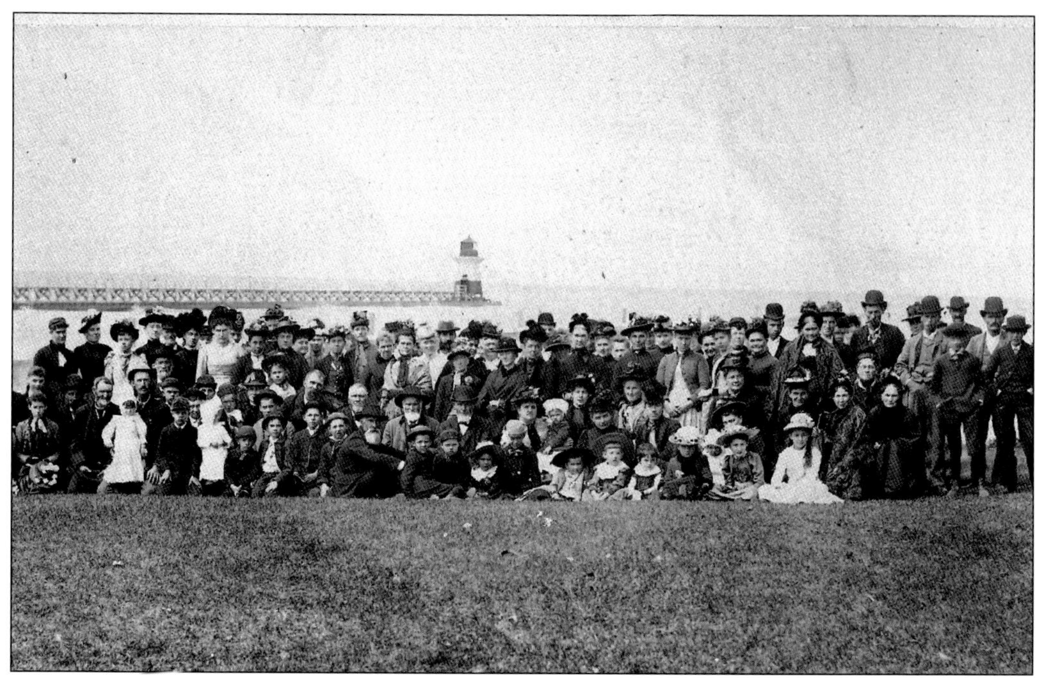

PICNIC AT POINT BREEZE. The Riches Corners Sunday school members enjoy a picnic at Point Breeze in this *c.* 1890 photograph. The lighthouse and pier are behind them. There was no church at Riches Corners, and the Sunday school was a community effort. (Courtesy of Orleans County Department of History.)

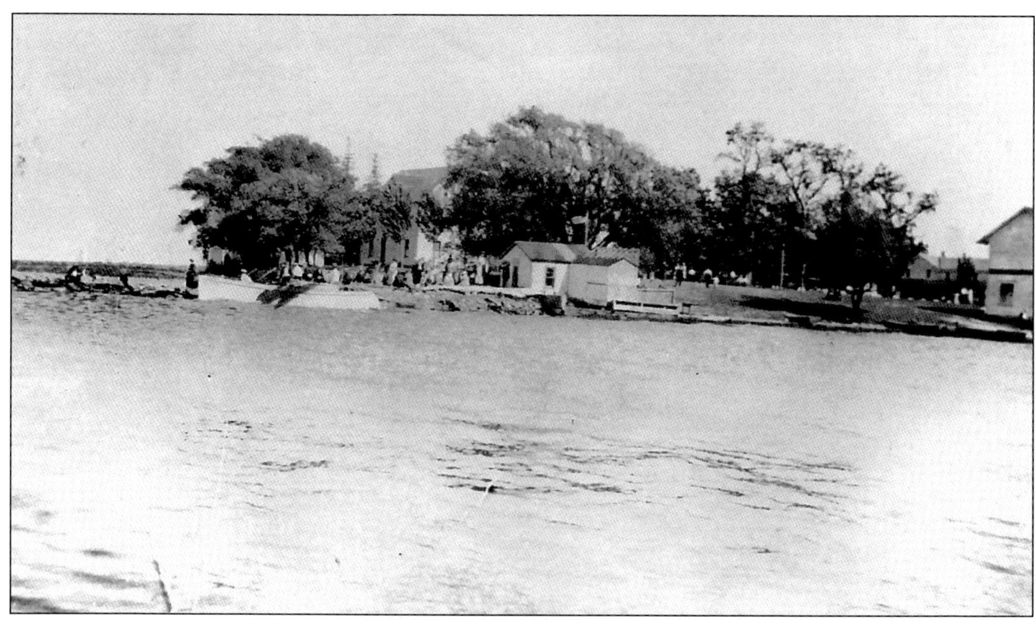

FUN IN THE SUN. Groups of people flocked to the shores of Lake Ontario and Oak Orchard Harbor during the summer months, as did this group in this 1900 photograph. (Courtesy of Orleans County Department of History.)

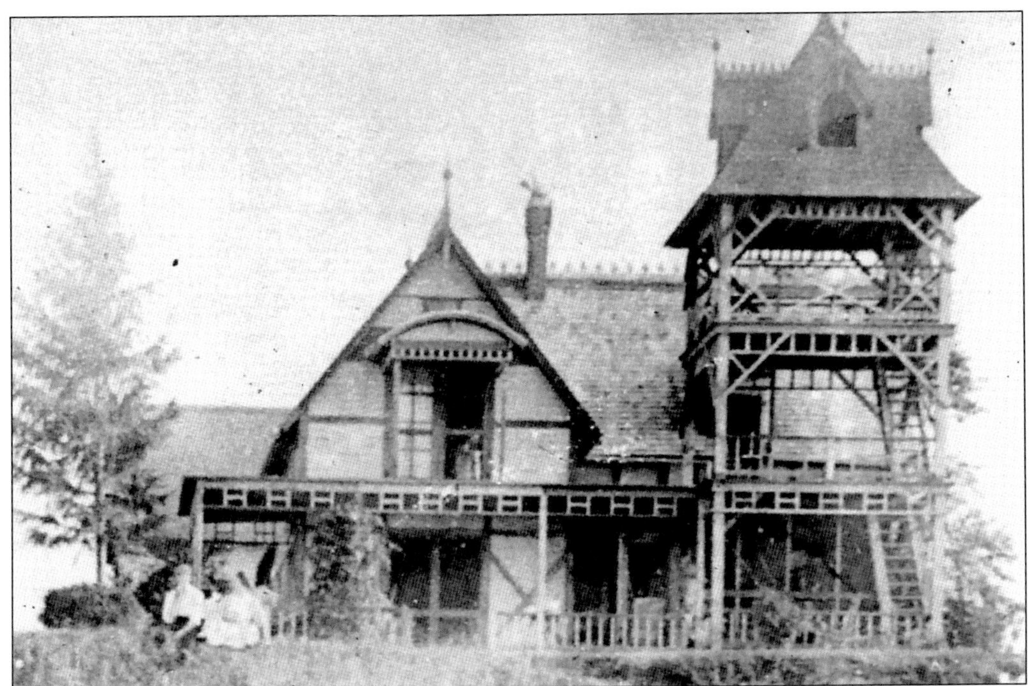

S. A. COOK COTTAGE. This cottage was the summer getaway for the famous furniture entrepreneur S. A. Cook of nearby Medina. Stick-style architecture was chosen for this private residence at Lakeside Bluff. (Courtesy of Orleans County Department of History.)

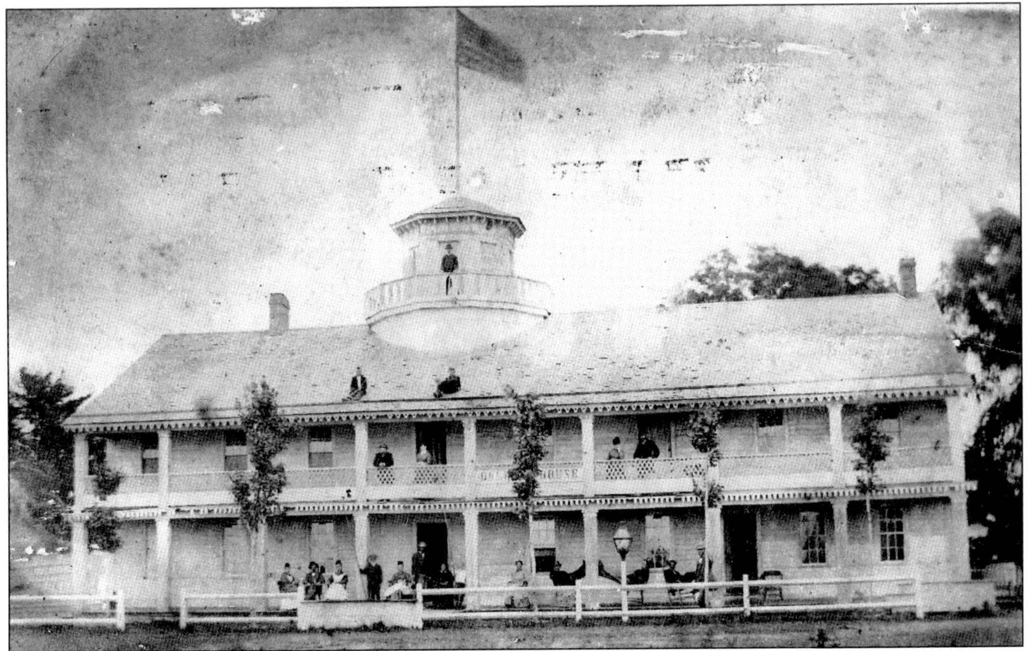

REST AND RELAXATION. The folks in this photograph, taken in 1897, enjoy a rest by the shores of Lake Ontario at Point Breeze. Called the Orleans House, this hotel burned on March 29, 1911. Note the men on the roof and the solitary man standing in front of the cupola. (Courtesy of Orleans County Department of History.)

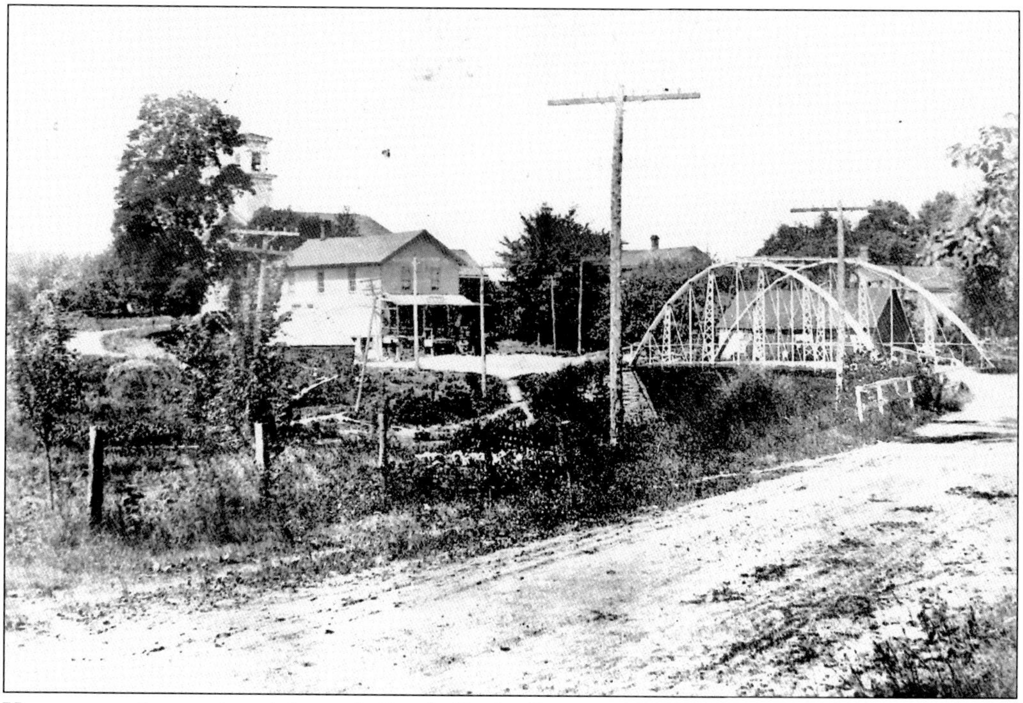

KUCKVILLE. Located on Johnson's Creek, Kuckville contained two stores, a blacksmith shop, a cooperage, and a church. Pictured are the store and the original bridge. (Courtesy of Winifred Miles Miller.)

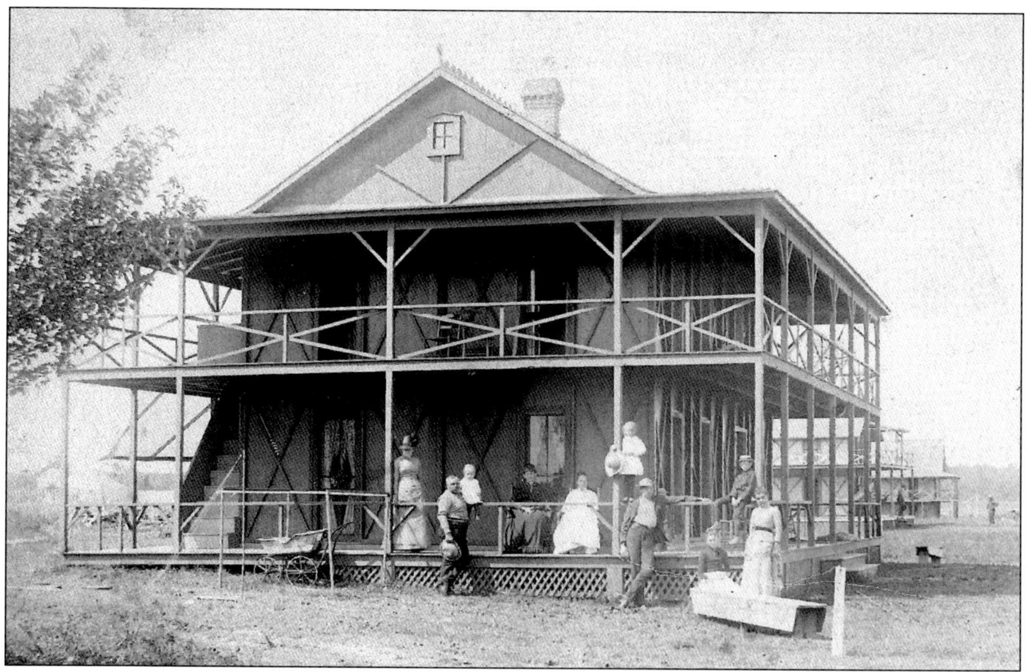

THE SIGNOR-WAGE COTTAGE. Shown is the Signor-Wage Cottage at Oak-Orchard-on-the-Lake. Judge Issac Signor is the man holding the baby. (Courtesy of Orleans County Department of History.)

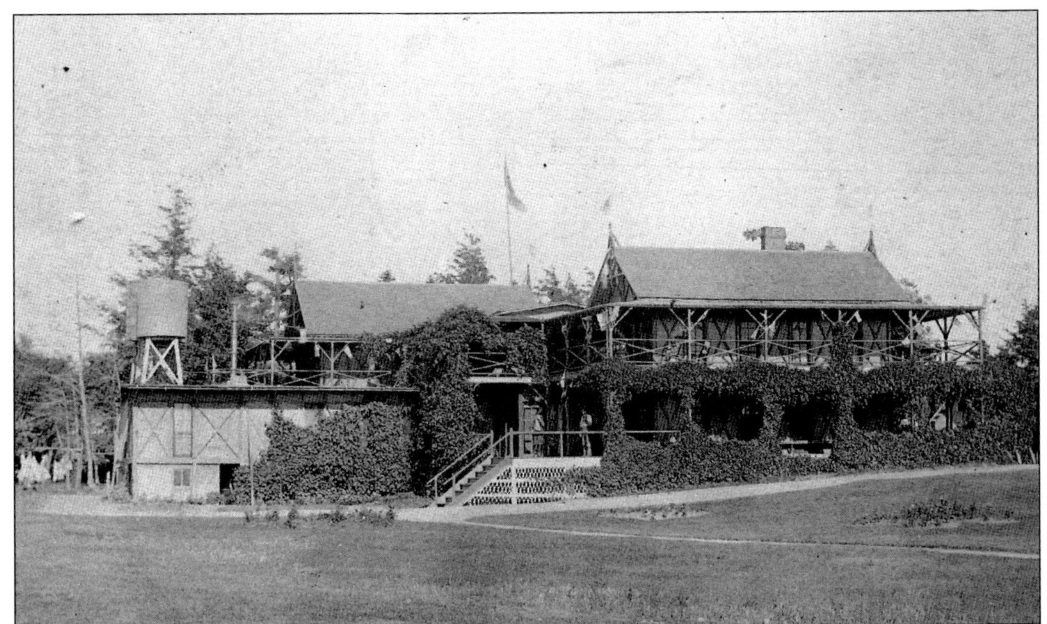

THE LAKESIDE PARK HOTEL. The sprawling stick-style resort was built in 1882 by Bruce Hoag. It contained a large dance hall and many guest rooms. Hoag also erected a bridge across the creek to get to the hotel. He beautified the grounds, added a pier, and constructed several cottages. The hotel was considered one of the finest resorts in western New York at the beginning of the 20th century. (Courtesy of Orleans County Department of History.)

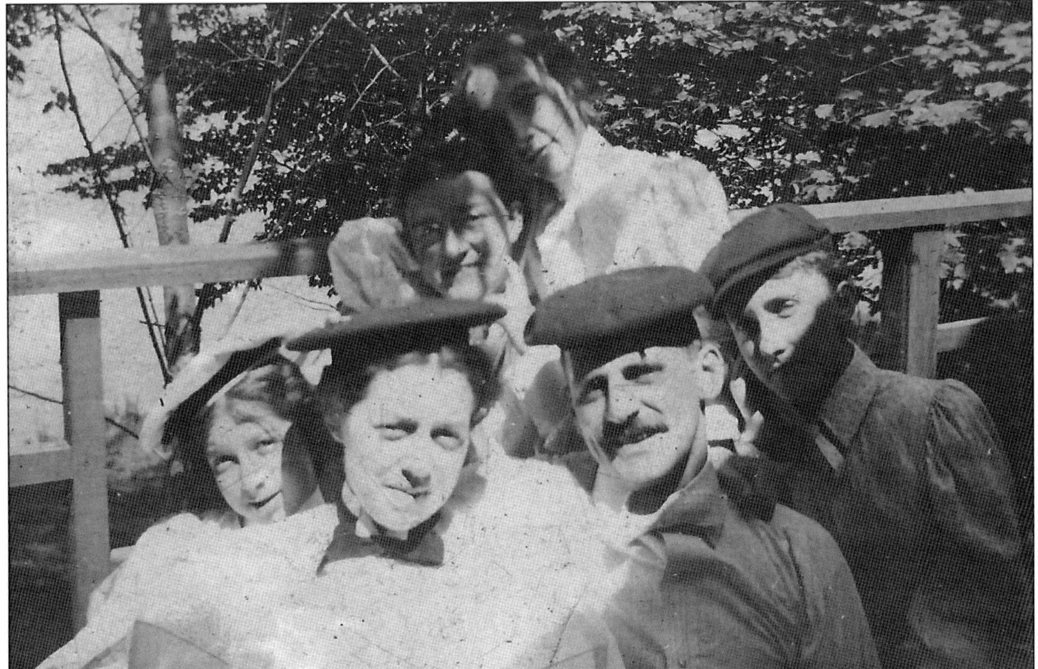

A DAY AT THE LAKE, C. 1900. Enjoying a day at the beach are, from left to right, (first row) Bess Keeney, Helen Wall, Dr. Belden, and Ollie Nott; (second row) Let and Fanny Stevens. (Courtesy of Orleans County Department of History.)

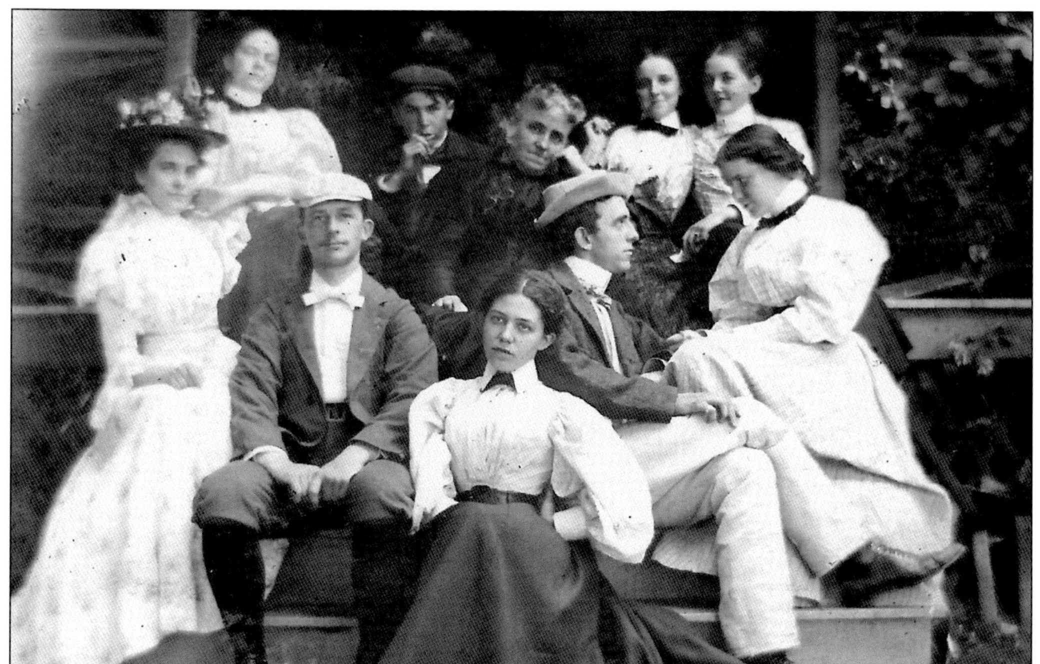

AT THE COTTAGE. Posing for a picture on the porch of O. H. Taylor's cottage at Lakeside Park are, from left to right, (first row) E. Irvin, Kit Taylor, Herbert Reed, and Babe Reynolds; (second row) Velma Blott (in long white dress), Bess Dye, George Spencer, Mrs. Taylor, Janet Smith, and Edith Baker. (Courtesy of Orleans County Department of History.)

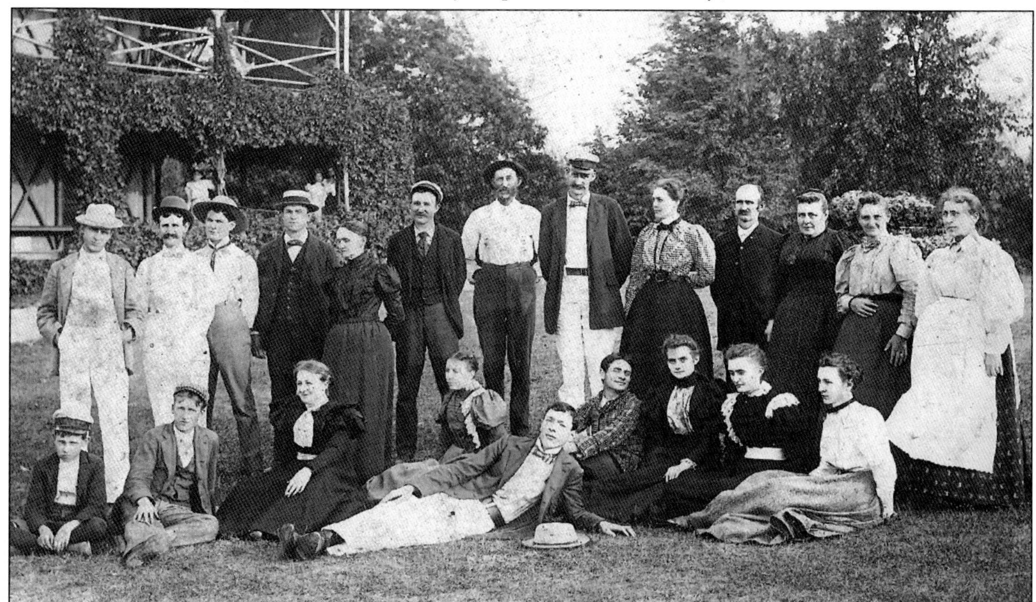

HAVING FUN BY THE LAKESIDE PARK HOTEL. A group of people enjoy a pleasant afternoon near the shores of Lake Ontario at Lakeside Beach around 1900. Most are unidentified. However, the man standing at extreme left is Wilkes Bolton. At extreme right is Mrs. Henry Bolton. The tall men in the center are Fred Kirsch (left) and Henry Bolton. (Courtesy of Orleans County Department of History.)

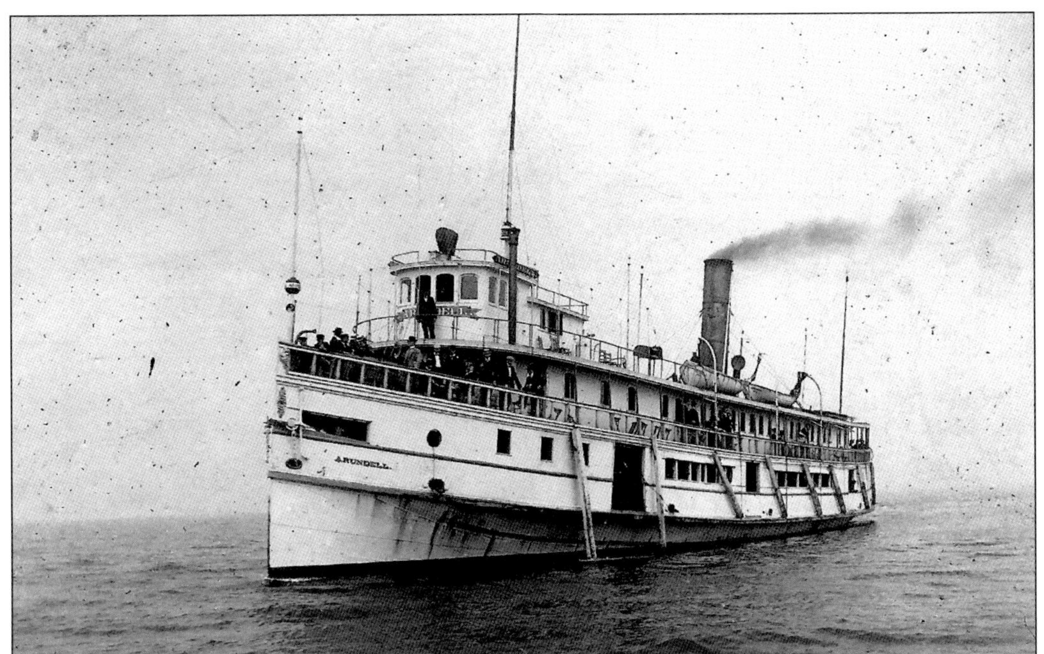

The Arundell, c. 1905. The *Arundell* was one of many excursion steamers that cruised Lake Ontario, taking passengers to and from Toronto, Olcott, Point Breeze, and Rochester. It was always filled for each town's annual Pioneer Days and picnic days during the summer. (Courtesy of Orleans County Department of History.)

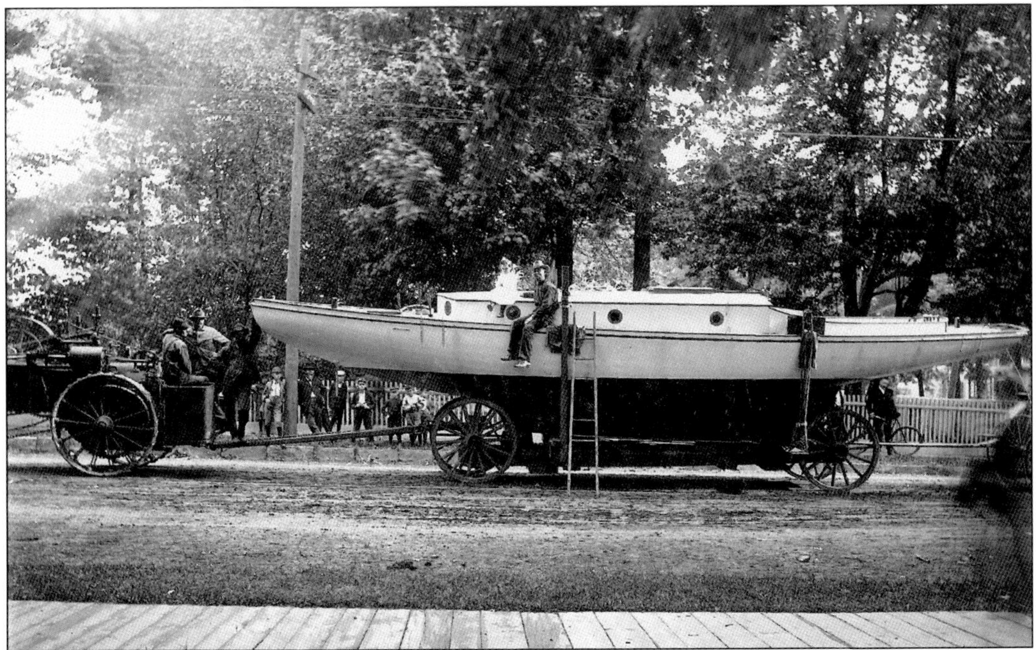

Hart Family's Boat, c. 1900. This sailboat, made for the Hart family, was built on the shores of Lake Ontario by shipbuilder Charles Reed, then hauled to the lake by a steam-powered vehicle and launched in the harbor at Point Breeze. (Courtesy of Orleans County Department of History.)

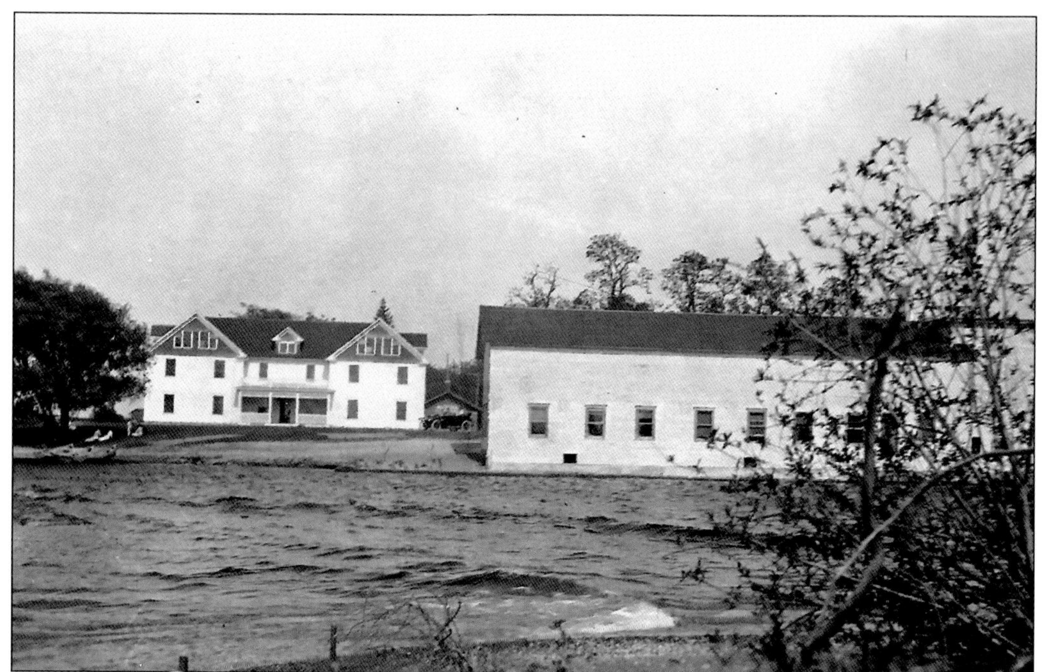

LAKELAND HOTEL. The Lakeland Hotel provided food, fun, and dancing to fun lovers for several decades. It was a dance hall in the 1950s and 1960s. It closed down for a while and was renovated and reopened as the Barbary Coast, but that is closed now. (Courtesy of Garland Miller.)

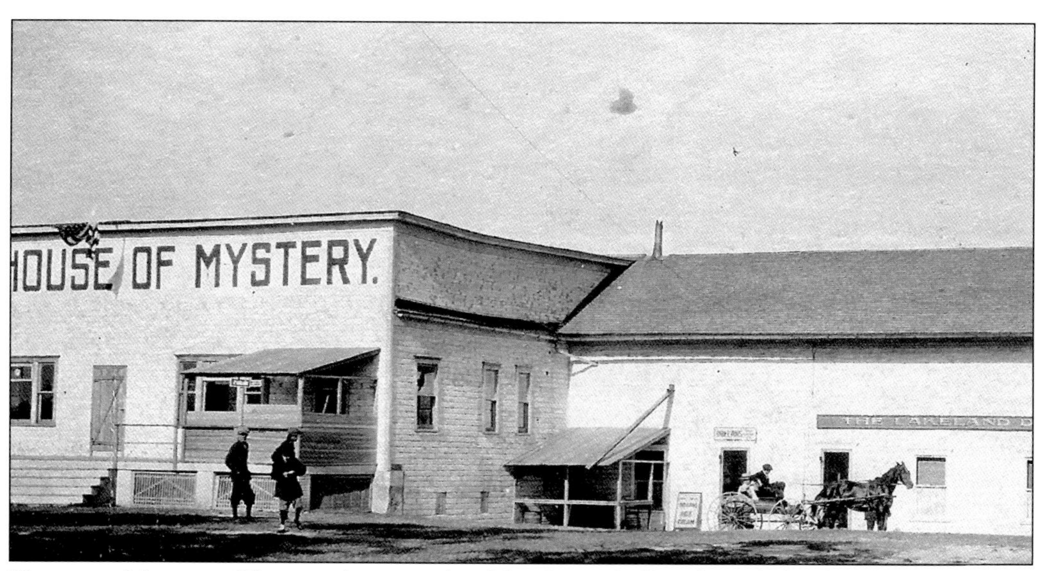

HOUSE OF MYSTERY. This was the east side of the dining hall at the Lakeland. Why it was called the House of Mystery remains a mystery to this day. (Courtesy of Sandy Tombari Freeman.)

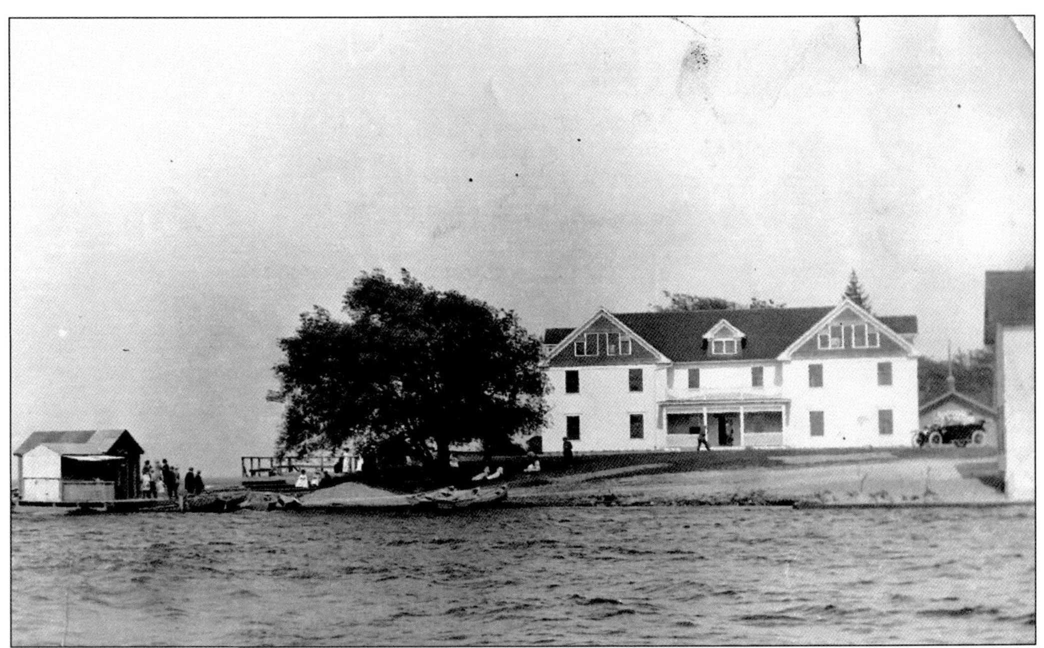

THE ROARING TWENTIES. Folks have a good time outside the Lakeland Hotel in this *c.* 1925 photograph. (Courtesy of Garland Miller.)

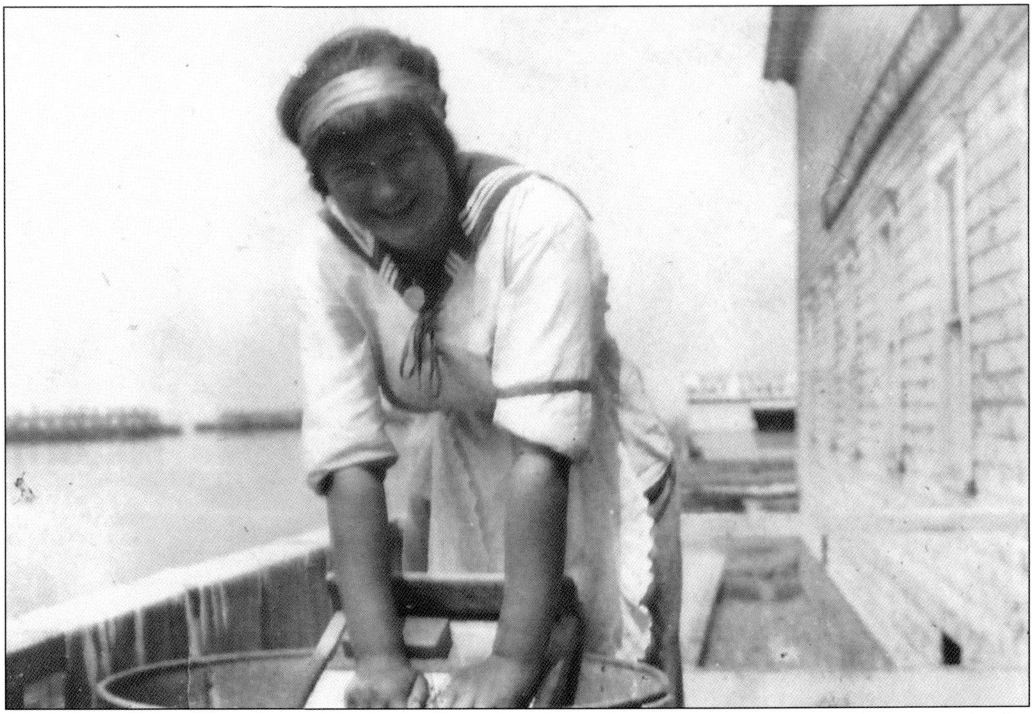

LAKELAND WAITRESS. Harriet Podgers Mattern uses a washboard to scrub napkins outside the Lakeland Hotel around 1915. (Courtesy of Marie Mattern Carlston.)

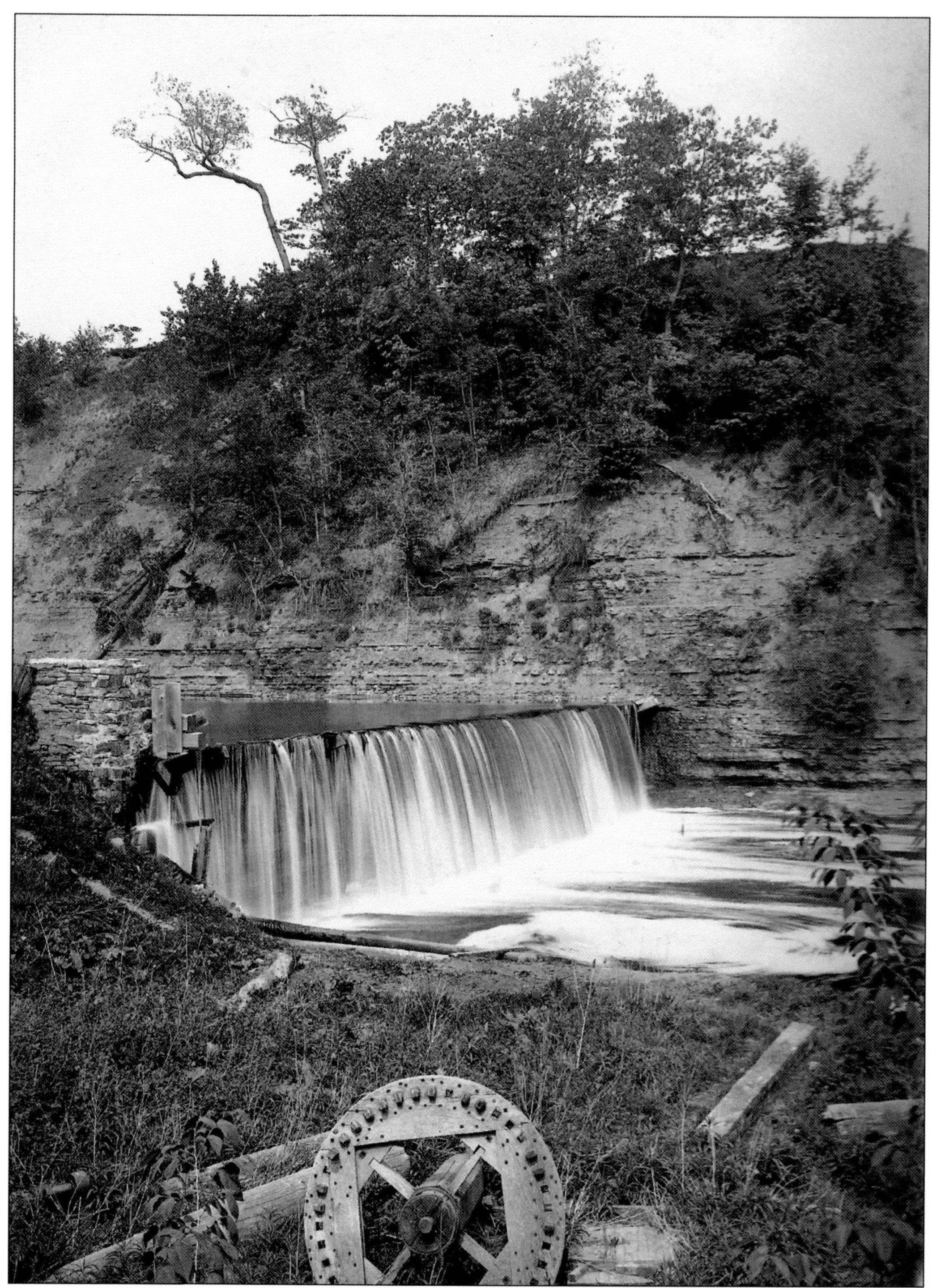

DAM FOR MILLPOND. This dam created a millpond to operate the mills at Waterport. It was located west of the current bridge. (Courtesy of Orleans County Department of History.)

Two

Early Years in and around Waterport

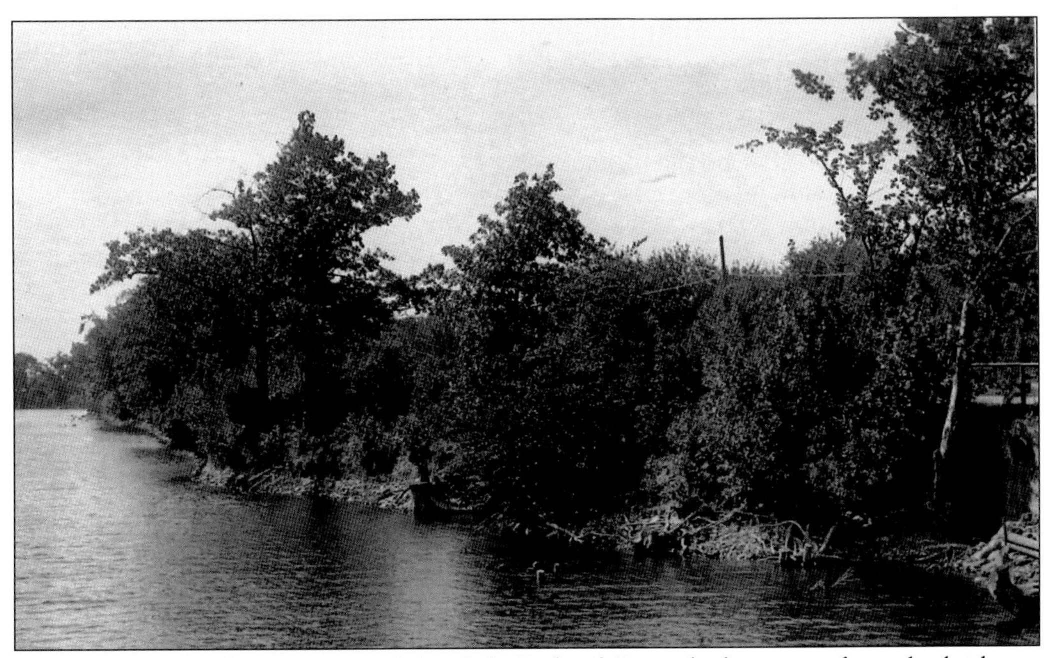

Looking West. This is a view of the Oak Orchard River, looking west from the bridge at Waterport. (Courtesy of John Sawyer.)

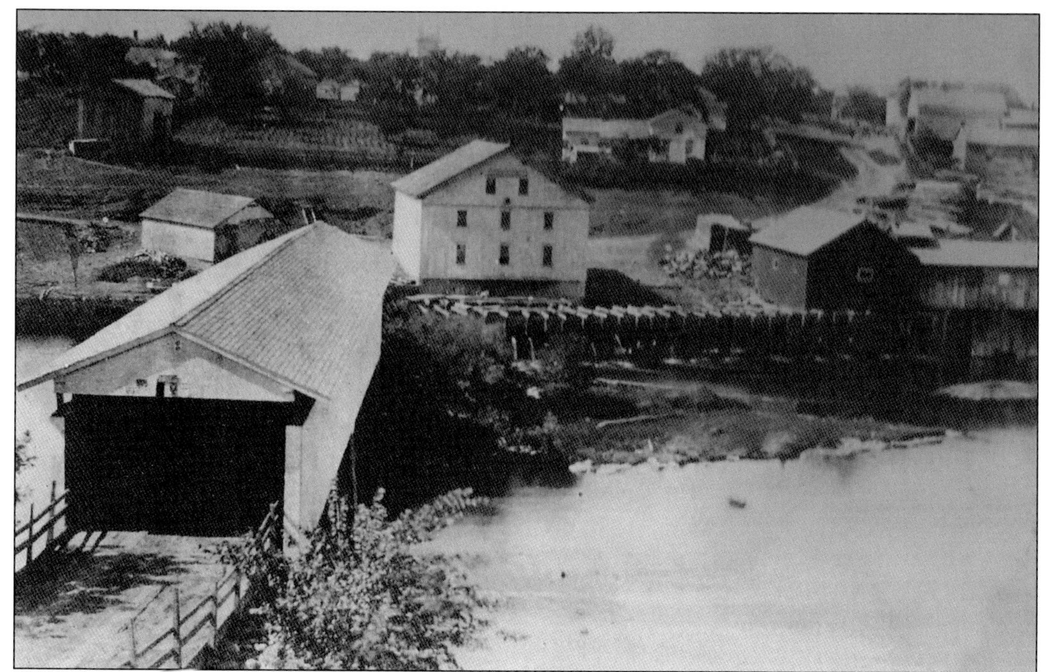

Kenyonville Bridge, c. 1875. In 1874, this 110-foot-long covered bridge was constructed at Kenyonville to span Oak Orchard Creek. It stood on three stone piers directly above a 10-foot dam, which provided a millrace for waterpower to run a gristmill and a sawmill owned by Barber Kenyon. The gristmill can be seen at far right. (Courtesy of Orleans County Department of History.)

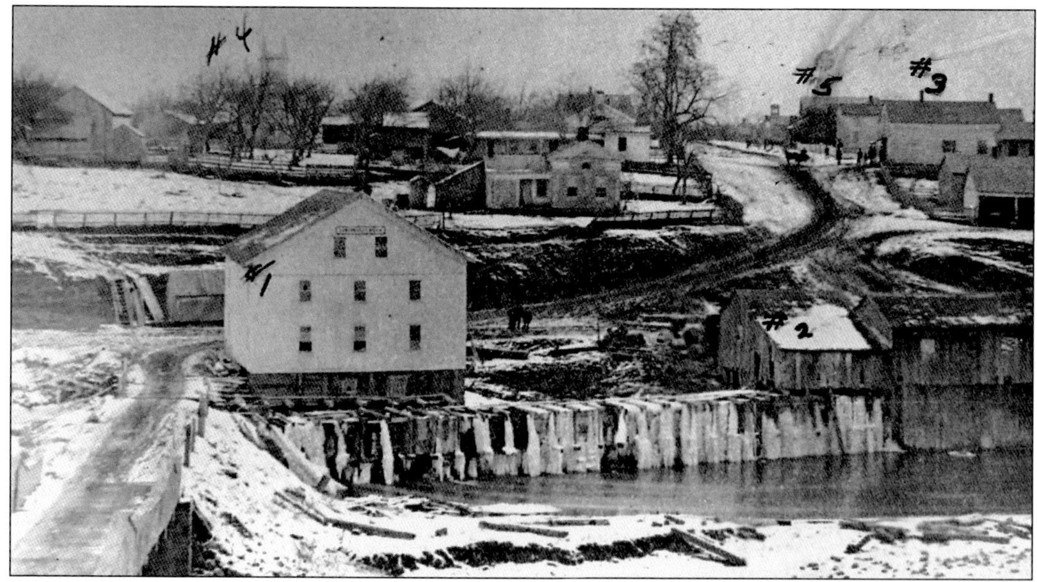

Kenyonville, c. 1872. Someone numbered this photograph, highlighting the points of interest of that era. The building at left, front, No. 1, is J. D. Fowler's custom mill; to its right is William Merrill's shingle mill; back right, No. 3, is Robert Potter's general store and post office; behind that, No. 5, is Leonard Wright's blacksmith shop; and at extreme left in the back is No. 4, the Methodist church. (Courtesy of Orleans County Department of History.)

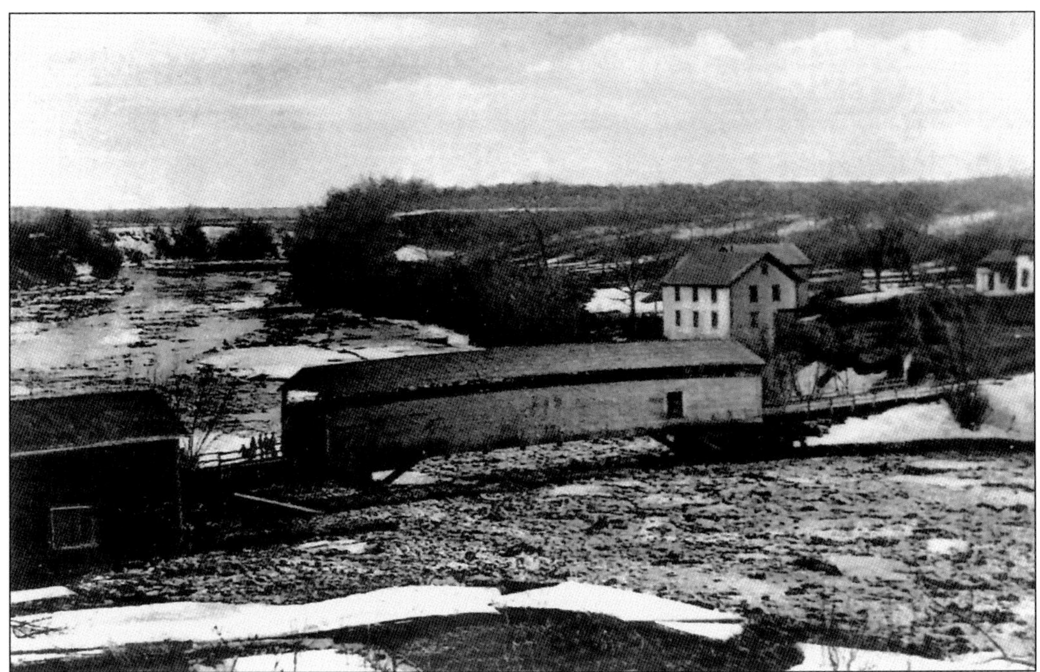

First Bridge. This is the covered bridge built at Two Bridges, looking south upsteam around 1907. (Courtesy of Mary Sage-Eisvang.)

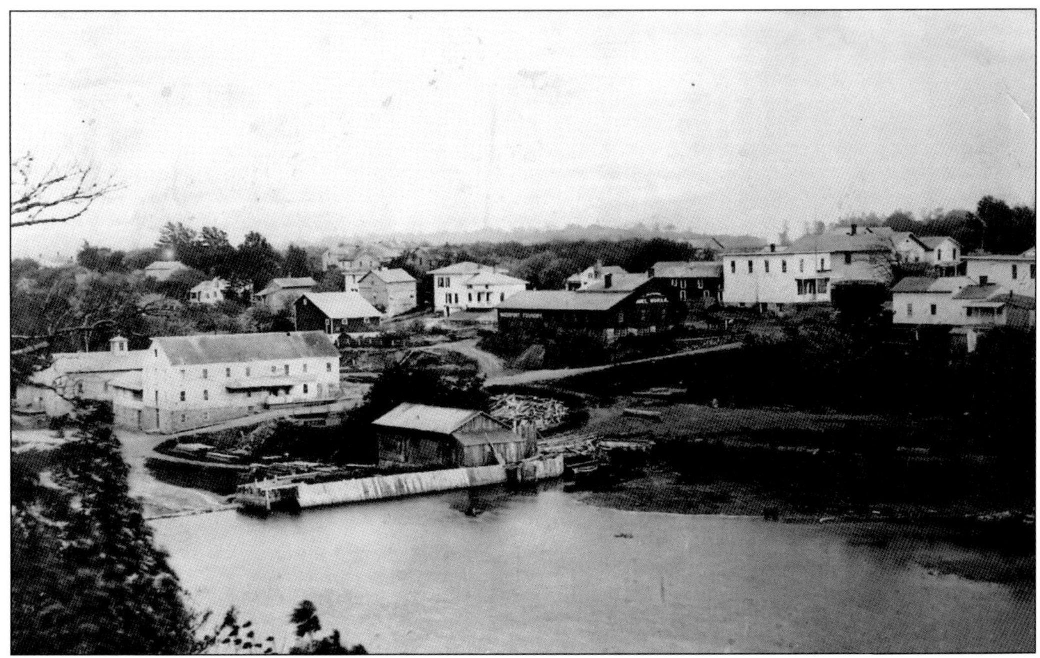

Waterport Hamlet, c. 1880. This view looks southeast into the hamlet of Waterport. Main Street runs horizontally through the center of the photograph, with the Waterport Foundry the dark building in the center. The foundry manufactured plows and cultivators and was a popular spot for area farmers. (Courtesy of Orleans County Department of History.)

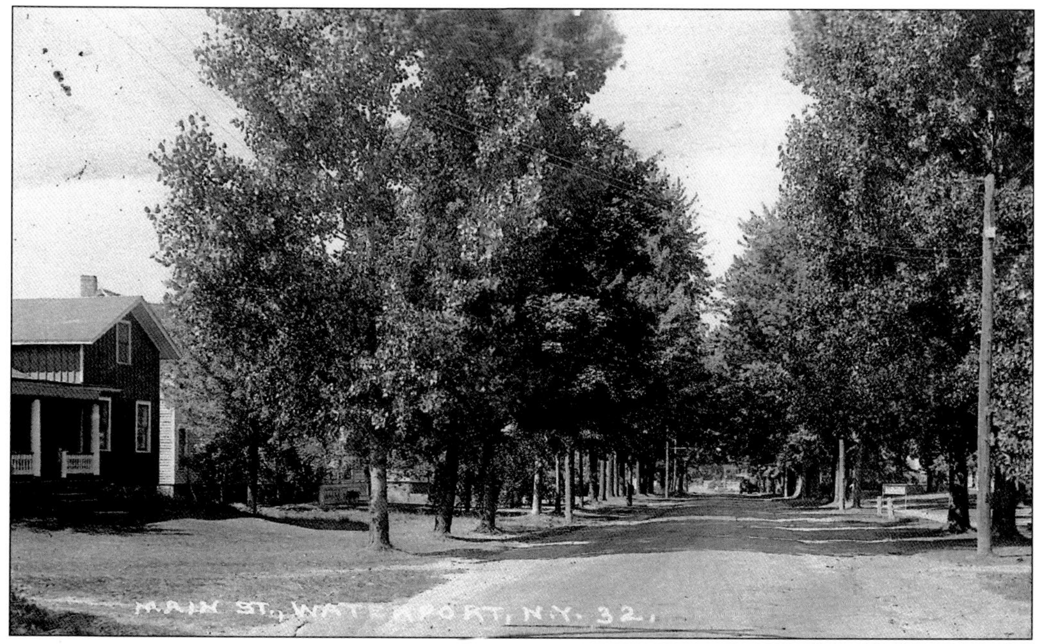

MAIN STREET, WATERPORT, C. 1920. This photograph shows Waterport's Main Street, looking south. (Courtesy of John Sawyer.)

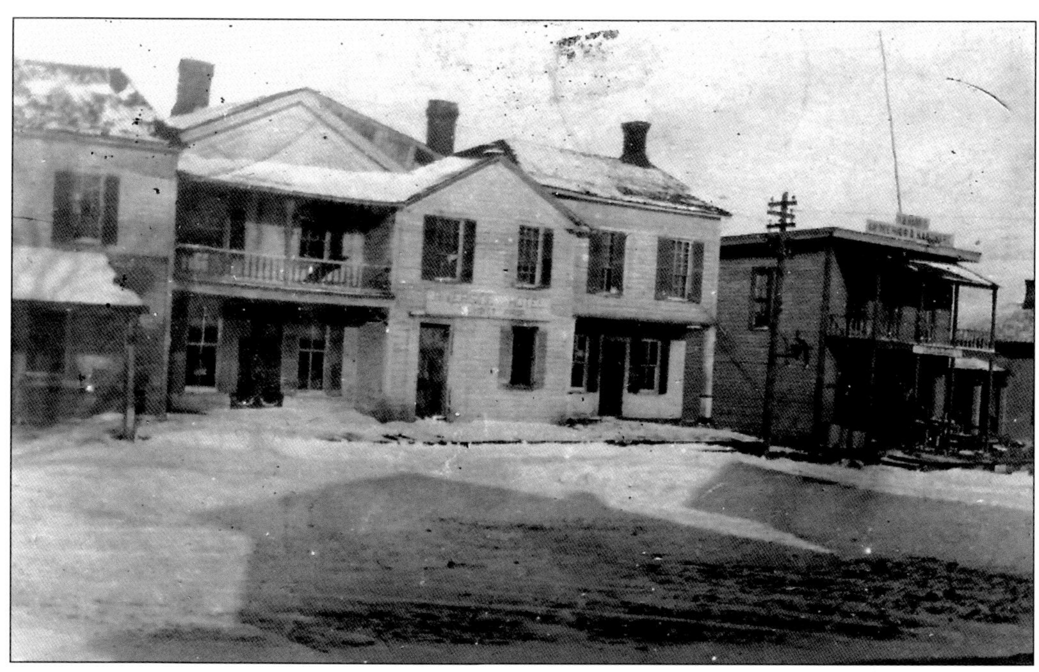

WATERPORT HOTEL. This hotel was very popular in Waterport until it burned in October 1907. When it started burning, the flames spread from building to building until most of the business section consisting of hotel, grocery store, meat market, harness shop, and several dwelling houses and other buildings were razed to the ground. (Courtesy of Orleans County Department of History.)

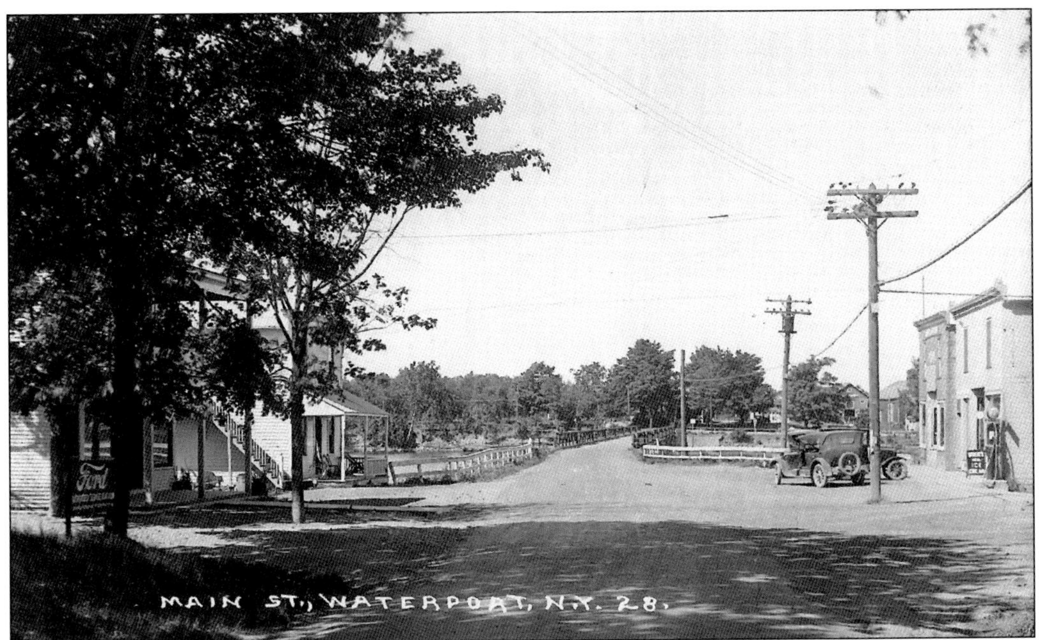

MAIN STREET, WATERPORT, c. 1920. This was the view looking north across the Waterport Bridge. Note the Model T Ford across the street from the Ford sign. (Courtesy of Orleans County Department of History.)

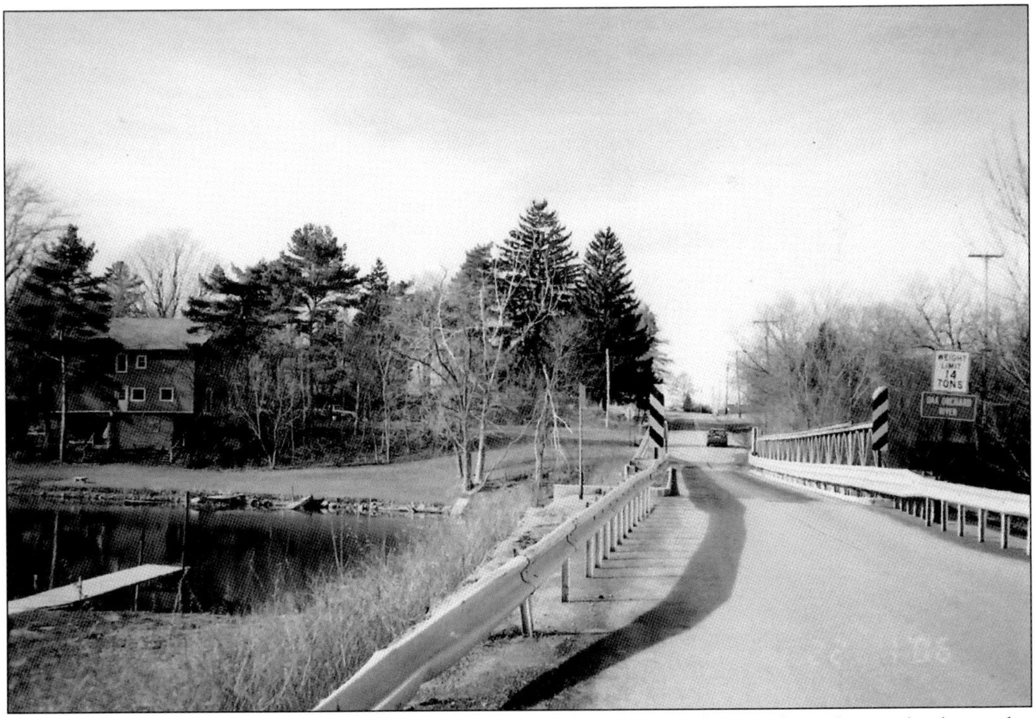

NOT MUCH HAS CHANGED. This bridge is in use today at the Bridges, located where the covered bridge used to be. A sign proclaims the crossing of the Oak Orchard River, and the vehicle must be under 14 tons. (Courtesy of Bud Canham.)

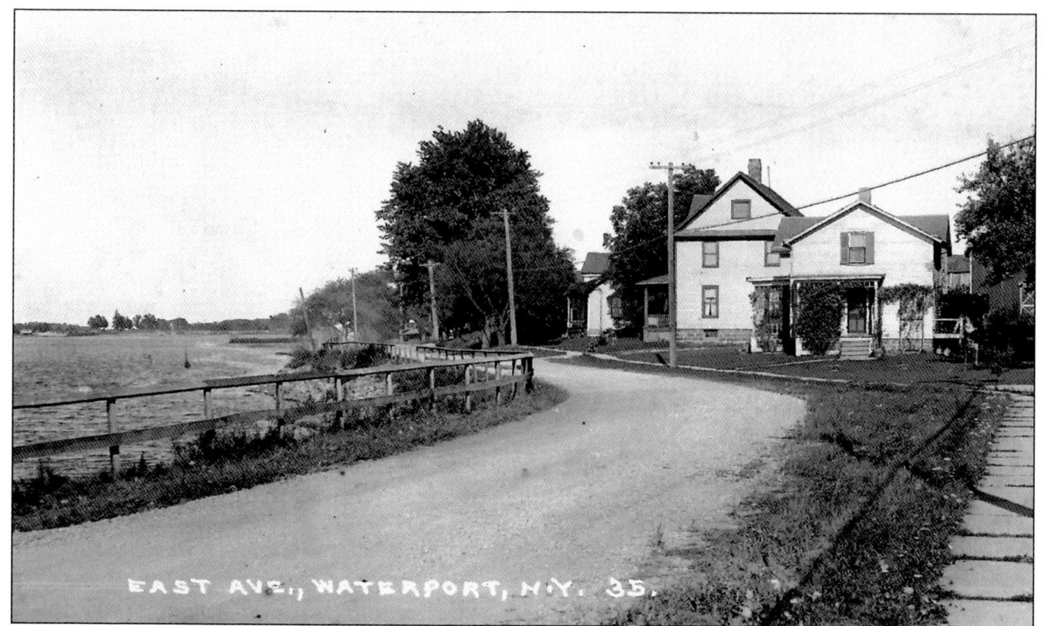

EAST AVENUE, WATERPORT, C. 1920. The eastward view of an area of the Oak Orchard Creek is referred to as Lake Alice. The name was given in memory of a daughter of A. L. Swett. She died in childhood. A. L. Swett Electric Light and Power Company constructed the Waterport Hydroelectric Plant in 1920. Now named the Waterport-Carlton Road, the view is much the same. (Courtesy of John Sawyer.)

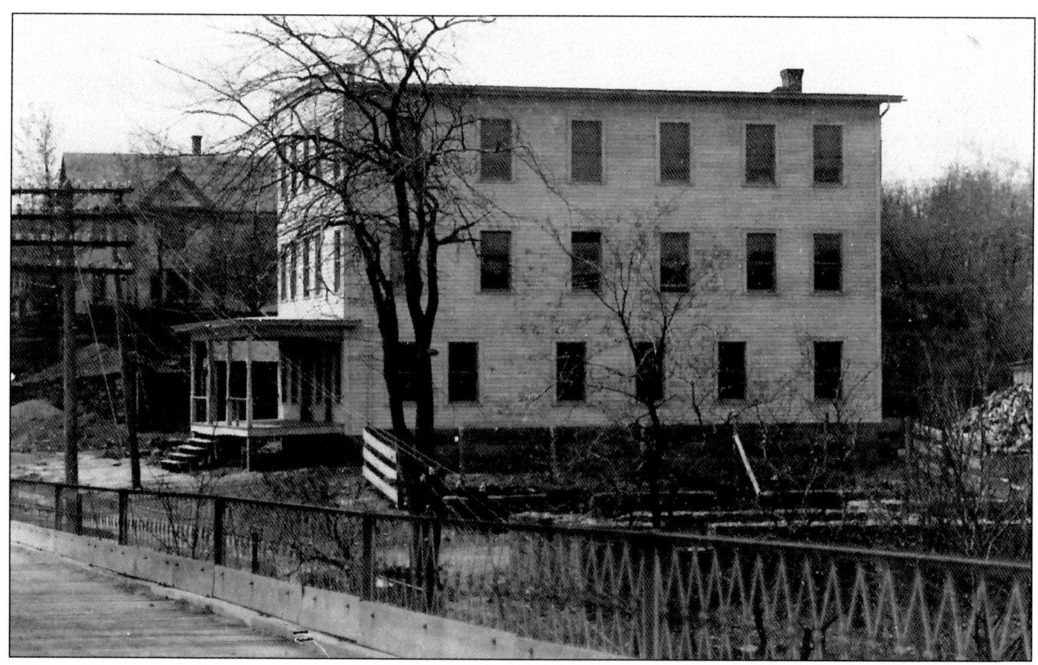

MAIN STREET, WATERPORT, C. 1910. This view is looking south across the Waterport Bridge. (Courtesy of Garland Miller.)

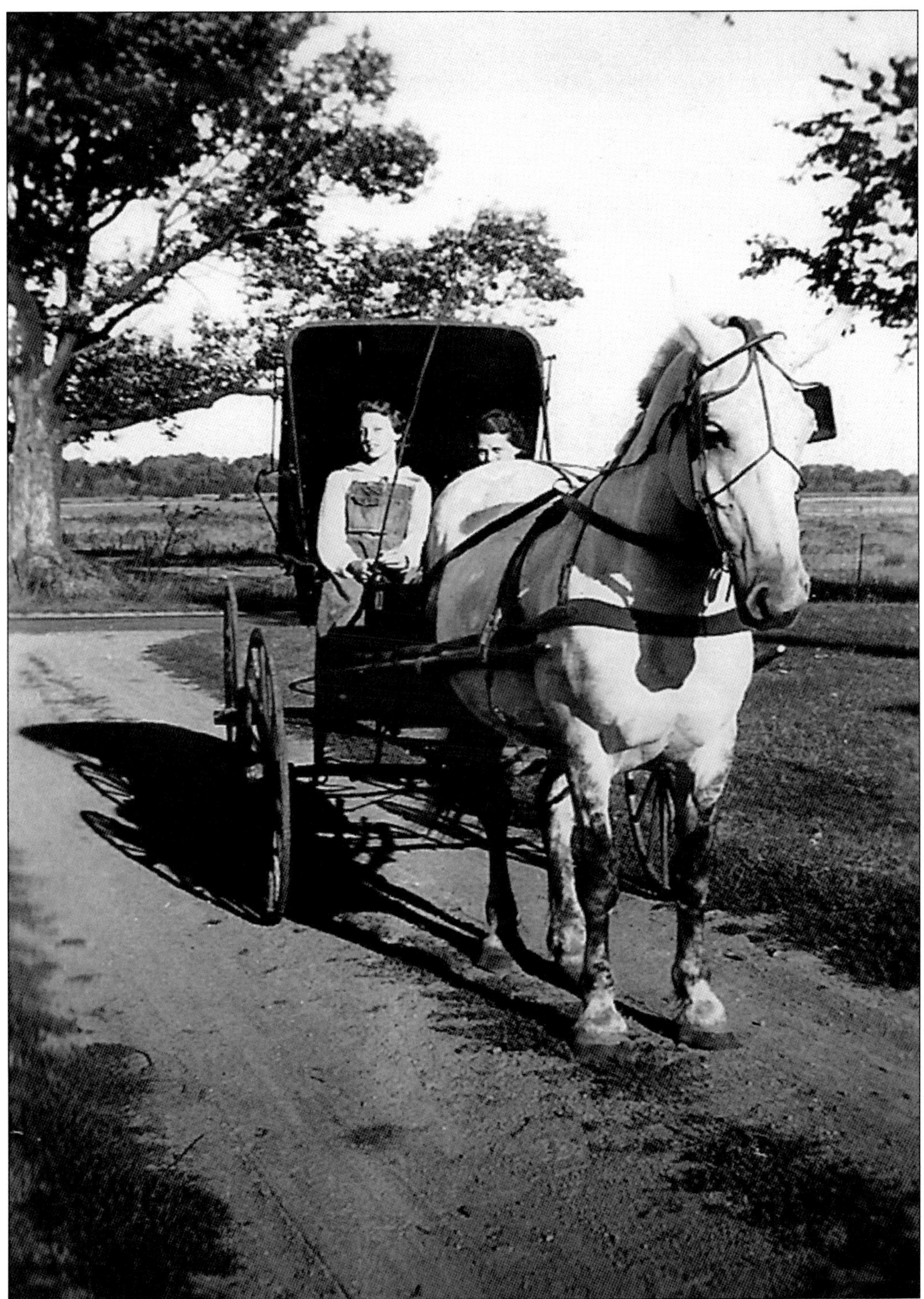

A Trip to Waterport. Gerry Miller and Gertrude Donnelly drive the carriage from Carlton Station to Waterport in 1935. Because of the sway in the bridge, the horse refused to cross. (Courtesy of Garland Miller.)

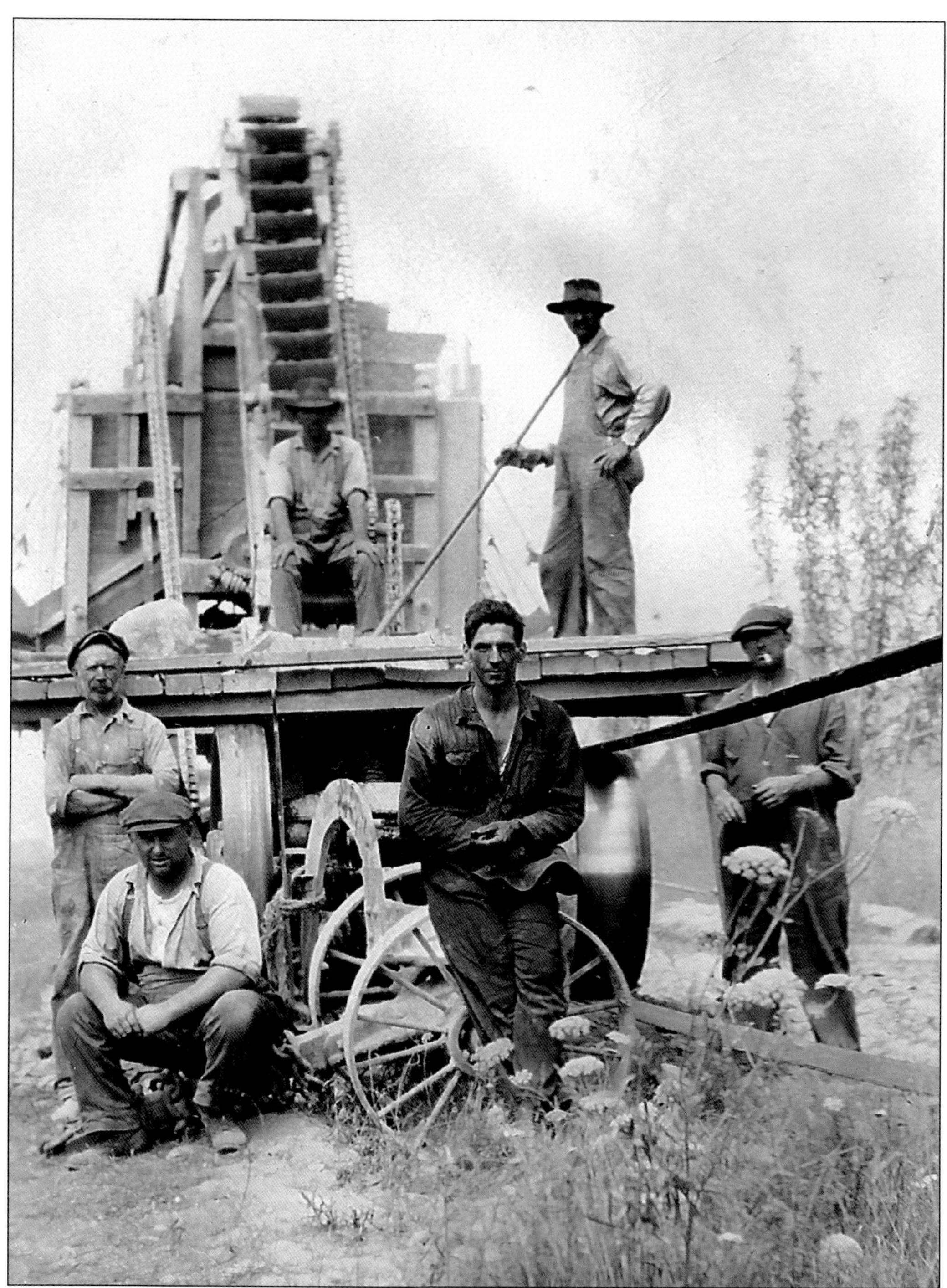

STONE CRUSHER. This is the same machine that appears in the photograph at right, but the people are of another generation. This is the front view of a stone crusher. The man on top is sitting on the conveyor that took rocks inside the machinery and split them into stones. Quarries were the mainstay in Carlton in the late 1800s to early 1900s, as much as farming or fishing. (Courtesy of Shirley Bennett Belson.)

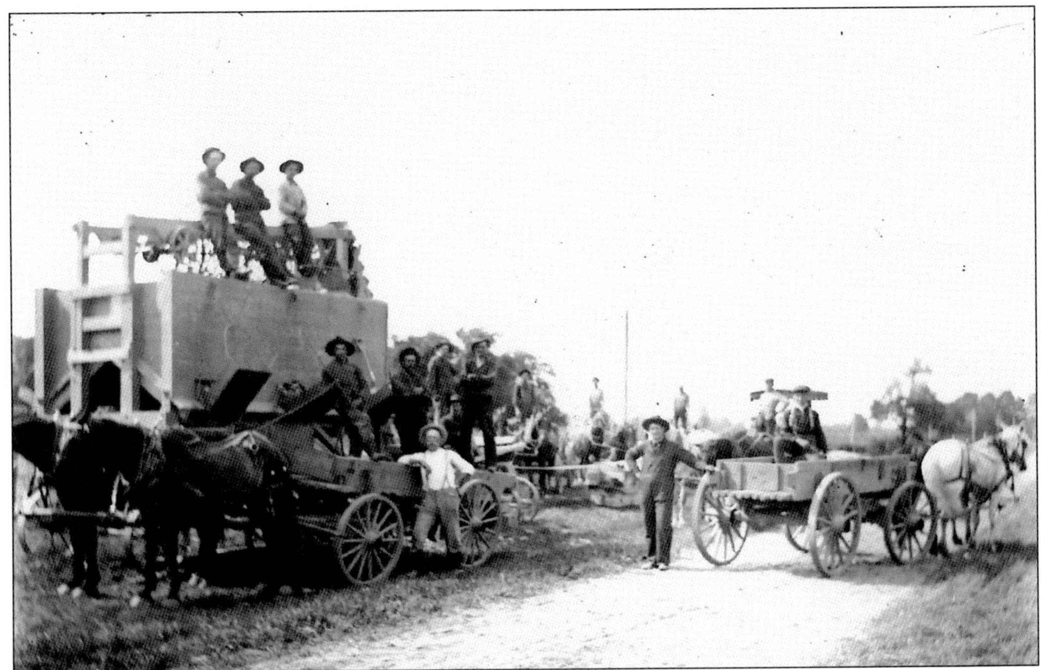

STONE CRUSHER, C. 1900. This photograph was taken from an old glass plate belonging to the ancestors of Cliff and Doris Kelly. It is the back view of a stone crusher, used by men working in the quarries in and around the Carlton area. It was run by chains. (Courtesy of Orleans County Department of History.)

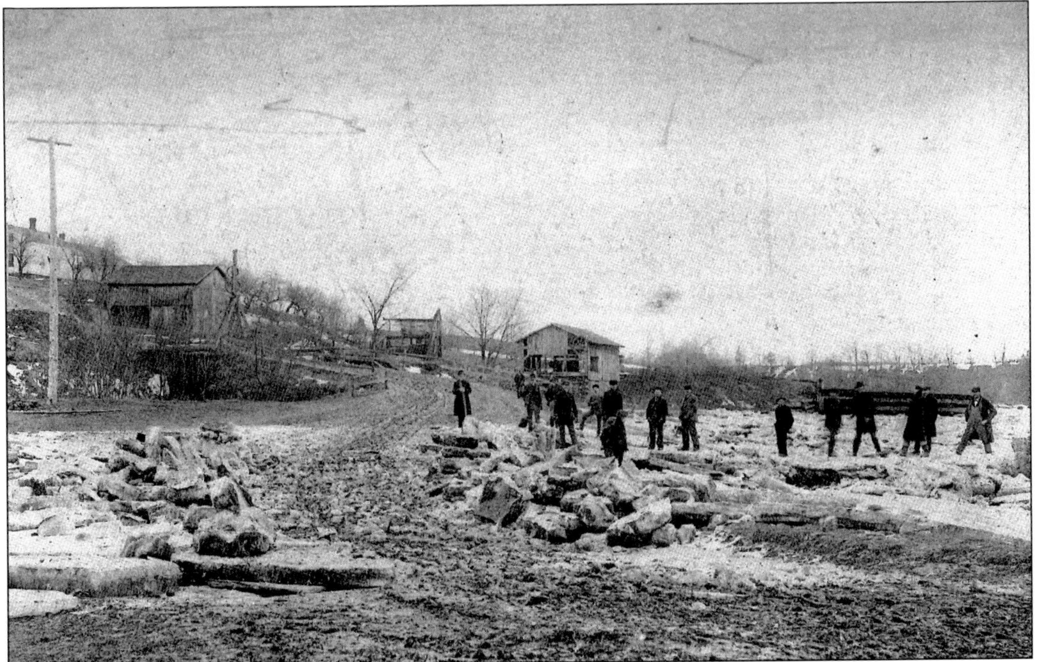

WORKING ON THE ROAD. This was the scene in Waterport around 1885, showing the old road before the high bridge was built above it. Perhaps they used a stone crusher to break up the large rocks into stone for the road base. (Courtesy of Orleans County Department of History.)

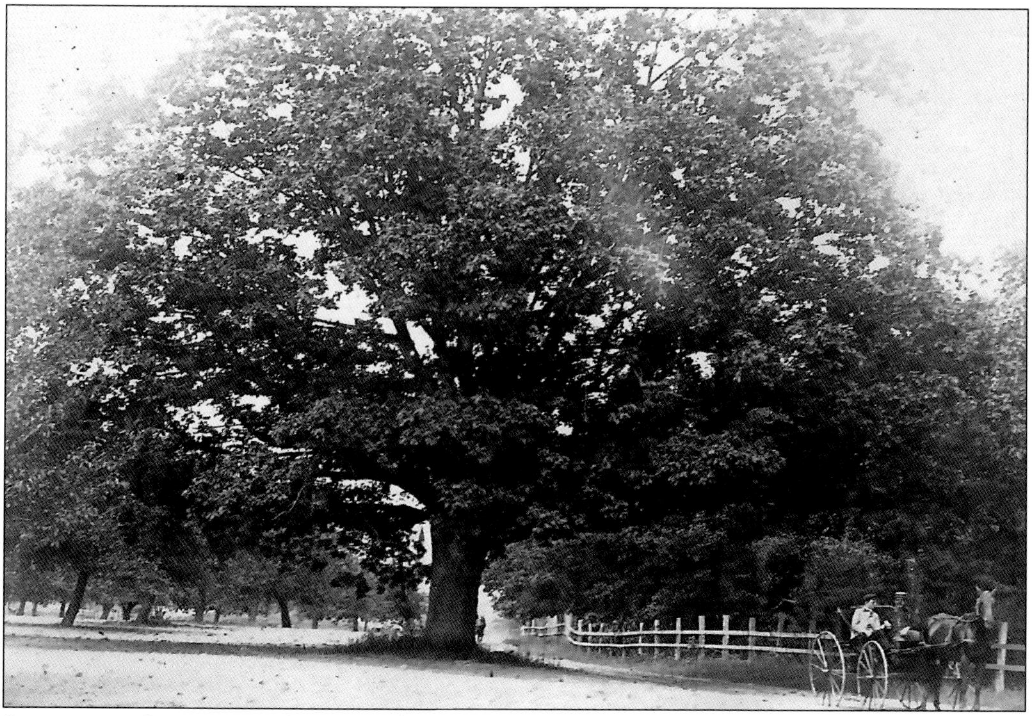

SPRAWLING OAK, 1897. This magnificent oak was located at the corner of Archbald Road and Route 18. (Courtesy of Orleans County Department of History.)

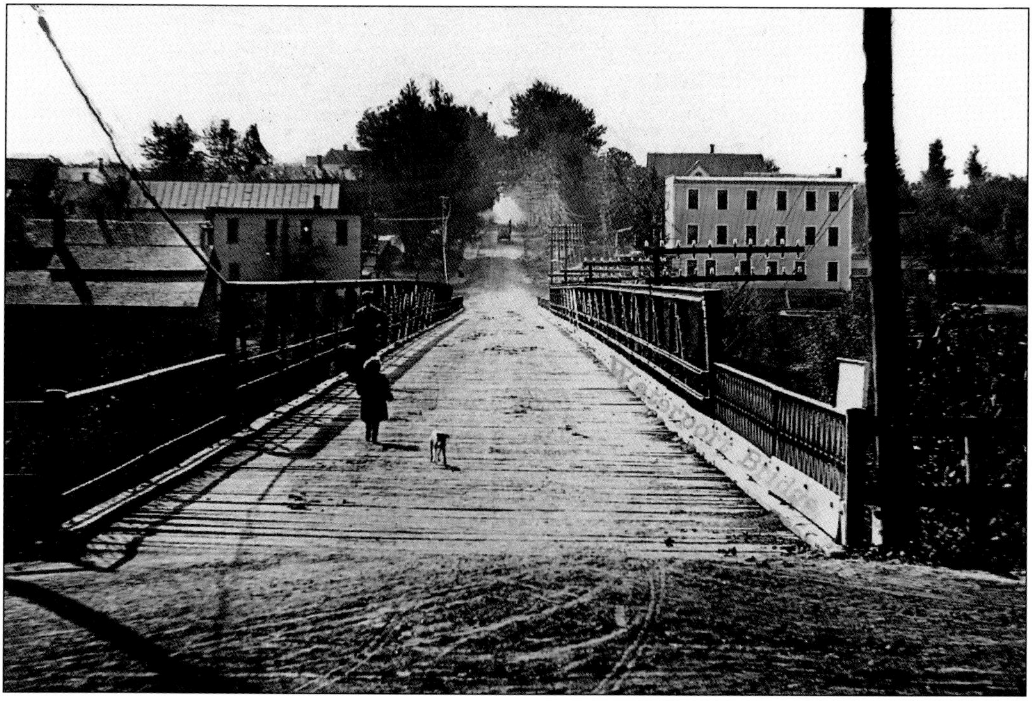

WALKING ACROSS THE WATERPORT BRIDGE. A man, a child, and a dog cross the old high bridge into Waterport around 1910. (Courtesy of Mike and Chris Elam.)

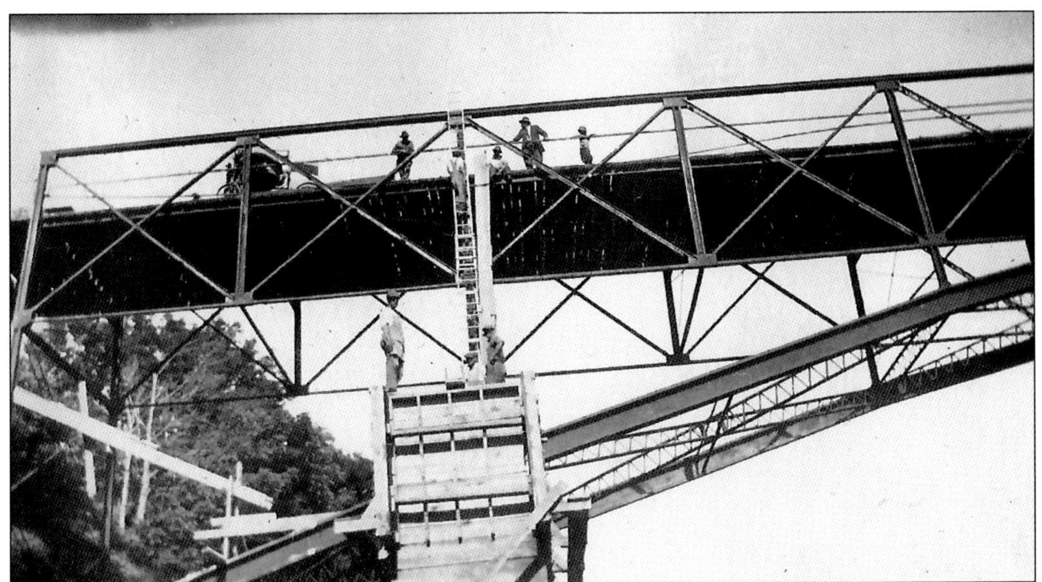

THE OLD WATERPORT BRIDGE, 1900–1918. Looking at the construction, the wooden planks, and the flimsiness of this bridge, it was easy to see why people, not to mention horses, were fearful of crossing. The old bridge is said to have weaved in high winds. (Courtesy of Jessica Matson.)

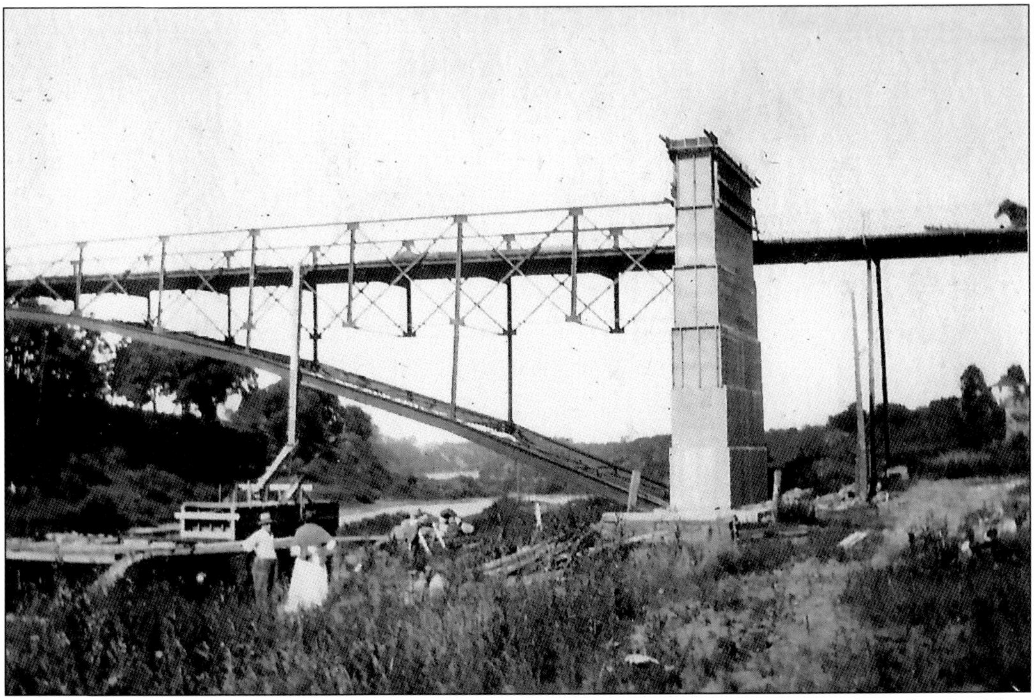

RECONSTRUCTION. Men work on the span of the bridge, which had a sway when finished but was the only way for people to cross Oak Orchard River. (Courtesy of Jessica Matson.)

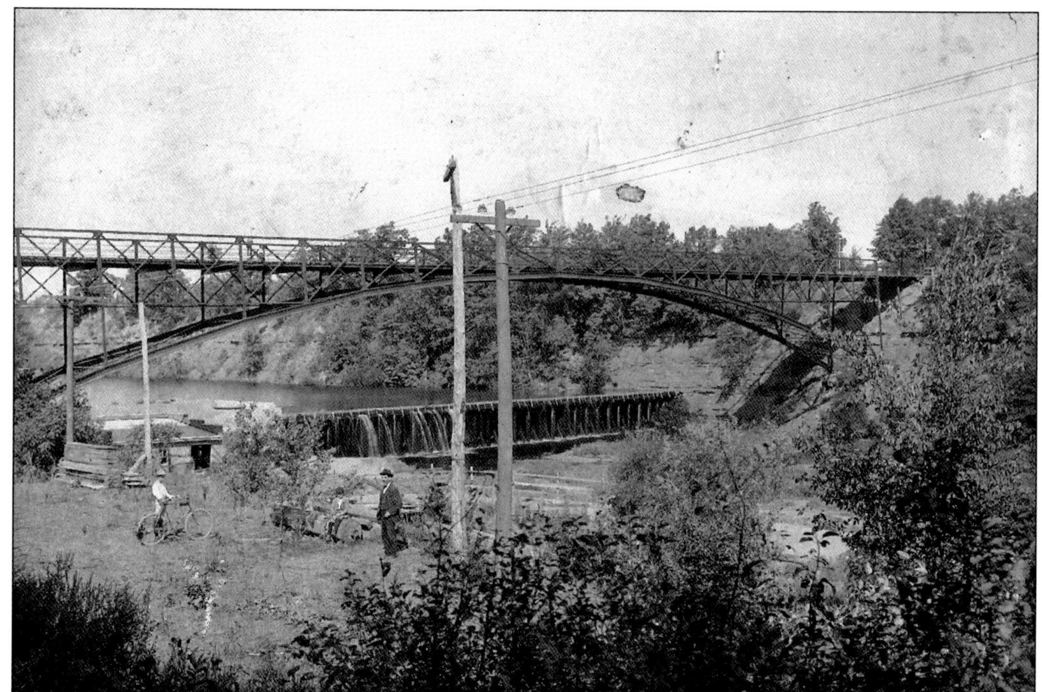

Two Views. The original Waterport Bridge was a sight to behold. In the photograph above, the waterfall below the bridge is meager, and men enjoy passing time on the bank. Note the boy with the bicycle. In the photograph below, the current seems stronger, and the water's flow is a more impressive sight. The Albion Power Company can be seen at left in both views. (Courtesy of Jessica Matson.)

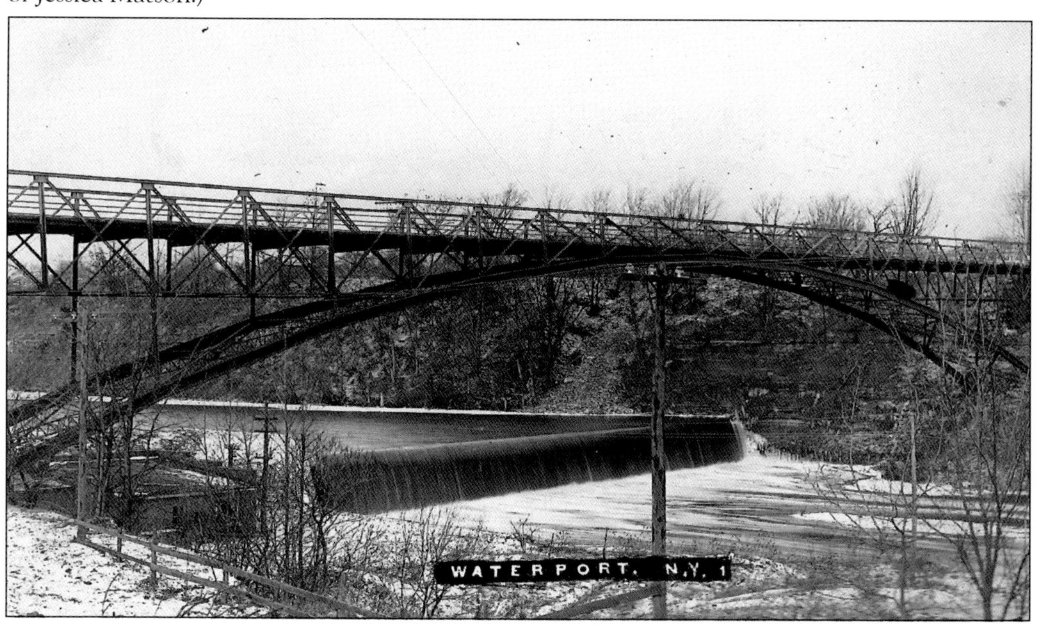

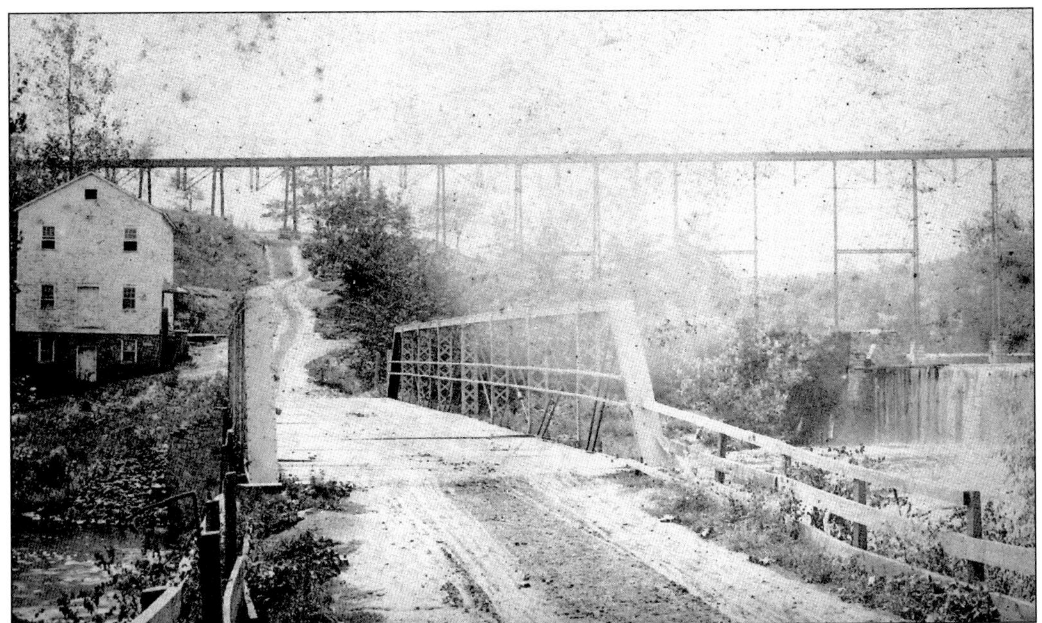

THE FIRST TRESTLE, 1890. This first railroad bridge, built in 1875, crossed Oak Orchard River. The first train crossed on November 18, 1875, and was driven by a local woman, Mrs. John Ross. Clark's Mill is at left, and the former Clark's Mill Road and bridge are no longer in existence. Today a different road sports the name Clark's Mill Road. (Courtesy of Orleans County Department of History.)

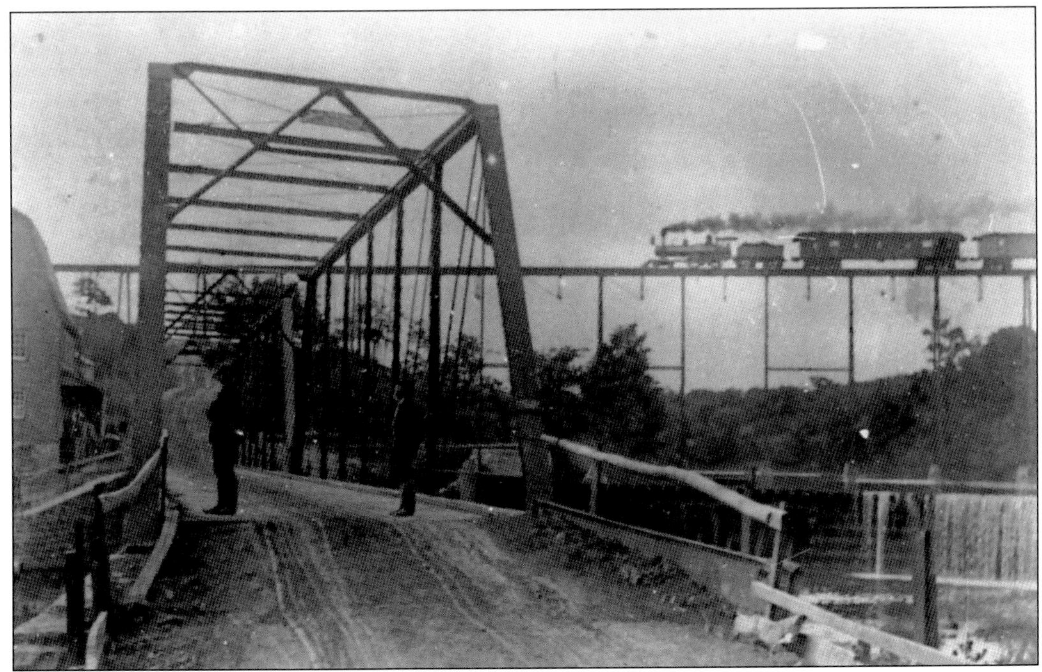

A PASSING TRAIN. People on the bridge seem more interested in what is going on at the mill to the left than in the train that is passing on the first trestle. This photograph was taken prior to 1892. (Courtesy of Orleans County Department of History.)

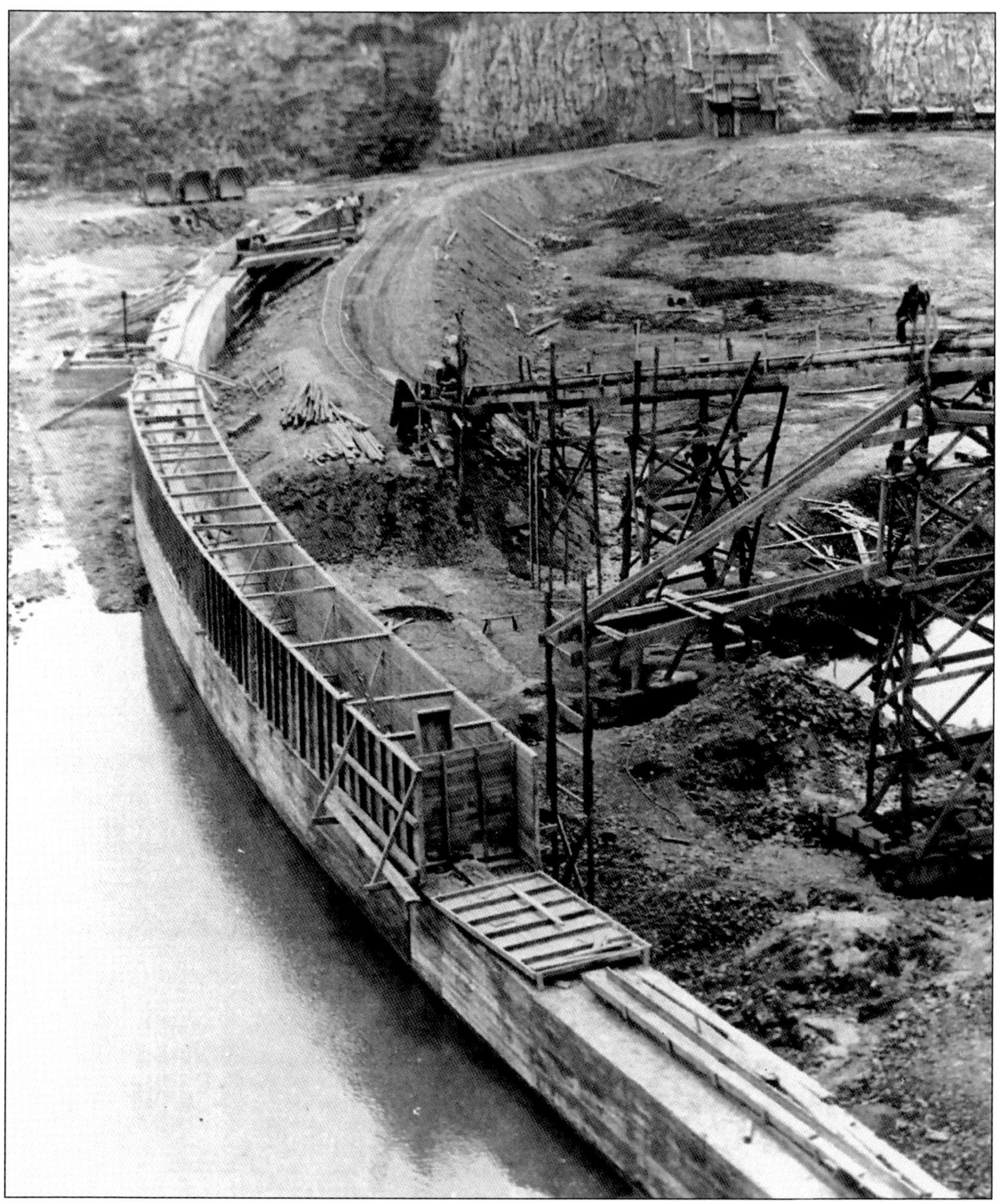

Building the Waterport Dam. The Waterport Dam was built between 1917 and 1919, with the power station completed by 1920. The dam provided power for Carlton and other local areas. It has had several owners over the years. (Courtesy of Mike and Chris Elam.)

Three

The Dam and New Trestle

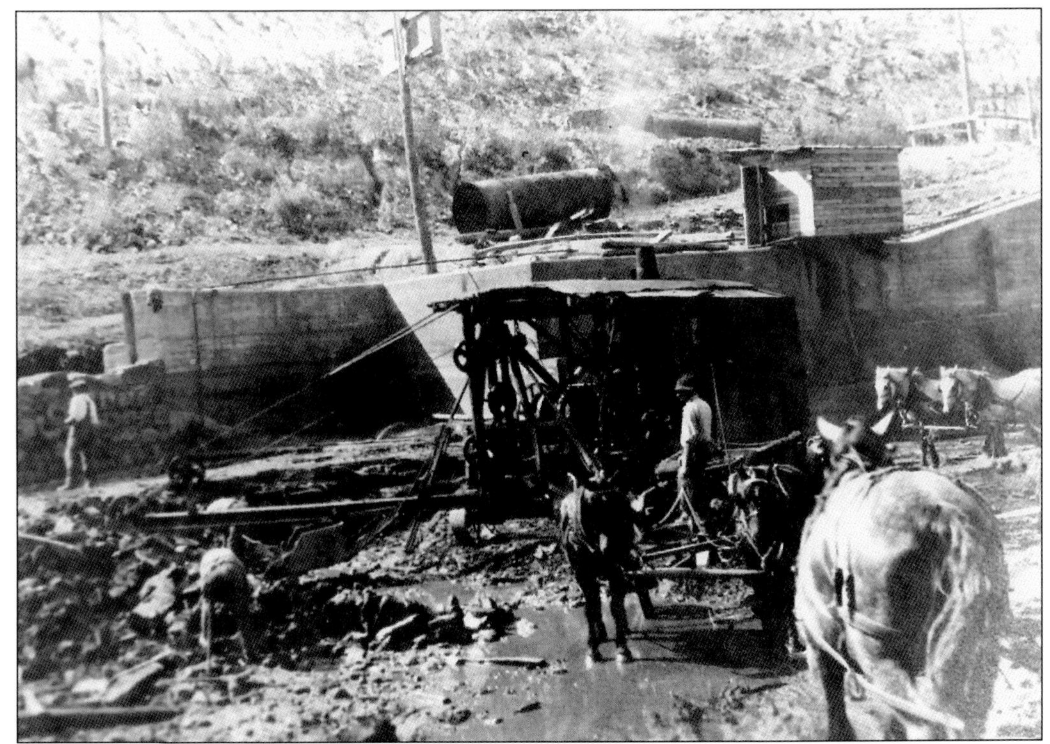

Lots of Horsepower. Horses, as well as steam shovels and equipment from a former century, were used to build the Waterport dam. (Courtesy of Mike and Chris Elam.)

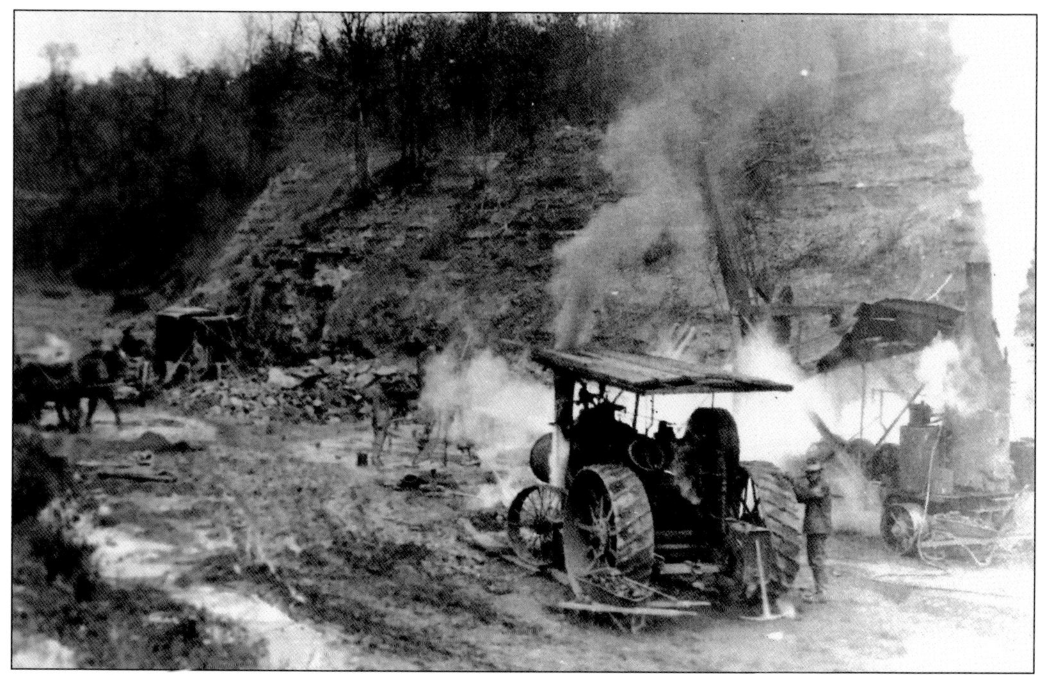

A LONG WAY TO GO. During the clearing of land for the Waterport Dam, horses patiently wait while work goes on around them. (Courtesy of Mike and Chris Elam.)

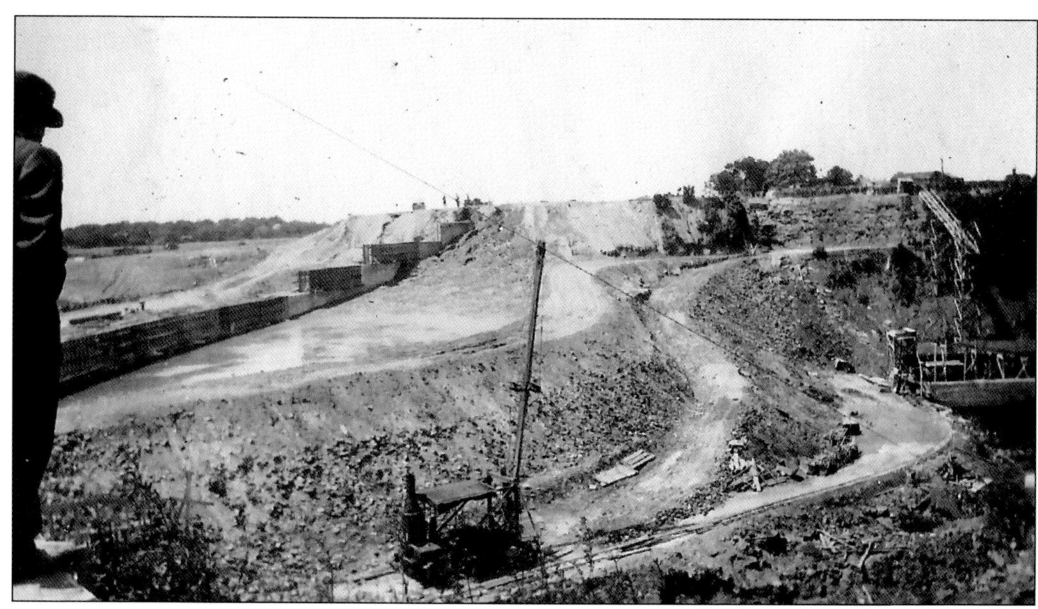

VISIBLE PROGRESS. Dirt has been cleared and smoothed, and a roadway is shaped as people prepare for the new dam at Waterport. (Courtesy of Jessica Matson.)

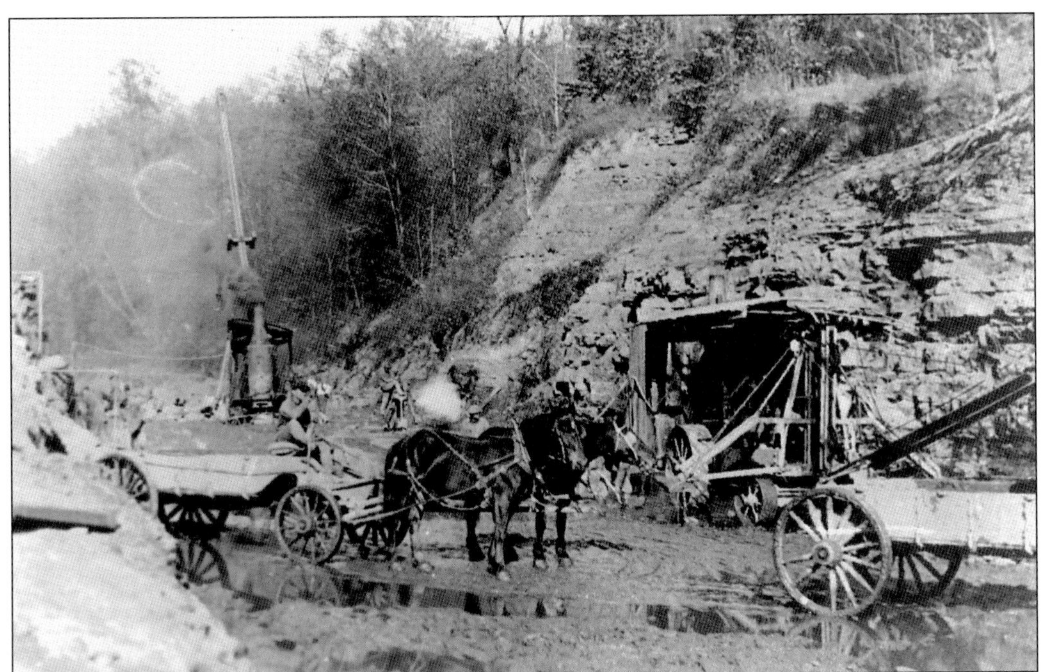

WAGONS AND EARLY MACHINES. Horses stand in front of a wagon during the clearing of land for the Waterport Dam. (Courtesy of Mike and Chris Elam.)

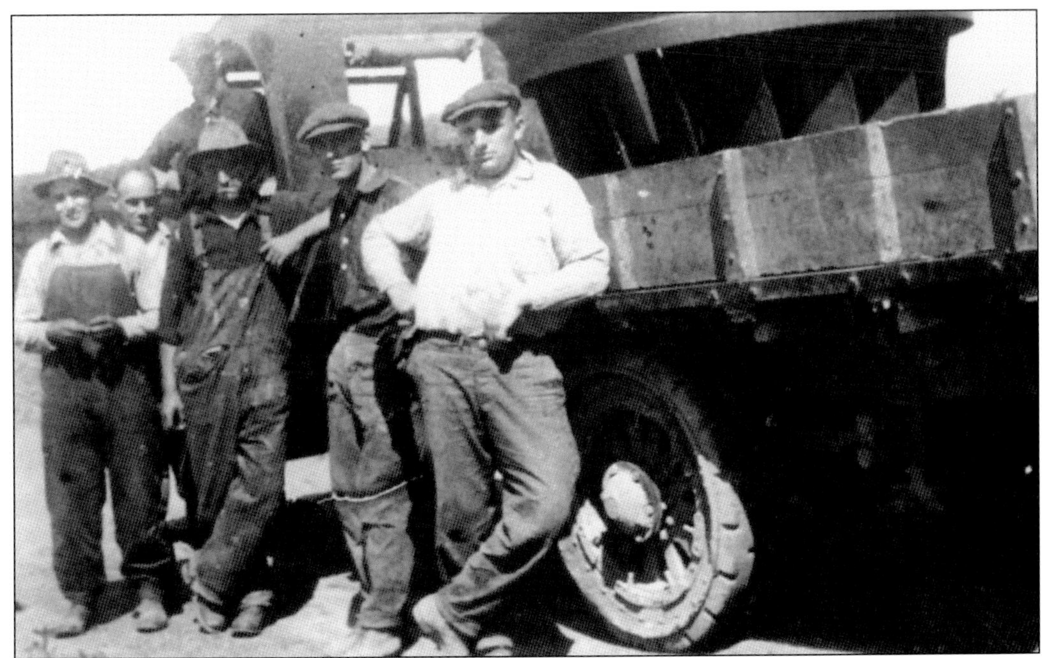

TAKING A BREAK. These unidentified workers rest by their truck during their job at the Waterport Dam project. (Courtesy of Mike and Chris Elam.)

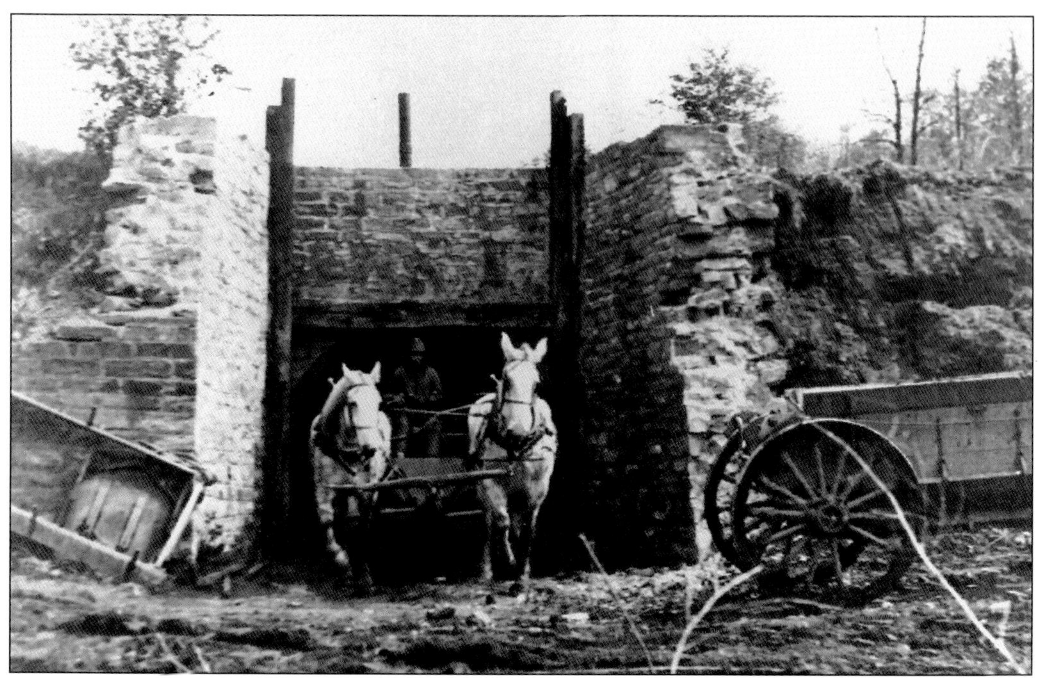

DRIVING OUT OF THE TUNNEL. A team of dapple gray horses pull drivers and a wagon from an inground tunnel on the grounds of the Waterport Dam project. (Courtesy of Mike and Chris Elam.)

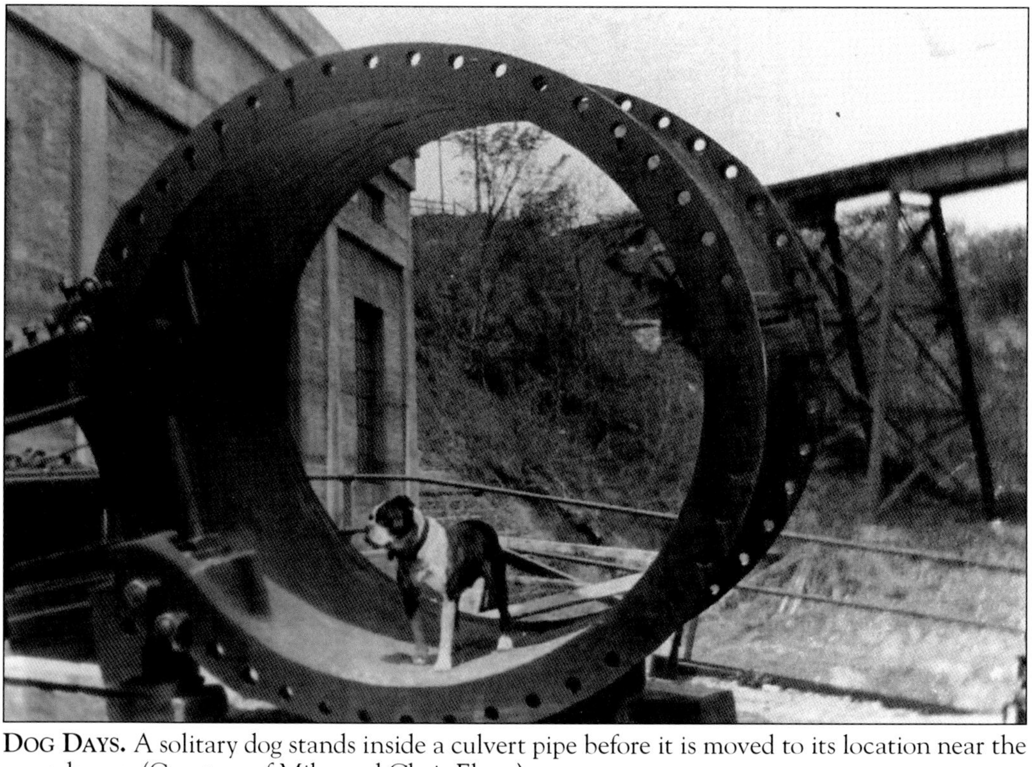

DOG DAYS. A solitary dog stands inside a culvert pipe before it is moved to its location near the powerhouse. (Courtesy of Mike and Chris Elam.)

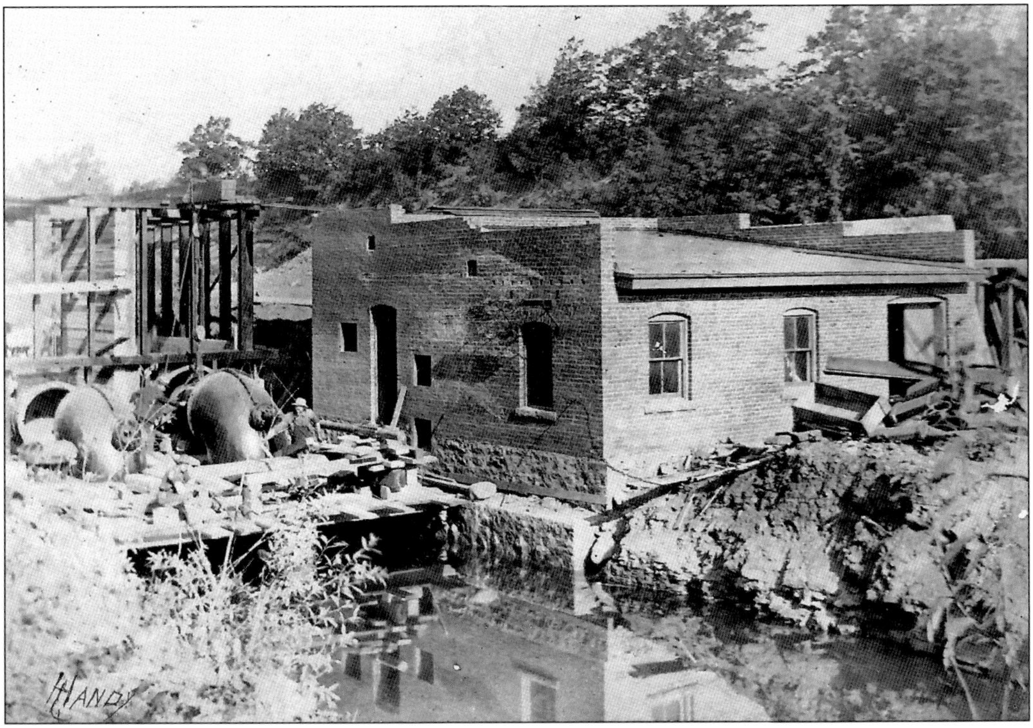

ORIGINAL POWERHOUSE. This building was west of the old Main Street Bridge in Waterport. (Courtesy of Orleans County Department of History.)

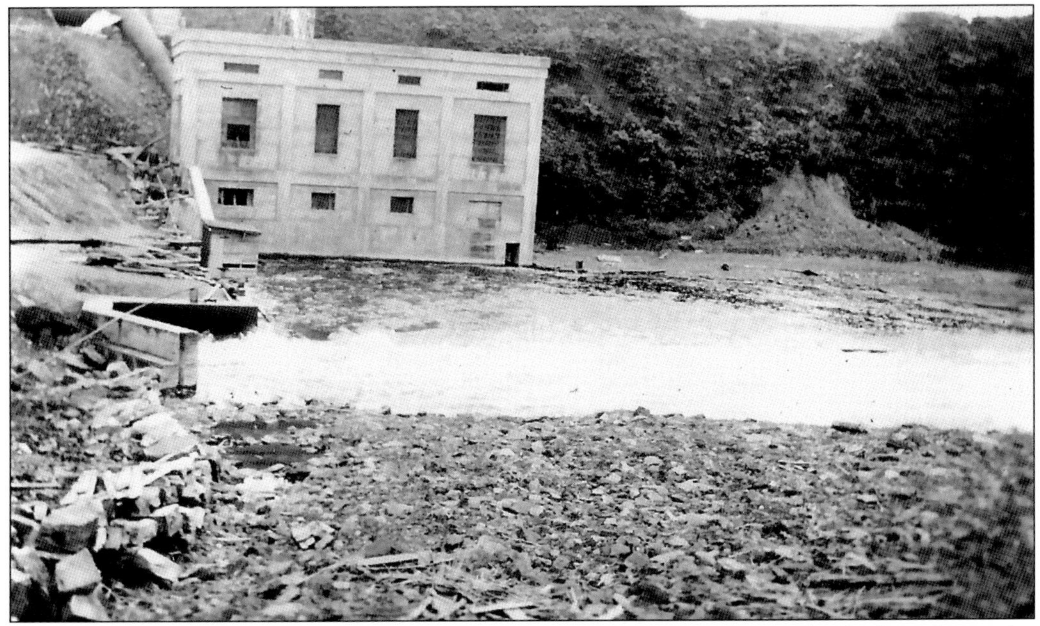

CONSTRUCTION NEARS COMPLETION. The powerhouse seems almost finished, and just the debris needs to be cleared up. (Courtesy of Jessica Matson.)

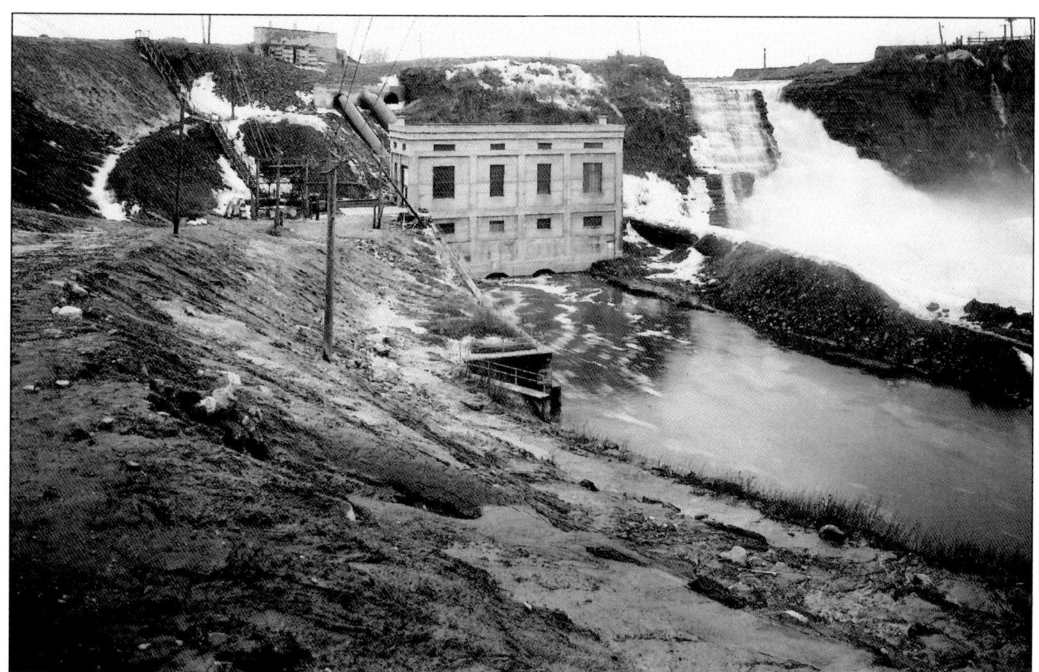

POWERHOUSE WORKING. Water flows freely over the finished Waterport Dam, and it swirls around the base of the powerhouse. (Courtesy of Orleans County Department of History.)

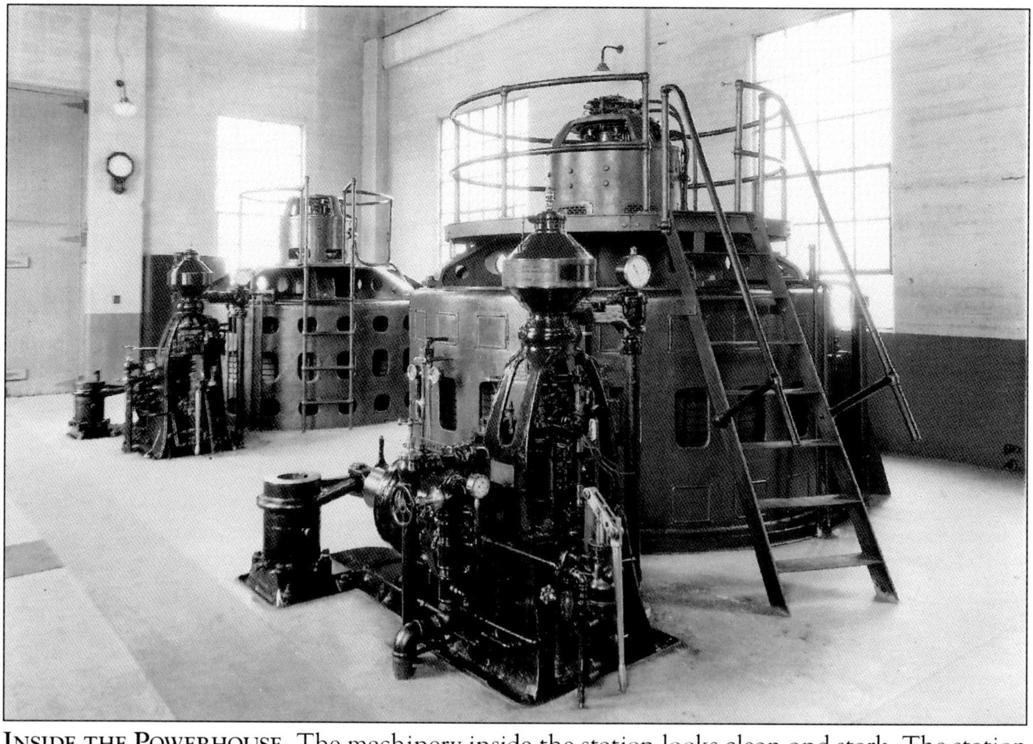

INSIDE THE POWERHOUSE. The machinery inside the station looks clean and stark. The station began pumping in 1925. (Courtesy of Orleans County Department of History.)

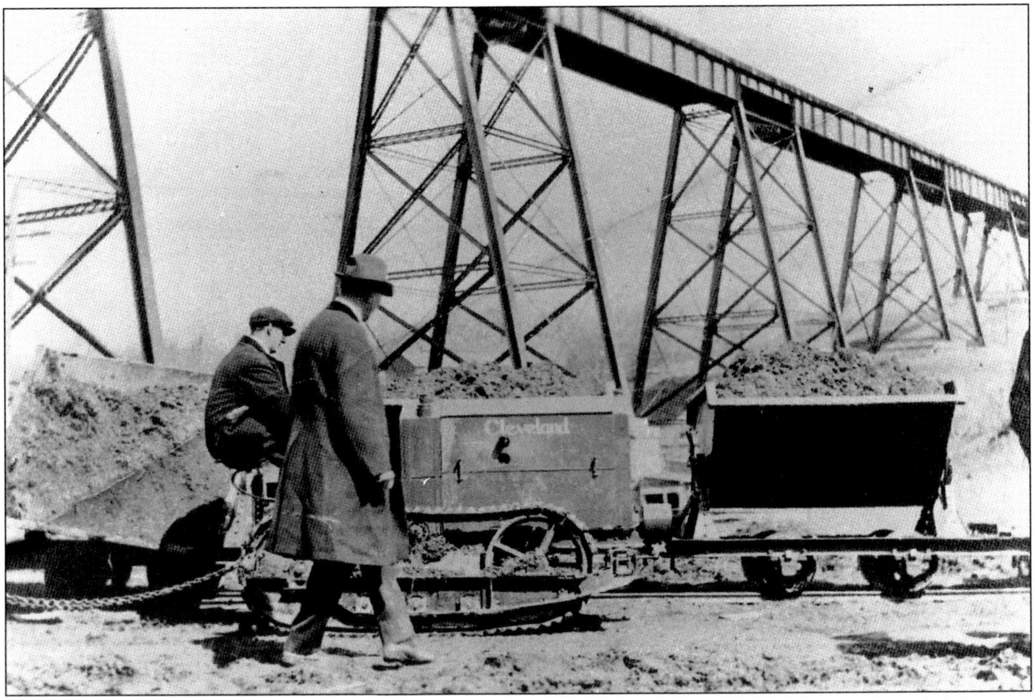

Small Rail Below the Trestle. Small railcars were used to haul dirt, rock, and debris in excavating the area below the trestle. (Courtesy of Orleans County Department of History.)

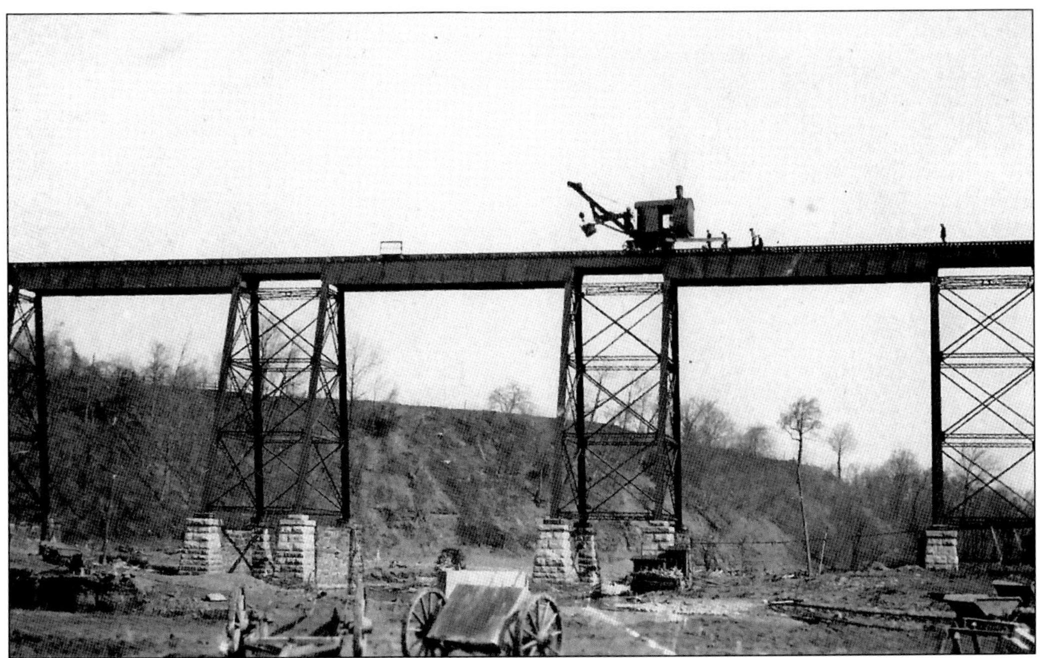

Putting Things in Their Place. A steam shovel is used to put pieces of rail and ties on the trestle. (Courtesy of Mike and Chris Elam.)

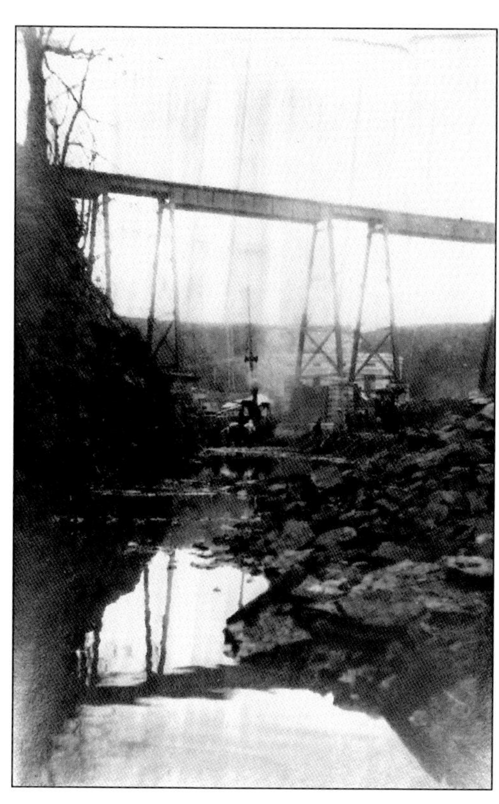

SEASONS OF CHANGE. Men continued to work on the dam and the trestle, whether it was warm or snowy. (Courtesy of Mike Elam and Jessica Matson.)

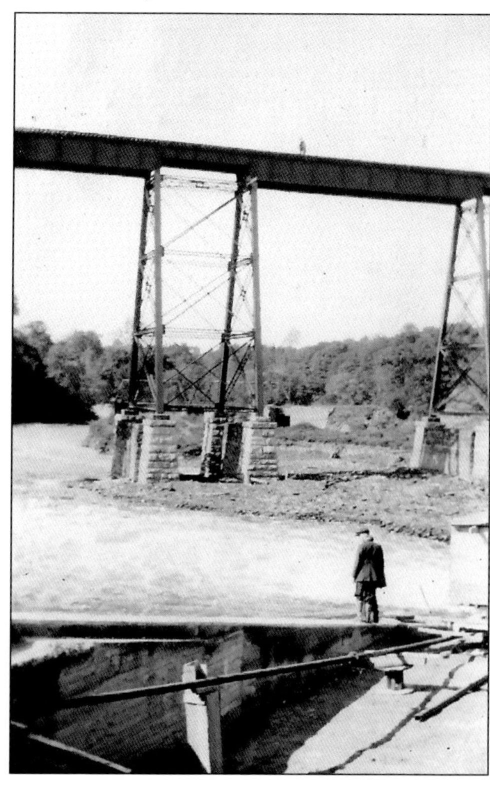

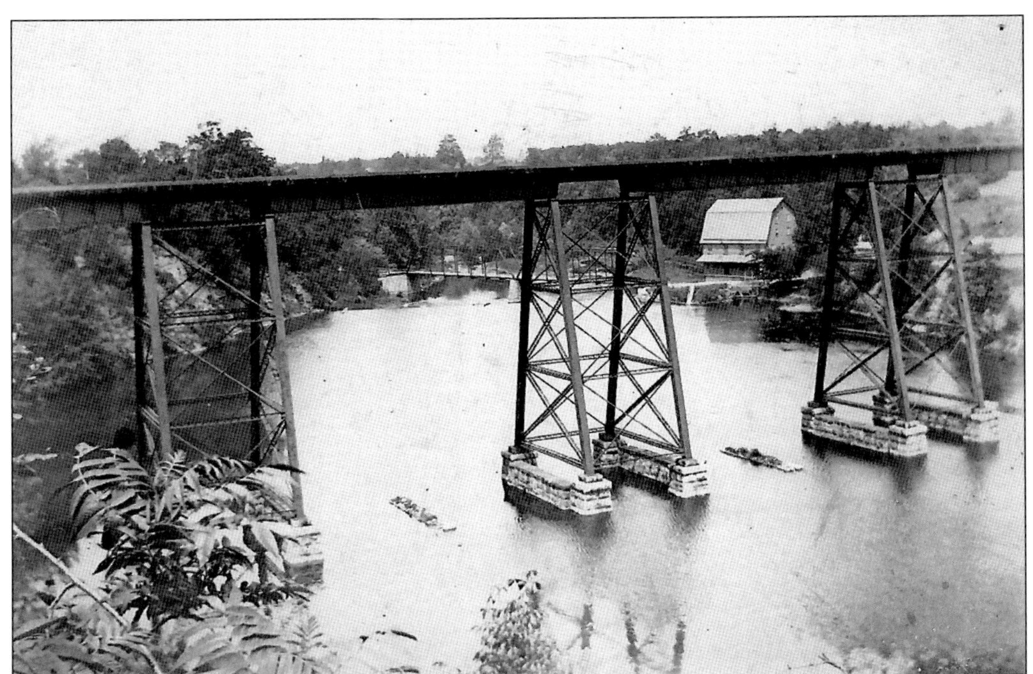

View of Clark's Mills. This beautiful view of the trestle and millpond shows Clark's Mills in the background. The mill, run by Woods and Lum, first milled Purity Flour. (Courtesy of Orleans County Department of History.)

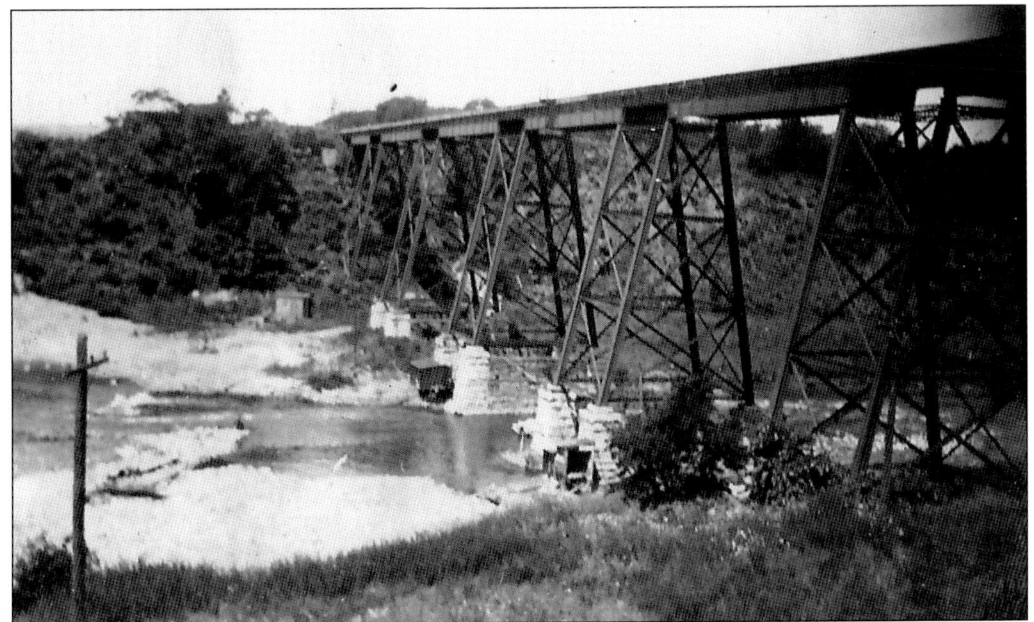

The Completed Trestle. This is an excellent view of the second Waterport trestle. Very solid when first completed, it carried trains of the Hojack Line from 1892 through 1978. (Courtesy of Jessica Matson.)

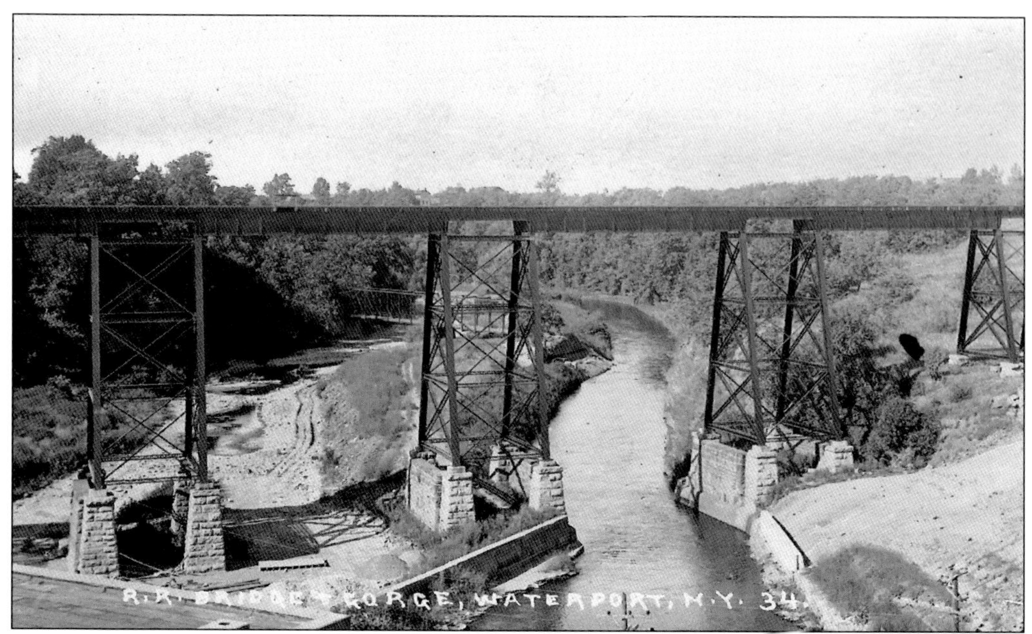

A TRANQUIL SCENE. The new trestle sits on a firm foundation, and by looking at the photograph, one would not know work was still being done. Behind the left base of the trestle's legs can be seen the double bridge leading to Clark's Mills. (Courtesy of Orleans County Department of History.)

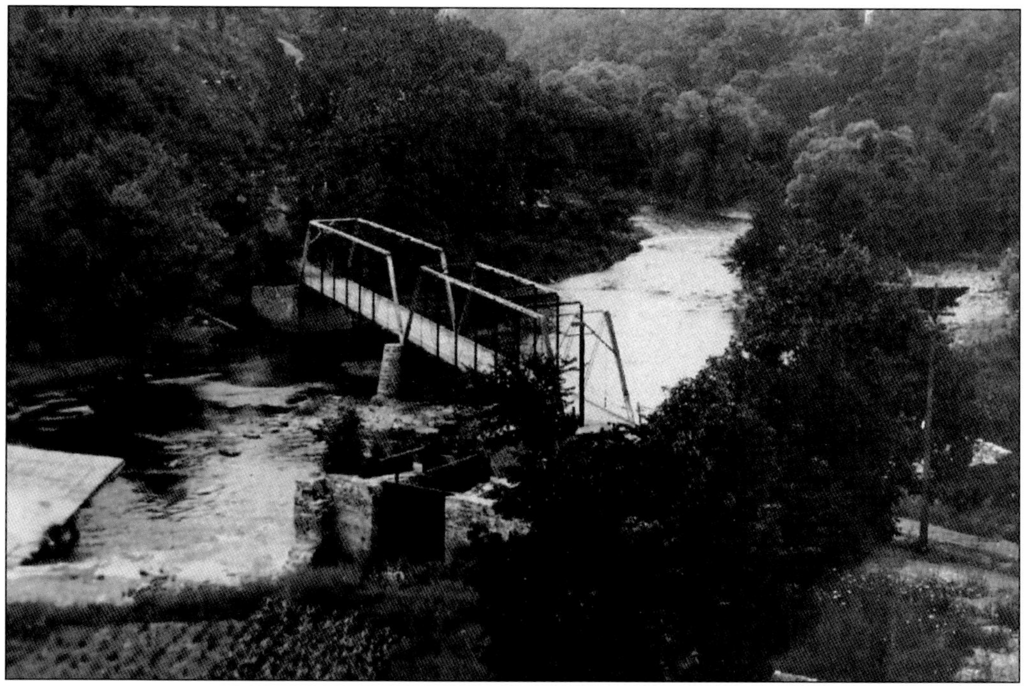

DOUBLE BRIDGE. This is a close-up view of the double bridge leading to Clark's Mills. In 1900, heavy rains caused the raceway to be washed away, which may be the reason the bridge in the top photograph appears to be going nowhere. (Courtesy of Mike and Chris Elam.)

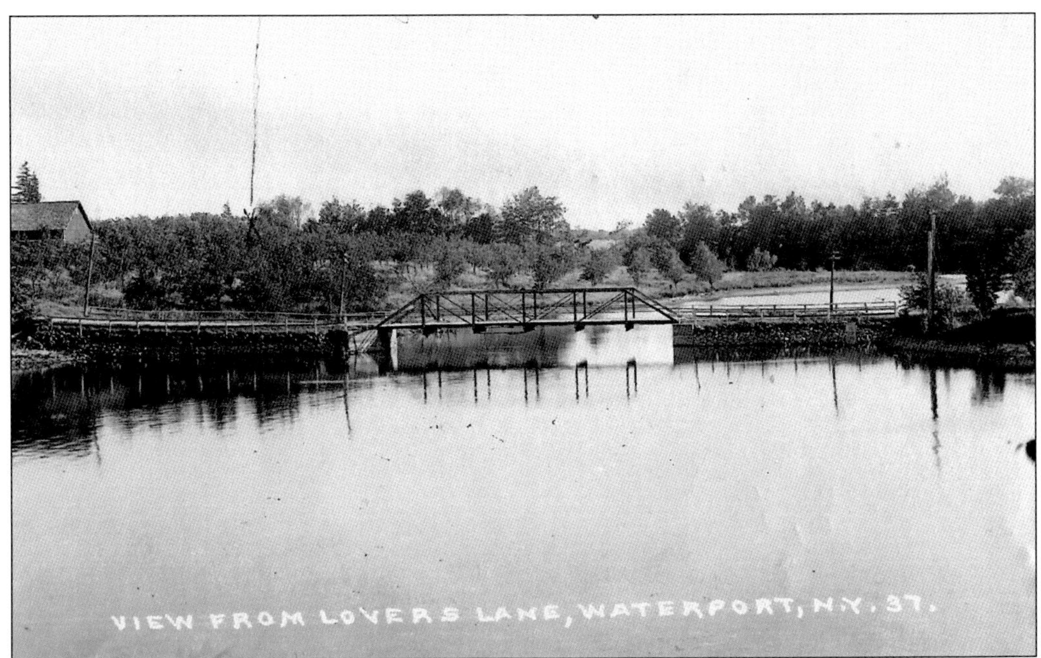

VIEW FROM LOVERS LANE. This is a tranquil scene of the bridge at Waterport that crossed Otter Creek. (Courtesy of Garland Miller.)

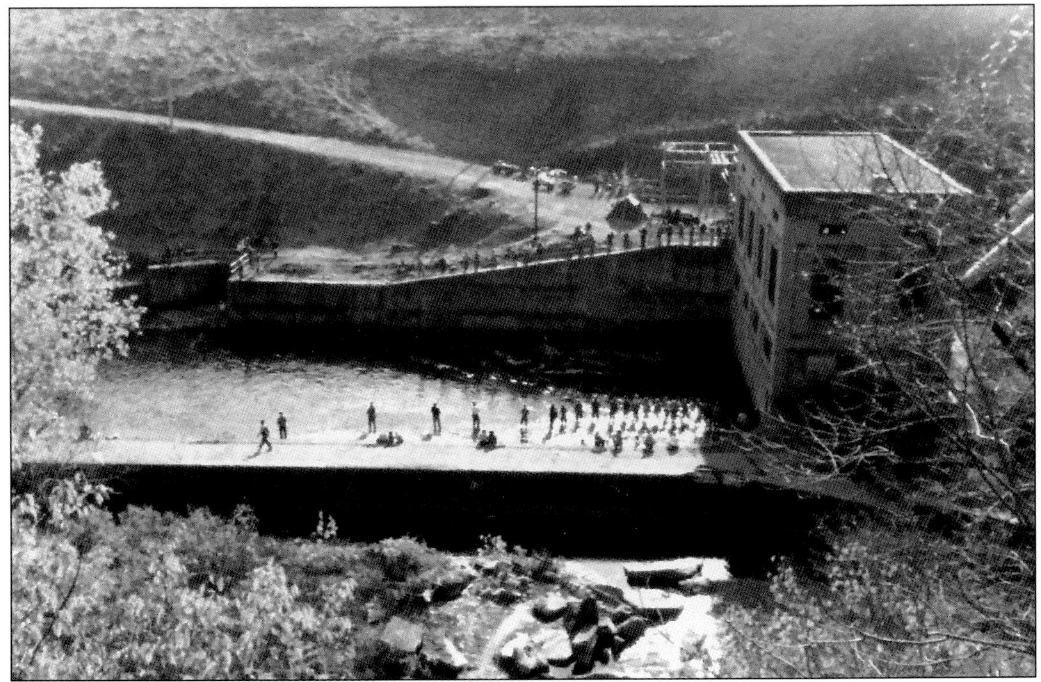

THE DAM TODAY. Fly fishermen enjoy the area immediately below the powerhouse today. Anglers travel great distances to try their luck at this spot, sometimes crowding it elbow to elbow. Salmon, brown trout, bass, and many more fish are found here. (Courtesy of Ashley Ward.)

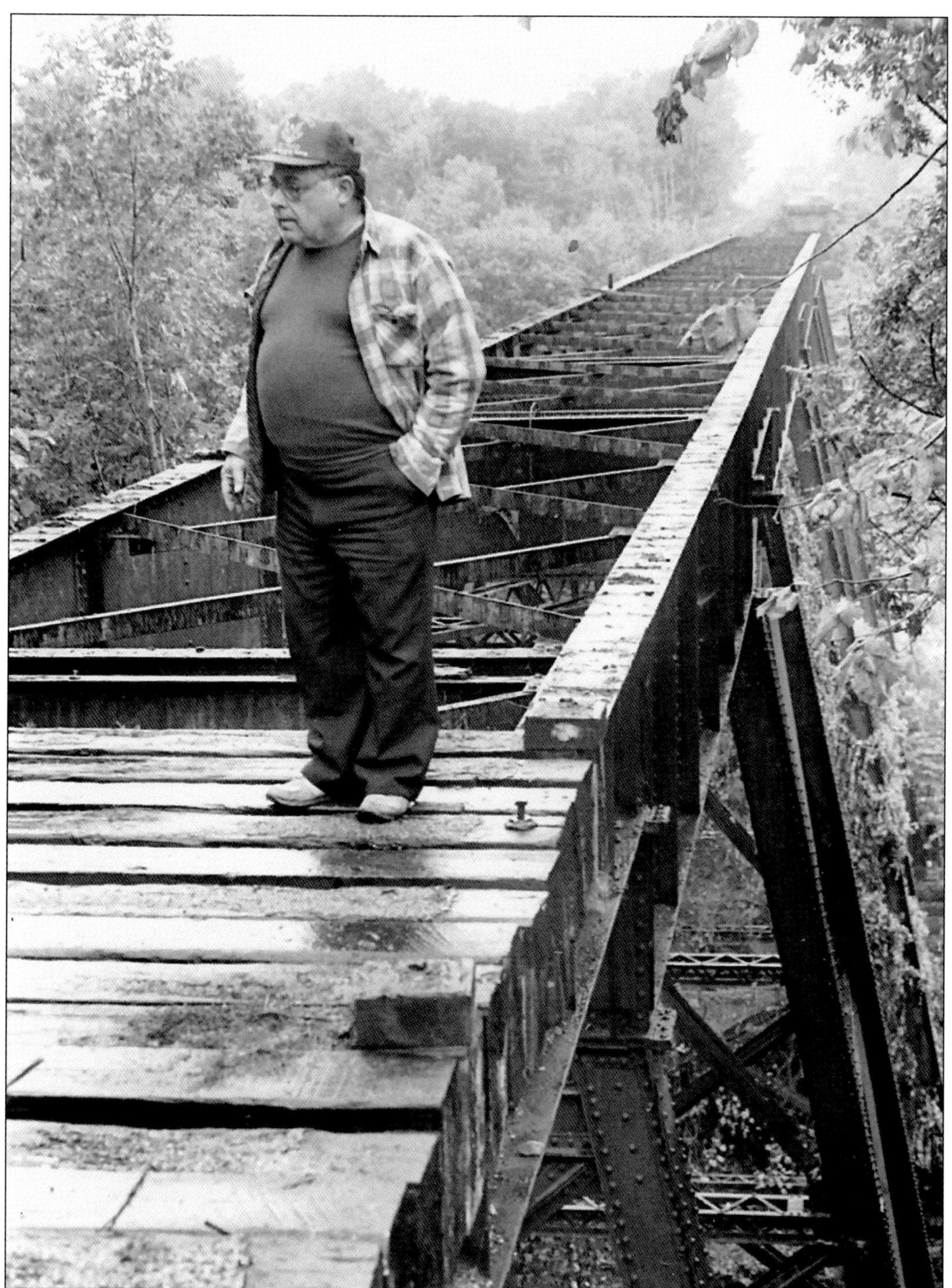

The Trestle Comes Down. Charles Pelleschi hired a Pennsylvania construction company to remove the 103-year-old structure. Pelleschi bought the land because he enjoyed fishing there on his many trips to Waterport. He had no use for the steel bridge on his newly acquired property so was also to sell its pieces for salvage. Contractor Jack Weakland, pictured here, was one of the last people to cross the trestle. (Courtesy of Douglas Miller.)

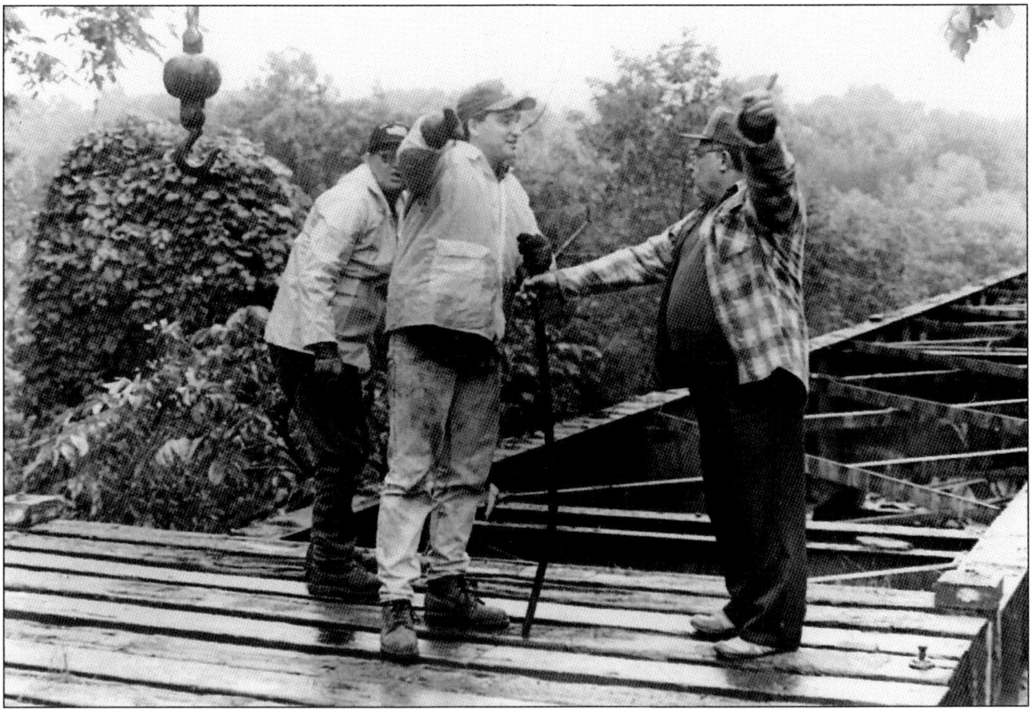

REMOVING THE TIES. The heavy ties were "hooked," hauled, and loaded for removal. A total of 400 of them were taken to Ricci Meadows Golf Course to be used for bridges and gardens on the 200-acre course. (Courtesy of Douglas Miller.)

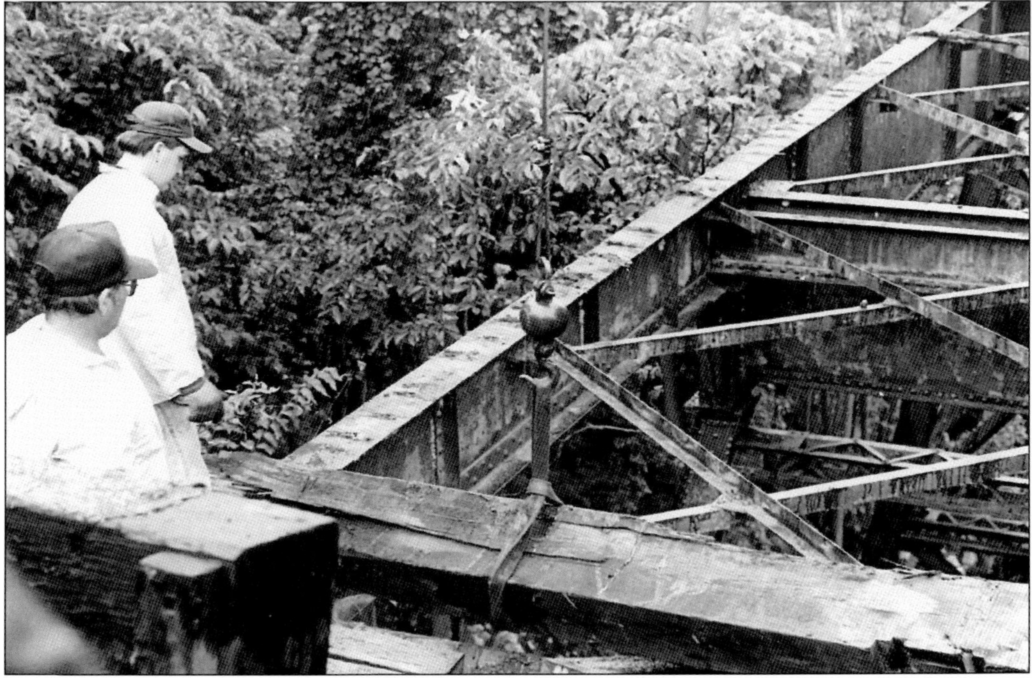

LIFTING A TIE. The strap is fastened around the railroad tie, and the hook lifts it up and off the metal framework of the trestle. (Courtesy of Douglas Miller.)

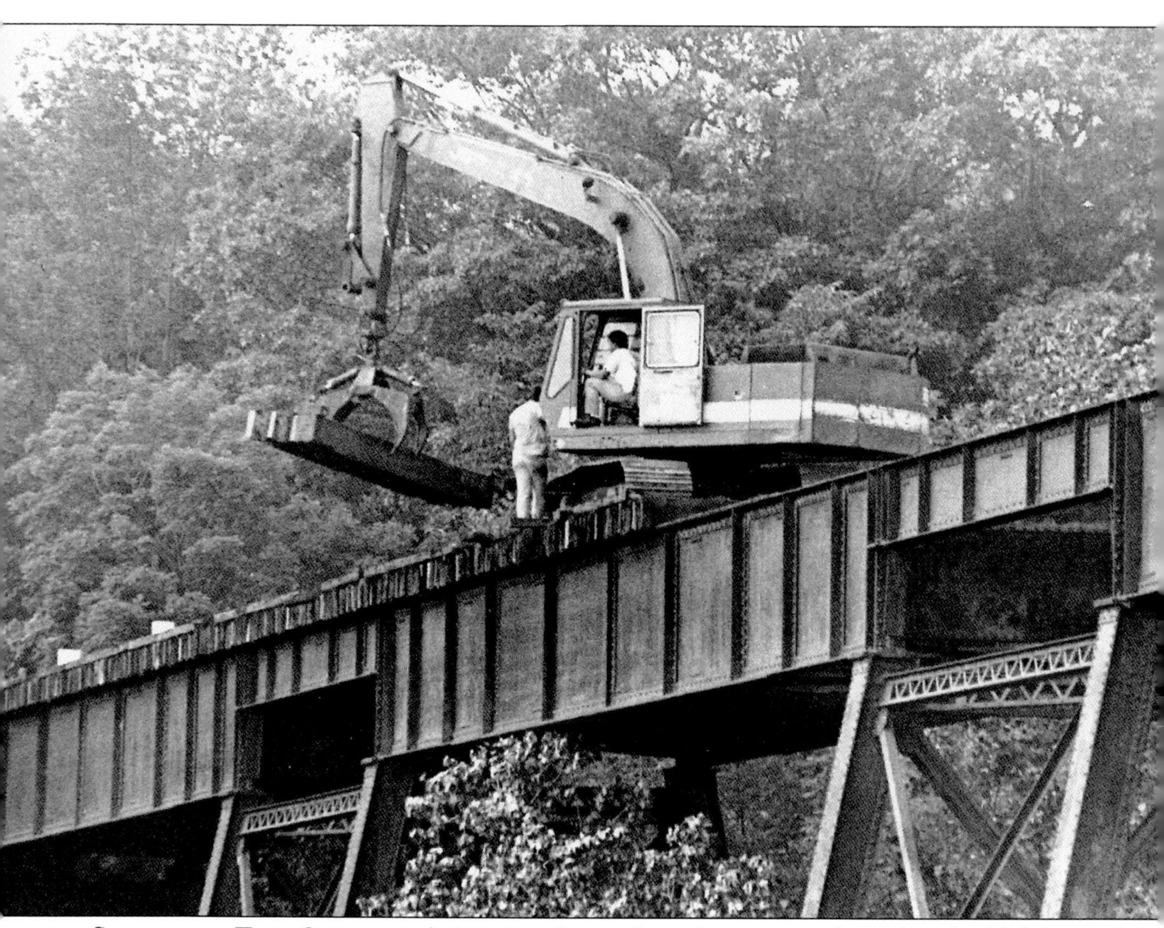

SAVING THE TIES. One can only imagine the perils workmen went through to build this great structure when one witnesses the nerves of steel necessary to harvest the salvage materials and take it down. The crane operators and other men must have had great confidence in each other. (Courtesy of Douglas Miller.)

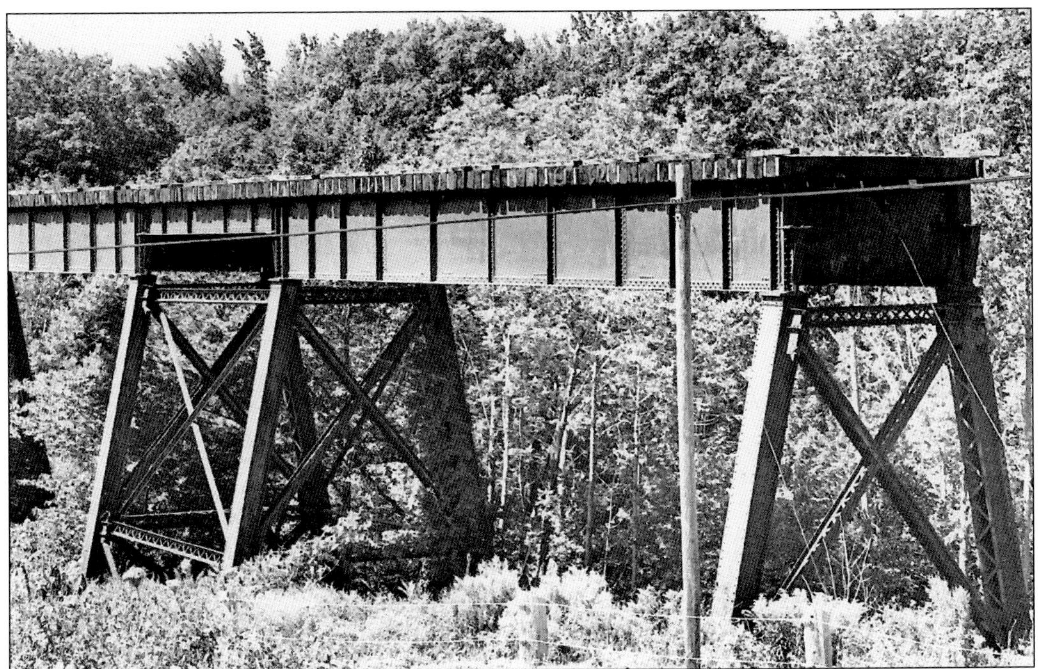

THE FINAL LENGTH. The trestle is all but gone in this photograph, with just a short section remaining to be taken down. (Courtesy of Douglas Miller.)

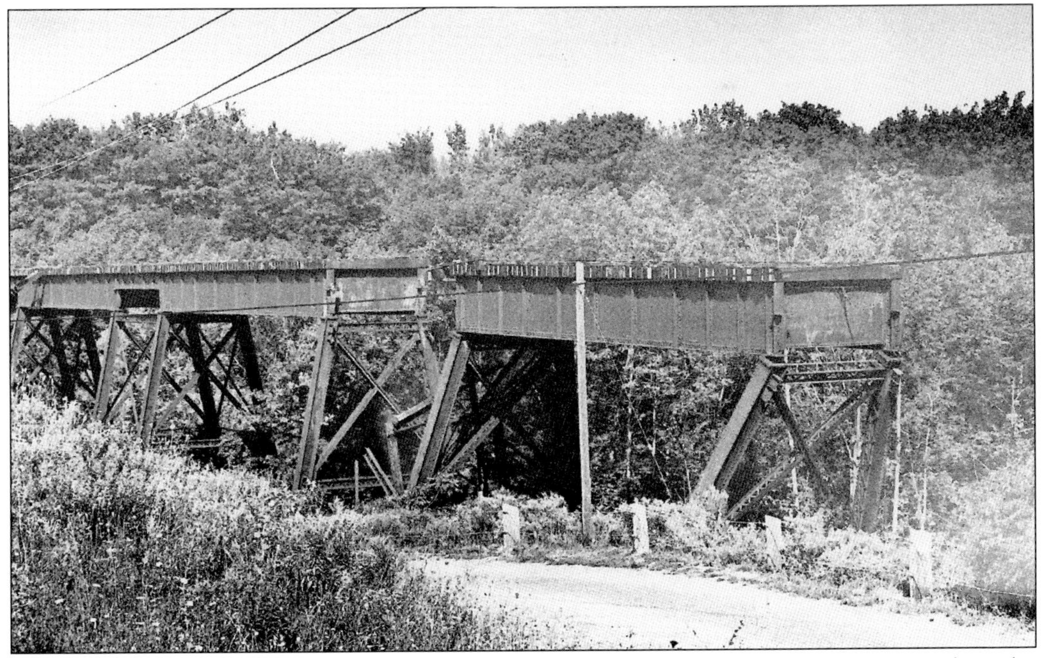

BUCKLING. The legs of the trestle begin to give way after the bolts have been loosened on the support structure above. (Courtesy of Douglas Miller.)

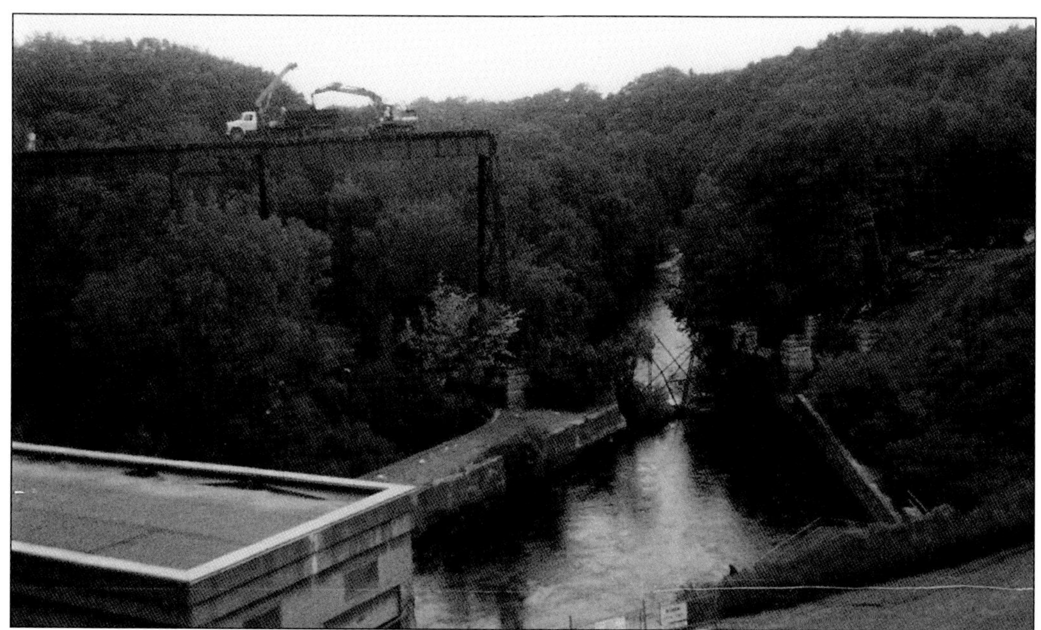

Half Gone. The trestle is halfway gone, as the crane sits precariously atop the structure, slowly dismantling it from middle to end. (Courtesy of Douglas Miller.).

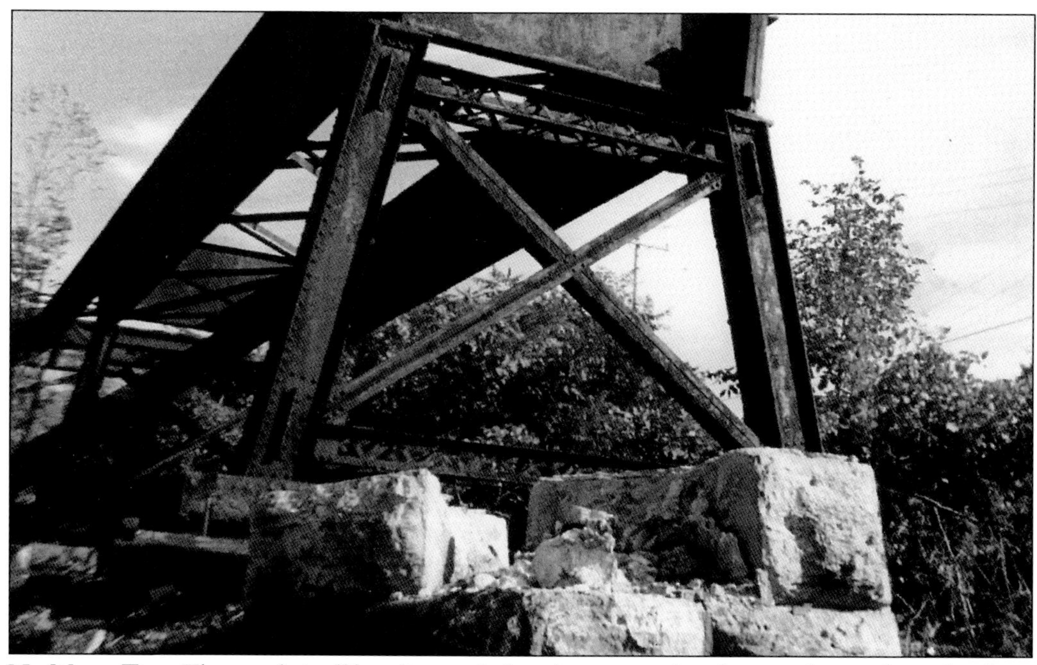

No More Ties. The trestle is all but dismantled in this view, taken from underneath on the short side of the structure. There is a geodetic benchmark located somewhere on the east abutment of the trestle. A benchmark is a very important point of reference for surveyors. There are only a few of them located around the county. (Courtesy of Douglas Miller.)

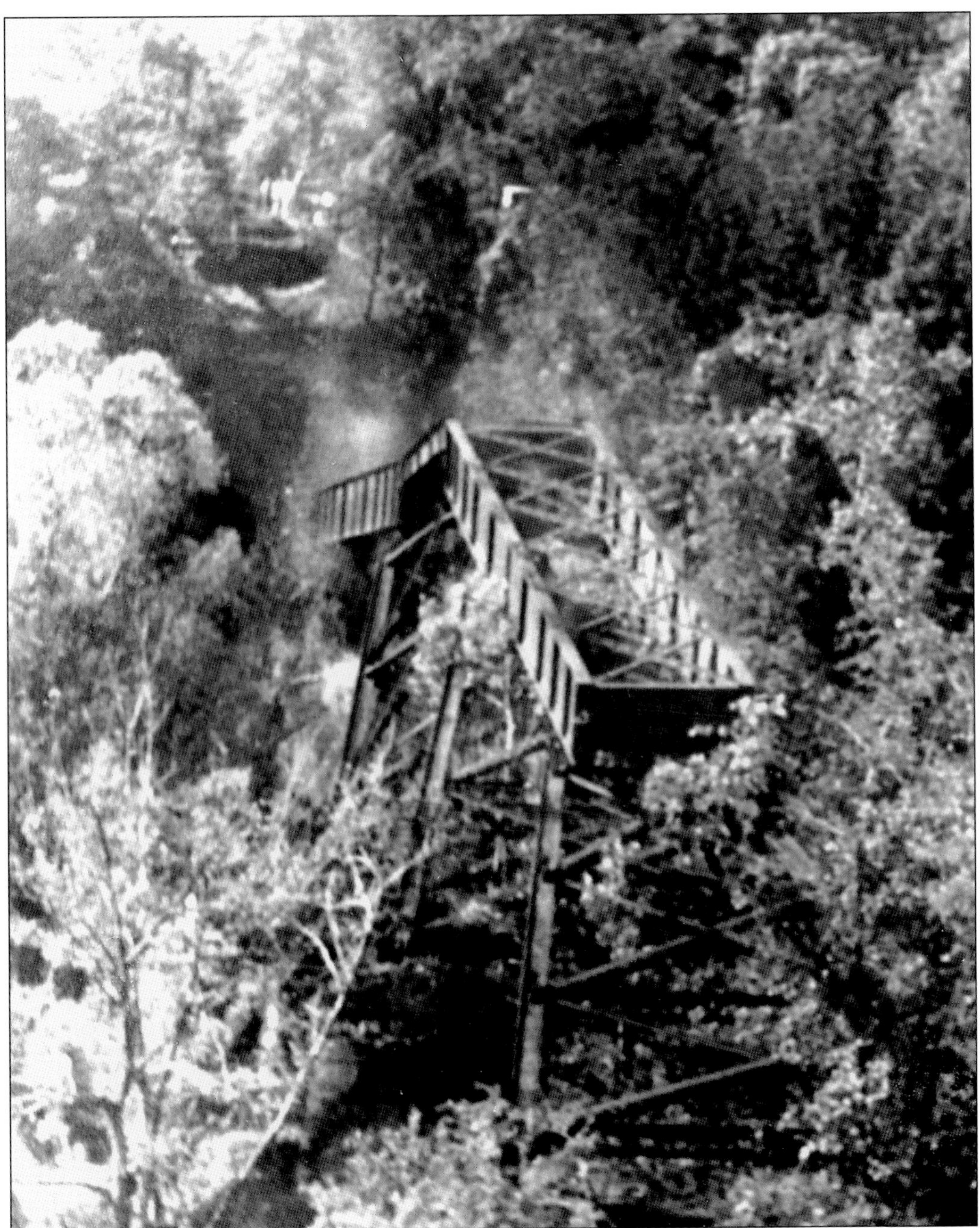

The Trestle Collapses. The final remnants of the trestle collapse and fall to the ground below, waiting for workers and equipment to come and take them away. The legendary Waterport trestle is now just a memory. No more will parents worry about their children playing on top of the dangerous structure, and no more will daredevils ride bicycles and motorcycles over the rotting boards. (Courtesy of Douglas Miller.)

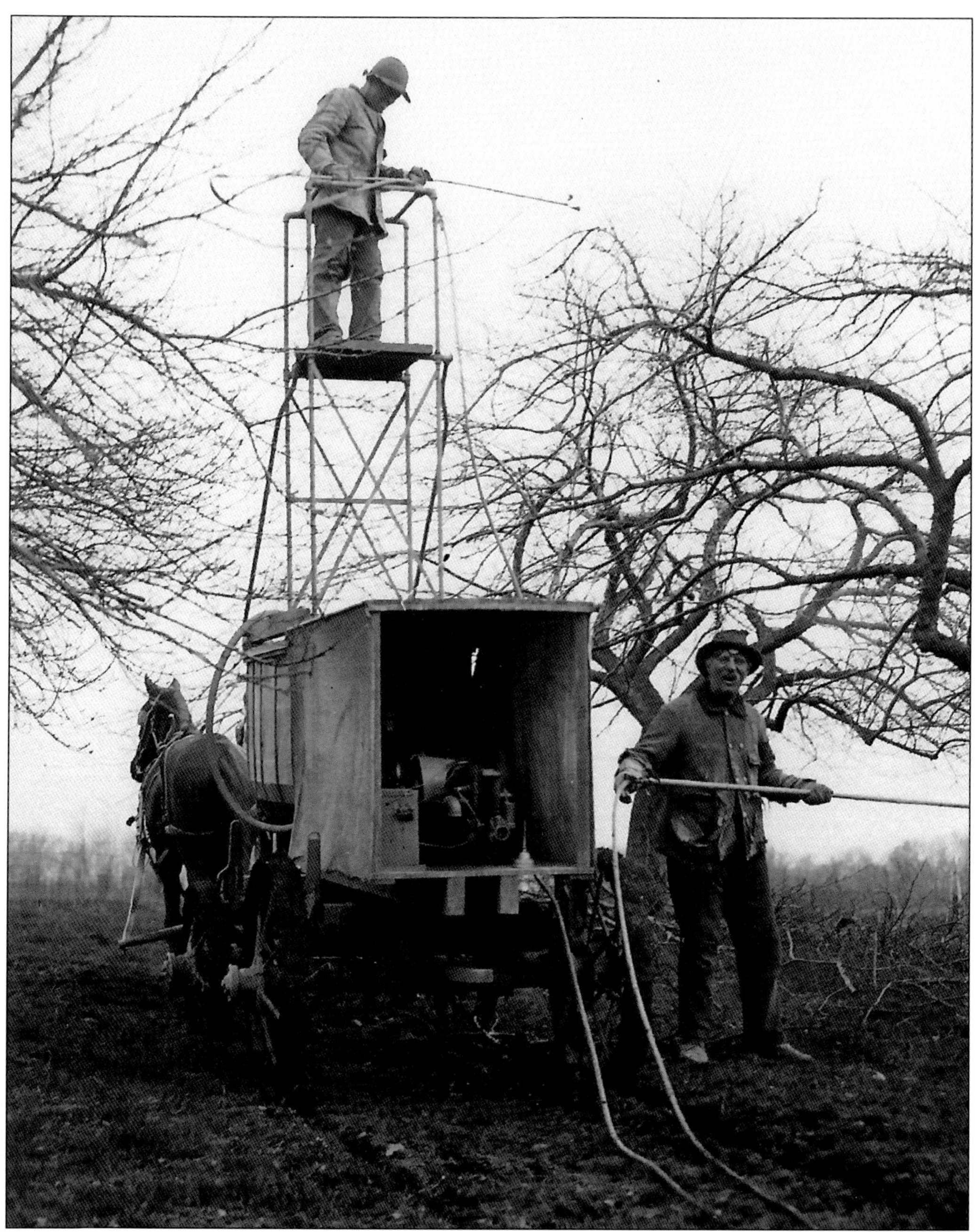

Spray Rig, c. the 1920s. Unidentified workers spray fruit at Meadow Brook Farm in Carlton. The farmers on the left seem confident in their equipment and their horses' temperament. (Courtesy of Pauline Kast Broadwell.)

Four

FARMING-SUSTAINED FAMILIES

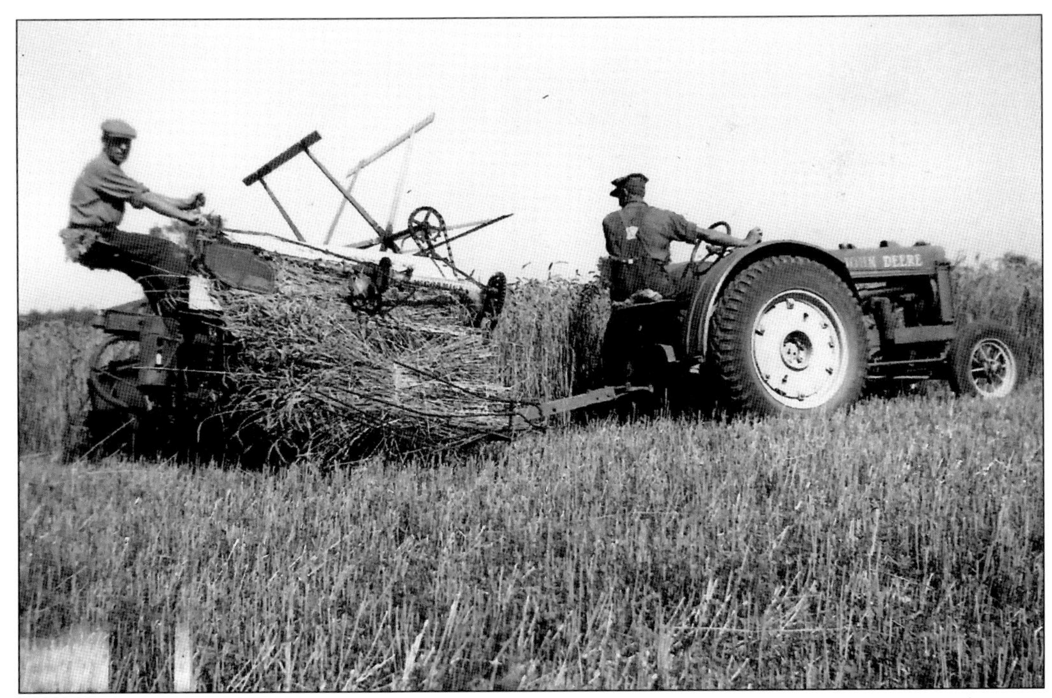

WHEAT HARVEST. Leon Curtis (left) and Gerald Miller are operating a "self-binder" to harvest their wheat. (Courtesy of Garland Miller.)

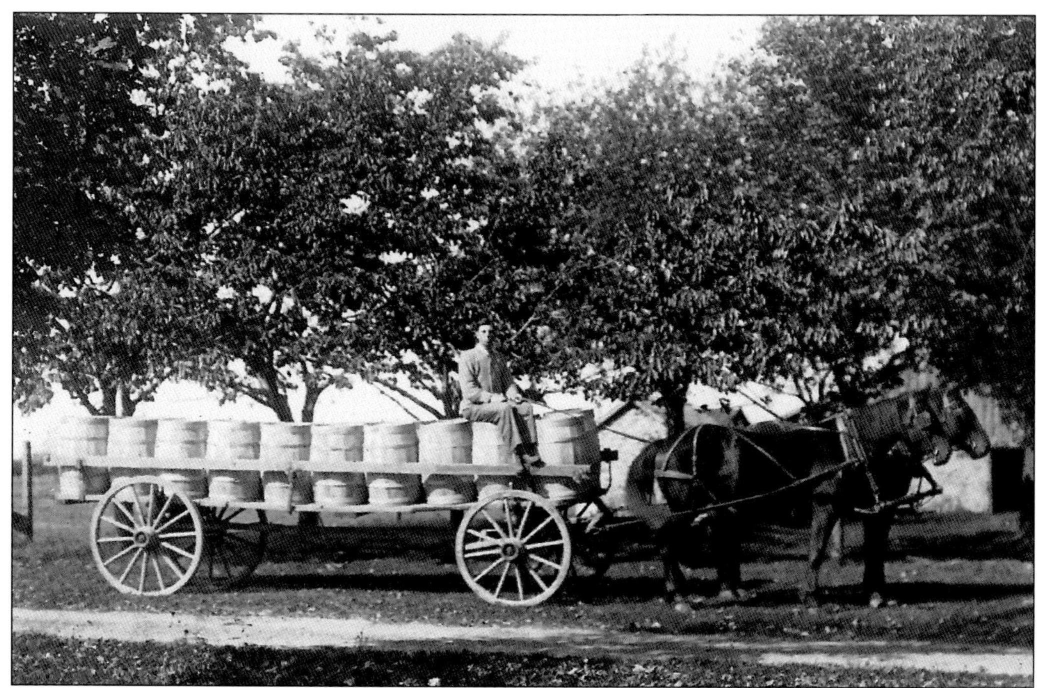

BARRELS TO MARKET. Using horse-drawn wagons for deliveries, many area farmers shipped via the railroad to places as far away as England. In earlier times, they shipped produce via lake schooners to Canada. Here Glen Broadwell appears proud to pose in 1927. (Courtesy of Pauline Kast Broadwell.)

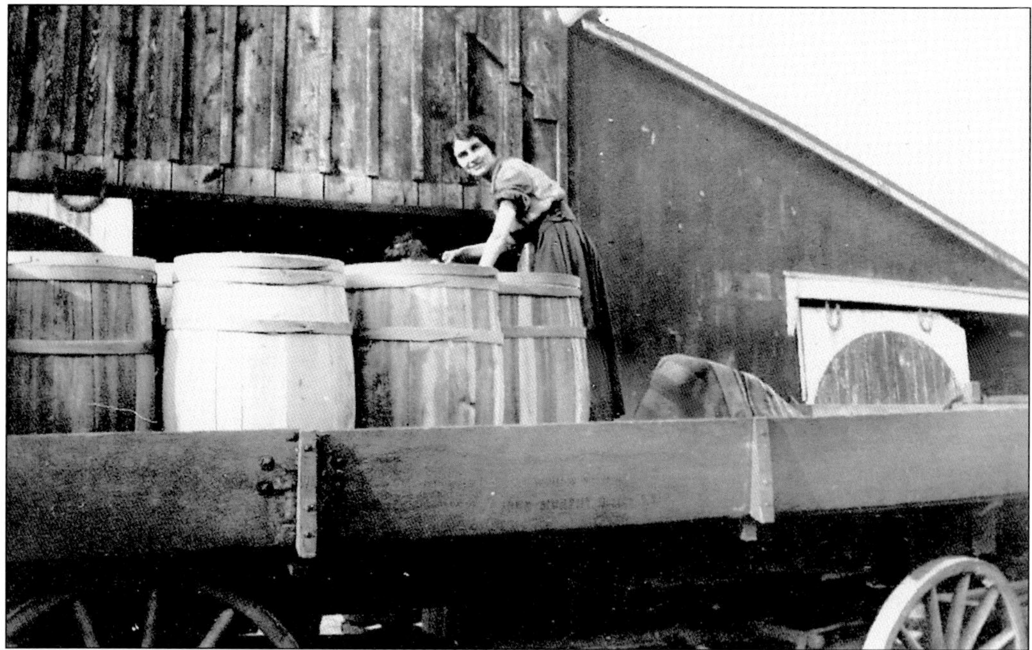

APPLE PACKING TIME. This unidentified worker helps pack apples. Women often worked on the farm and then in the house as well. Perhaps farm life was the origin of the expression "A woman's work is never done." (Courtesy of Pauline Kast Broadwell.)

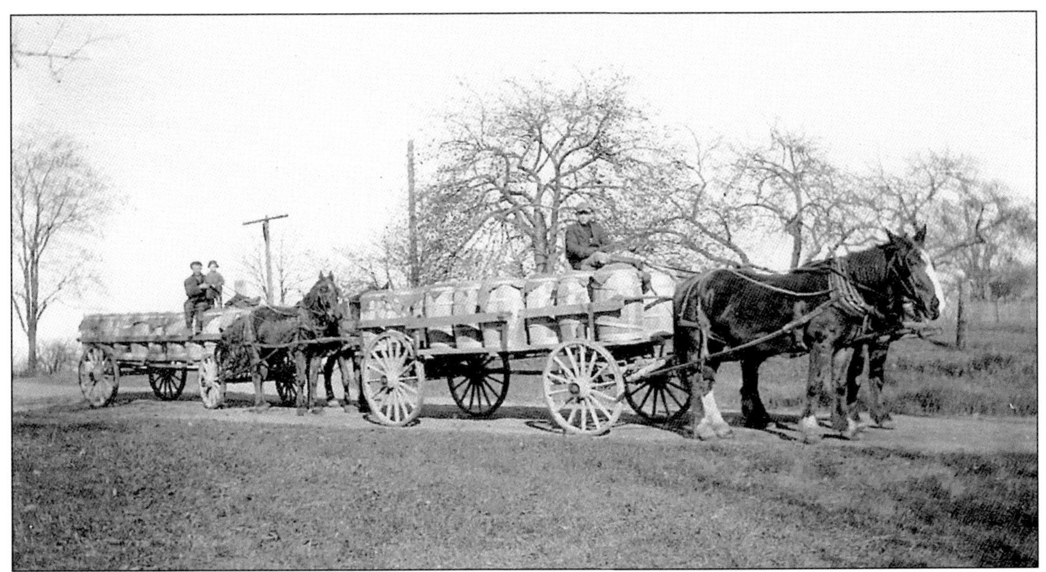

APPLES TO MARKET. The Broadwell teams were likely headed to the Hojack Line to ship these barrels of apples to places far away. (Courtesy of Pauline Kast Broadwell.)

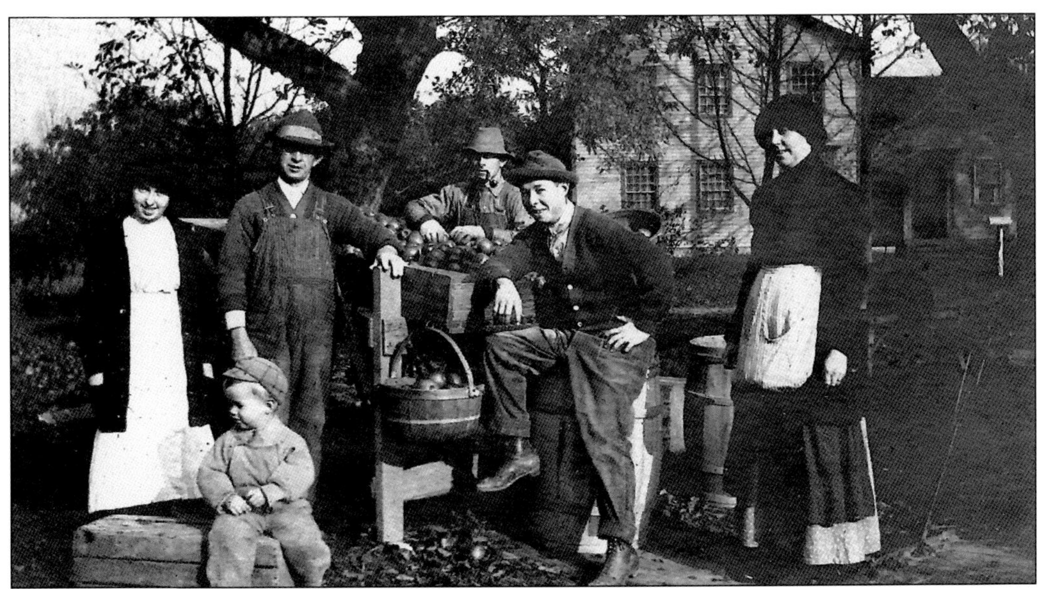

HARVEST FAMILY. Hundreds of apples were sorted before barrels were filled for shipment. Note the important role the village cooper filled. (Courtesy of Jessica Matson.)

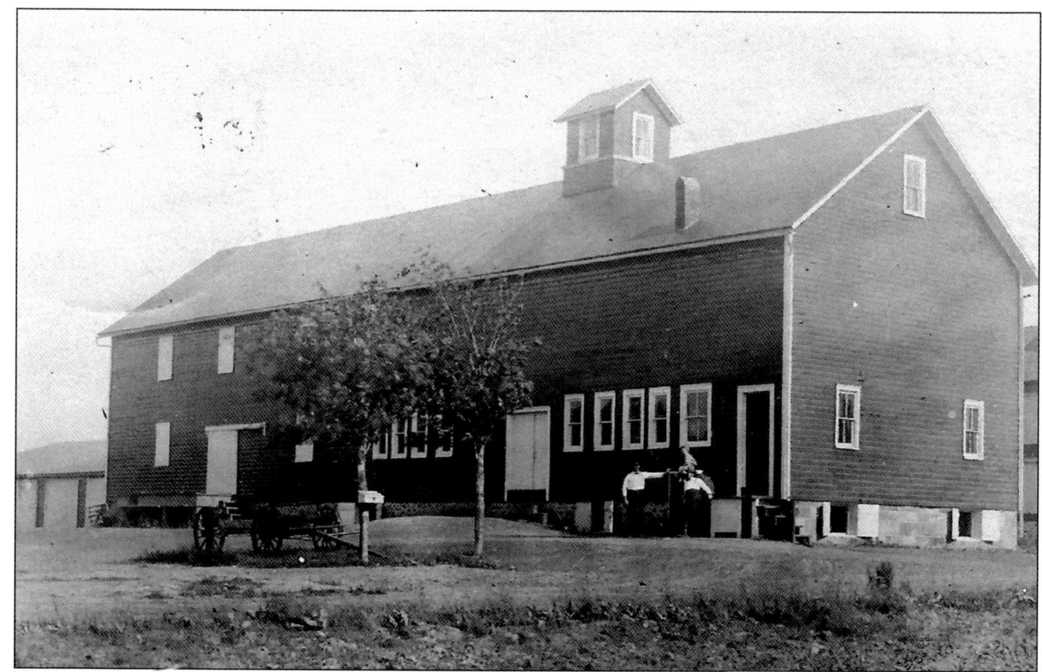

Harris Warehouse. It was November 7, 1906, and a lovely fall day in Carlton. The apples were harvested, and many folks prepared for winter. (Courtesy of Orleans County Department of History.)

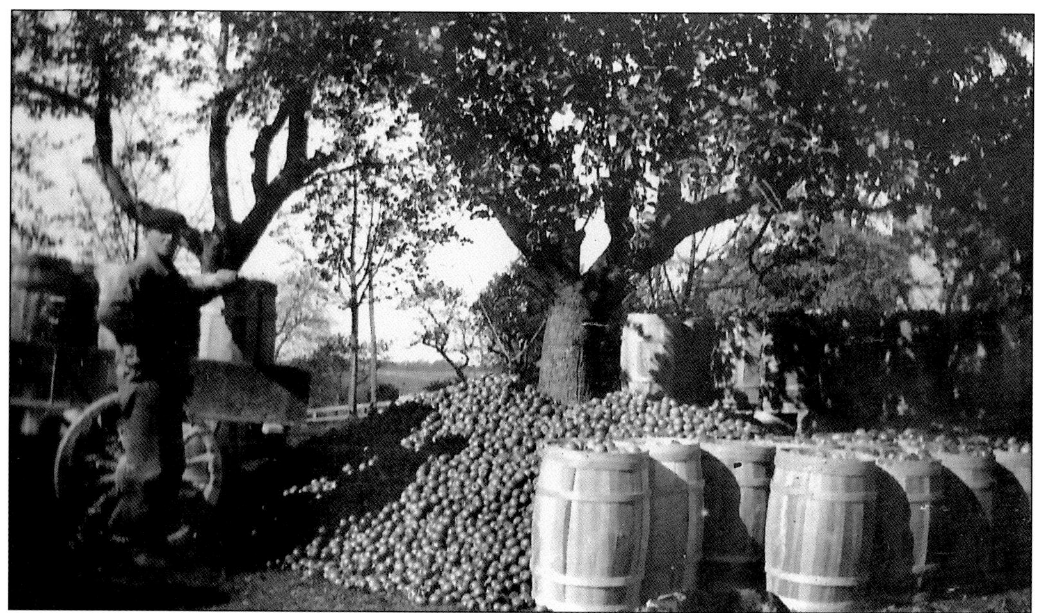

Apples Galore. A farmhand stands beside the tractor overlooking hundreds of apples below the tree at the Matson Farm around 1920. (Courtesy of Jessica Matson.)

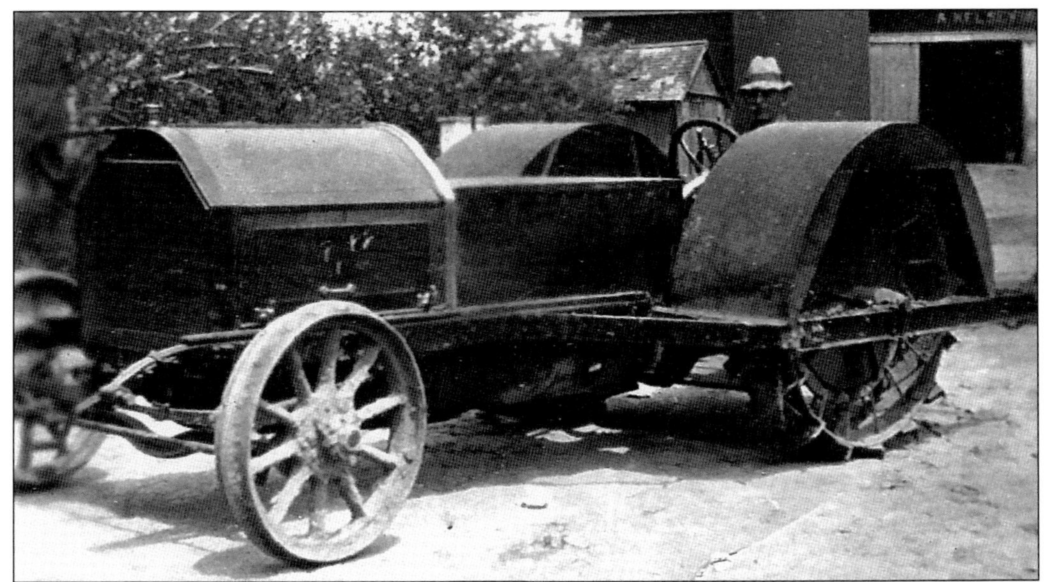

GRANDPA ON THE TRACTOR. Robert Kelsey poses on his iron machine around 1915. (Courtesy of David Kelsey.)

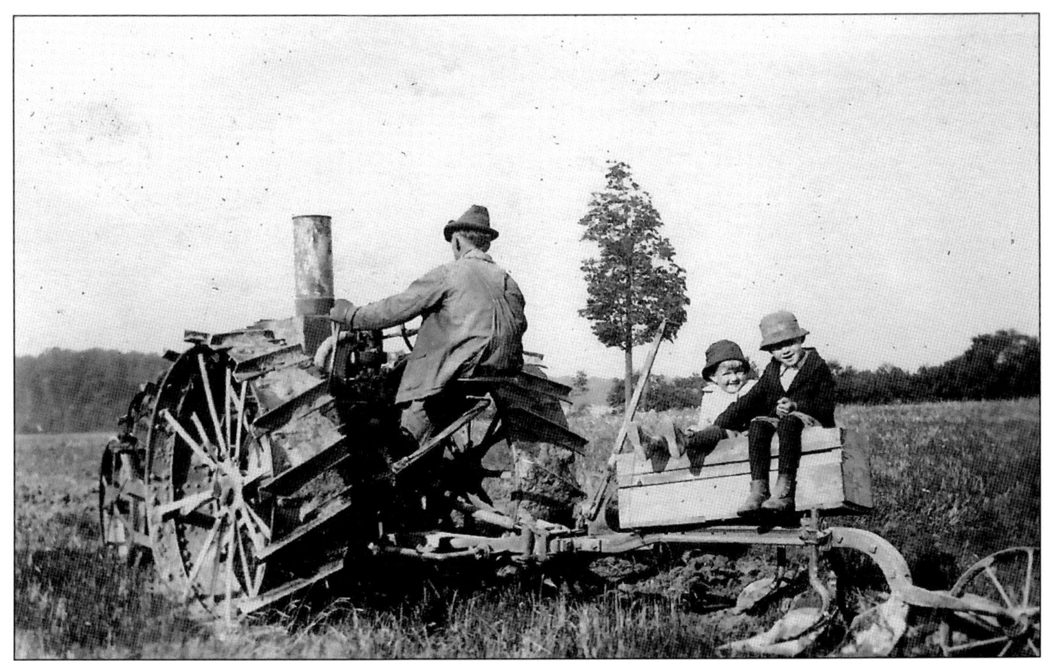

RIDING ALONG. Farm living often meant children accompanied a parent for the day on the farm. This is Herman Newton with his sons, Clair (left) and Donald. (Courtesy of Jessica Matson.)

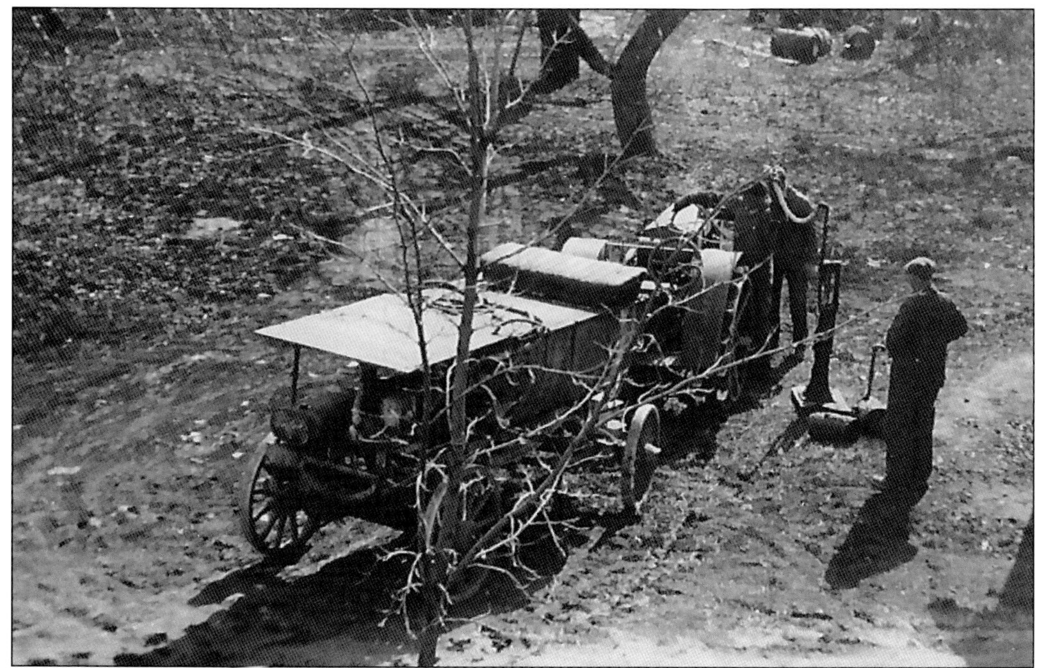

SPRAY RIG. This contraption was modern for its time, around 1910. (Courtesy of Pauline Kast Broadwell.)

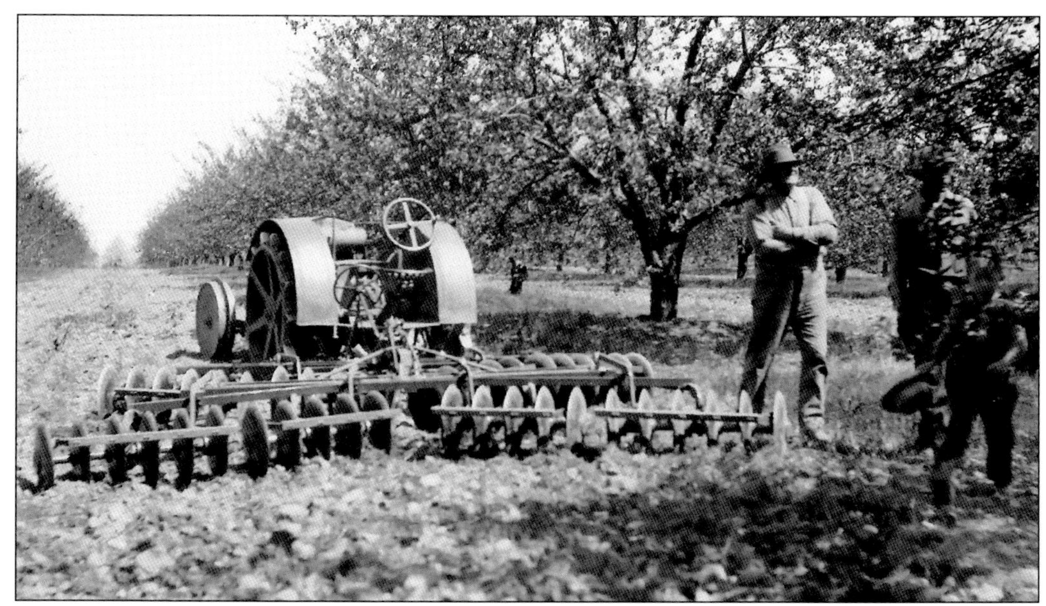

DISKING THE FIELDS. These unidentified workers enjoy an afternoon of farming in the sun around 1910. (Courtesy of Pauline Kast Broadwell.)

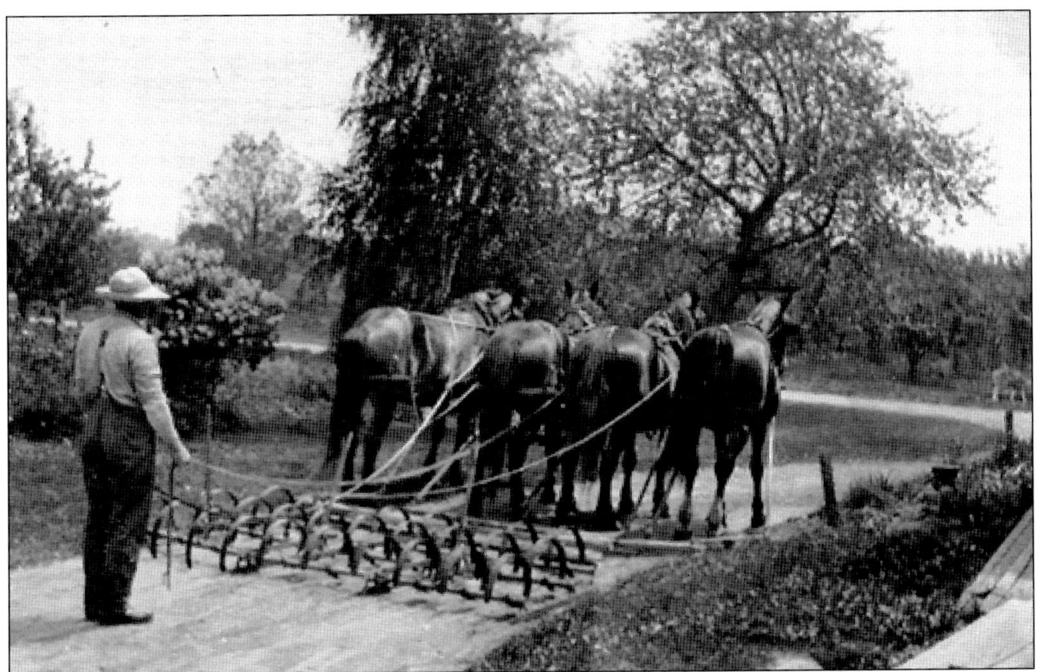

FOUR-HORSE DISK. One of the hired hands on the Broadwell Farm works a team of horses to disk up fields. Although farmers had tractors after 1910, some preferred horses until the 1950s. (Courtesy of Pauline Kast Broadwell.)

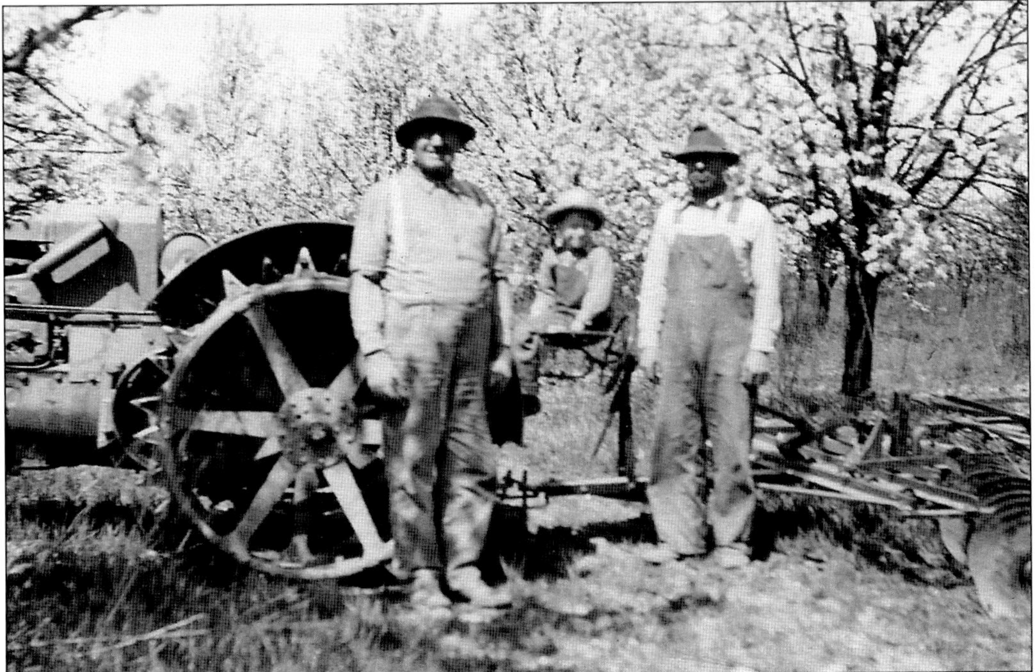

THE OLD TRACTOR. This tractor was a relic when this photograph was taken in 1930, but as long as tractors ran, farmers used them. From left to right are Frank, baby Franklin, and Glen Broadwell. (Courtesy of Pauline Kast Broadwell.)

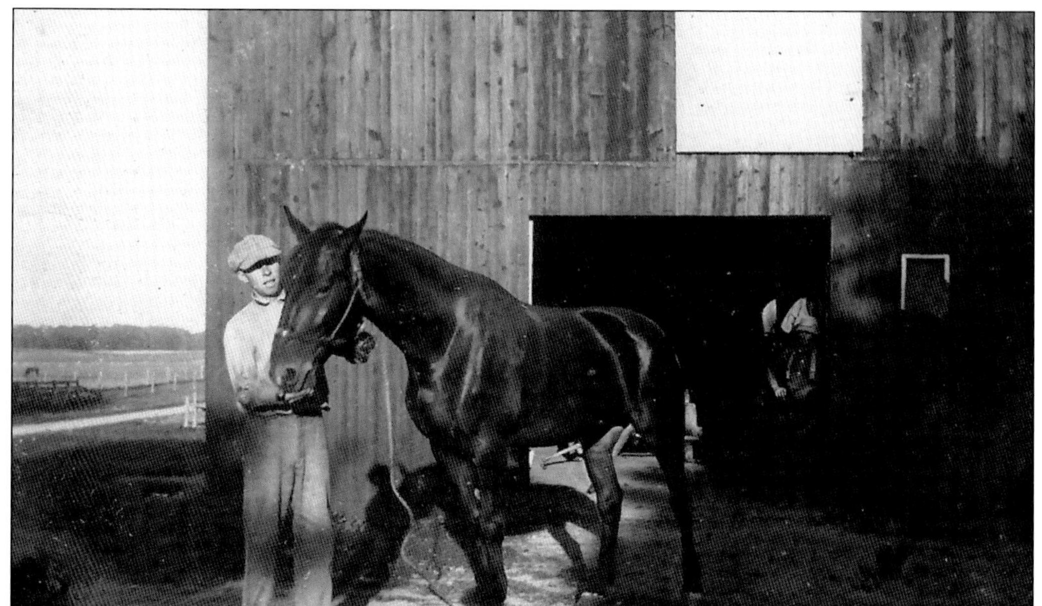

FINE EQUINE. A horse tender poses with a horse at a stable near Clark's Mills. Note the horse in the field to the left of the barn. Horses were treasured commodities long after the automobile, especially in the country. (Courtesy of Jessica Matson.)

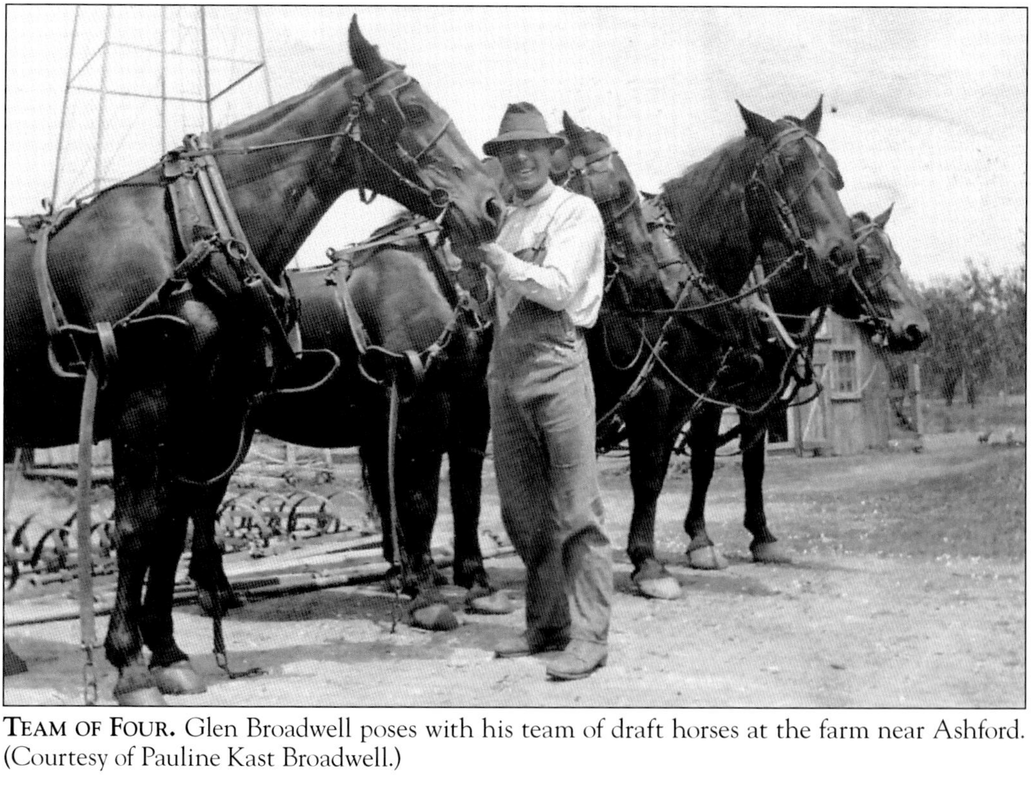

TEAM OF FOUR. Glen Broadwell poses with his team of draft horses at the farm near Ashford. (Courtesy of Pauline Kast Broadwell.)

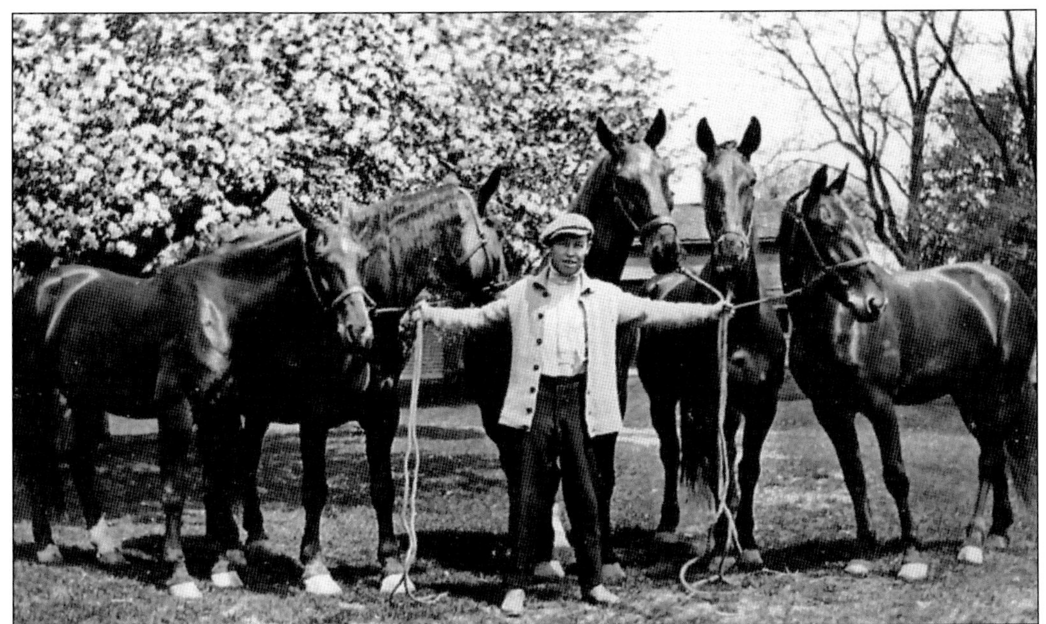

Holding the Reins. These are five impeccably groomed horses belonging to the Ives family, seen here around 1930. (Courtesy of Jessica Matson.)

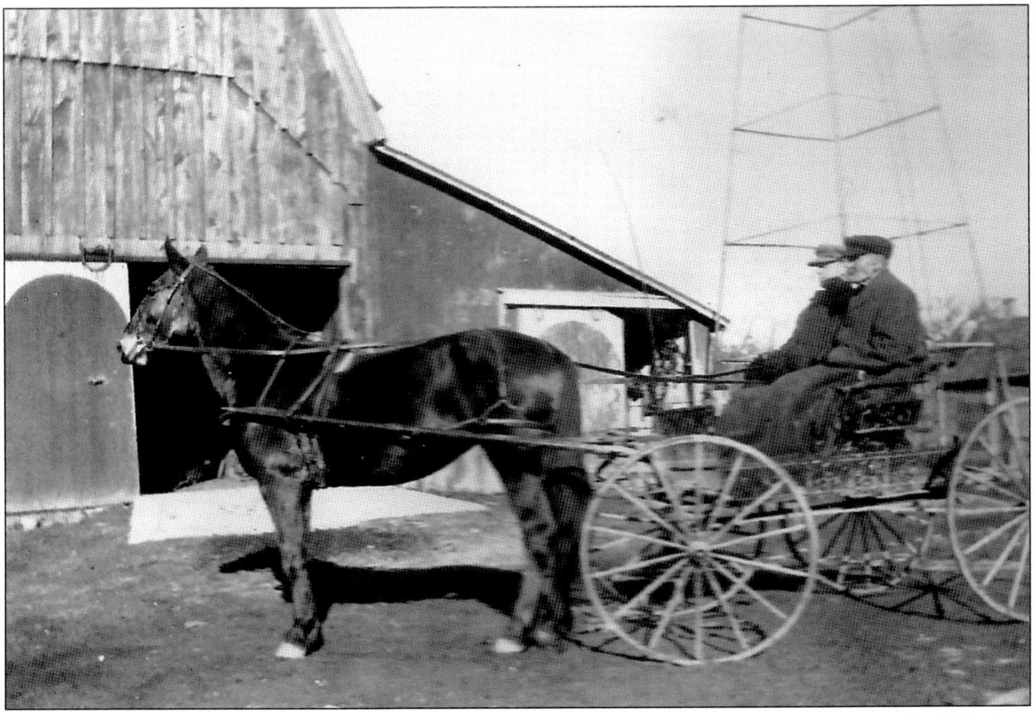

Going to Town. Frank and Glen Broadwell pose in front of the barn and windmill before leaving for town. (Courtesy of Pauline Kast Broadwell.)

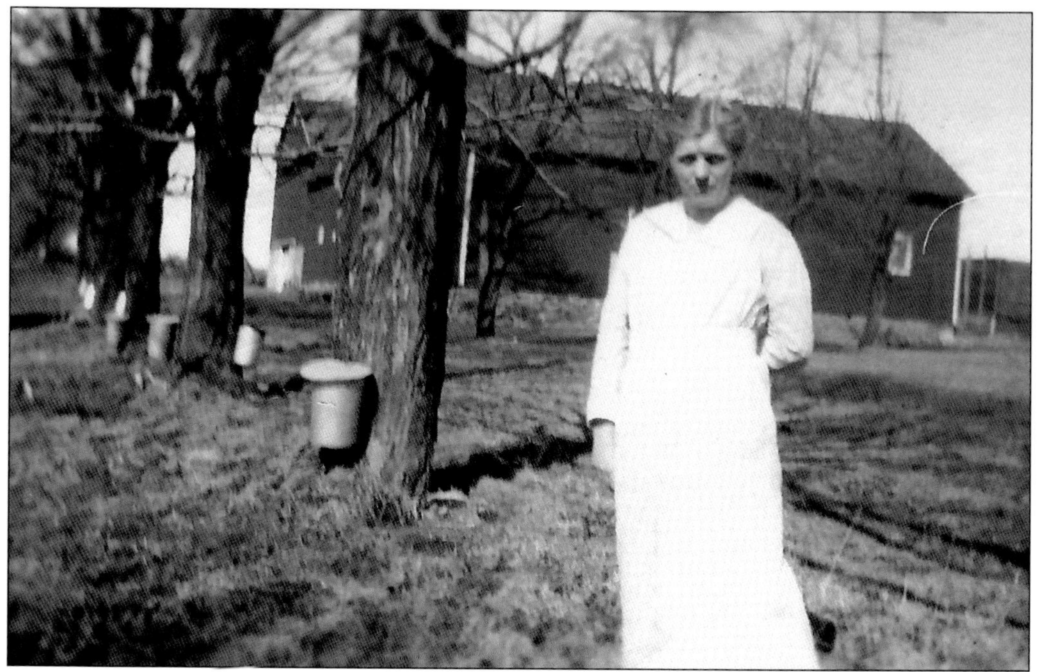

SAP BUCKETS. Grandma Rath tends her sap buckets that will fill with sap to be boiled down into delicious maple syrup and candies. Approximately 35 gallons of sap are needed to cook down into 1 gallon of syrup. (Courtesy of David Kelsey.)

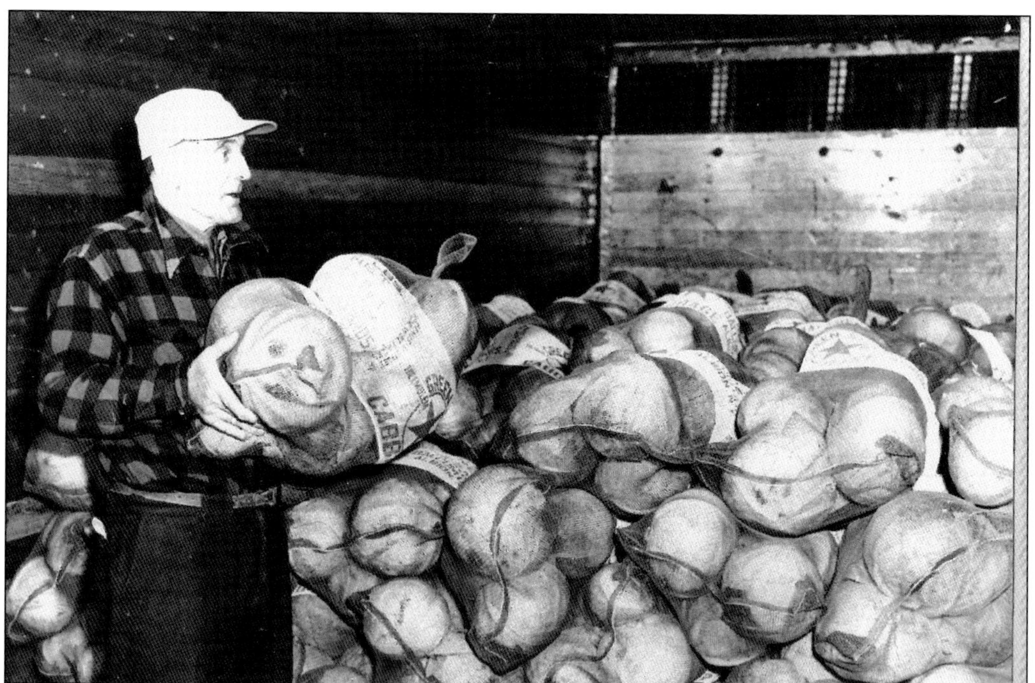

LOTS OF CABBAGE. These heads of cabbage are fine examples of the quality vegetables Carlton farmers produce. Considered a "cold crop," cabbage grows and stores well in this area. (Courtesy of David Kelsey.)

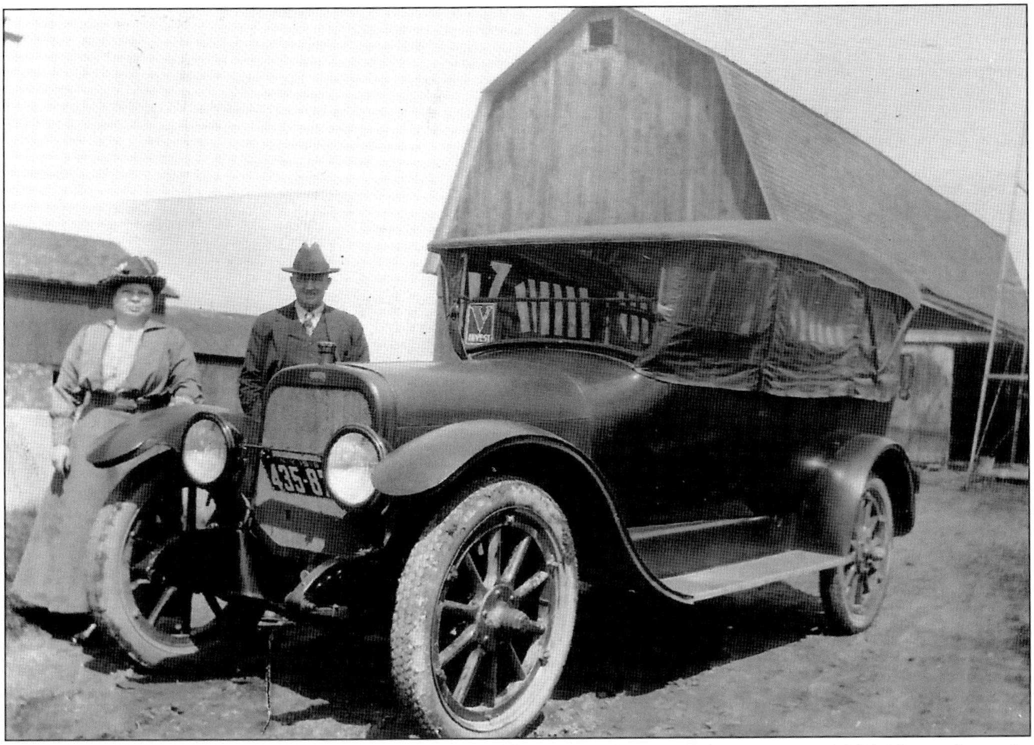

RIDING IN STYLE. Vinnie and Frank Broadwell pose in front of their car in 1919. Note the side curtains on the windows. This was a step up from a horse and carriage. (Courtesy of Pauline Kast Broadwell.)

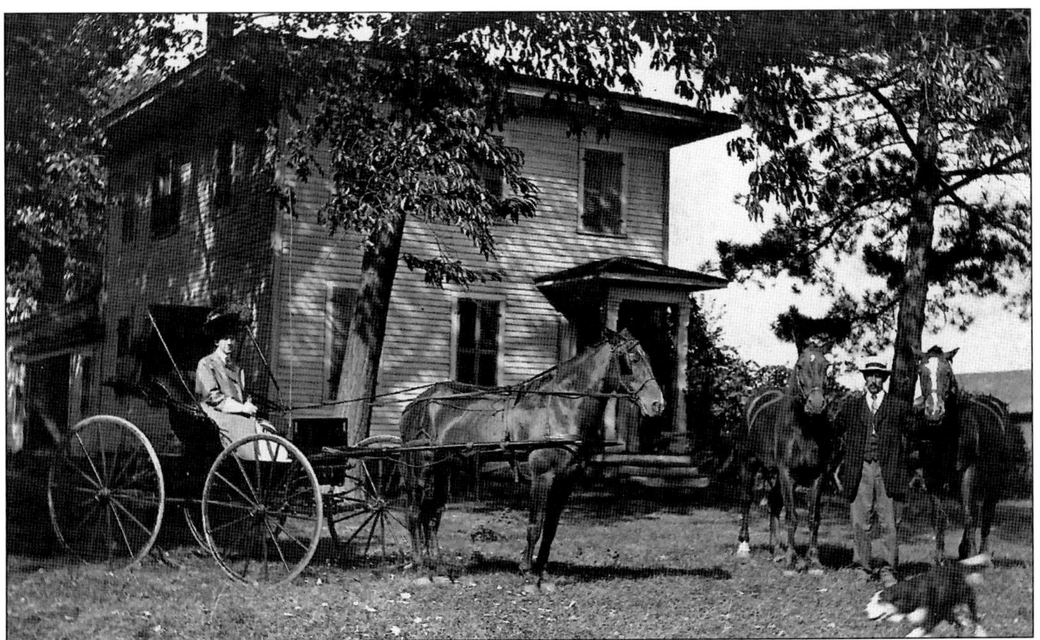

PREFERRING HORSES. This couple enjoys using their horses and riding in the carriage at their home near the Bridges around 1900. (Courtesy of Garland Miller.)

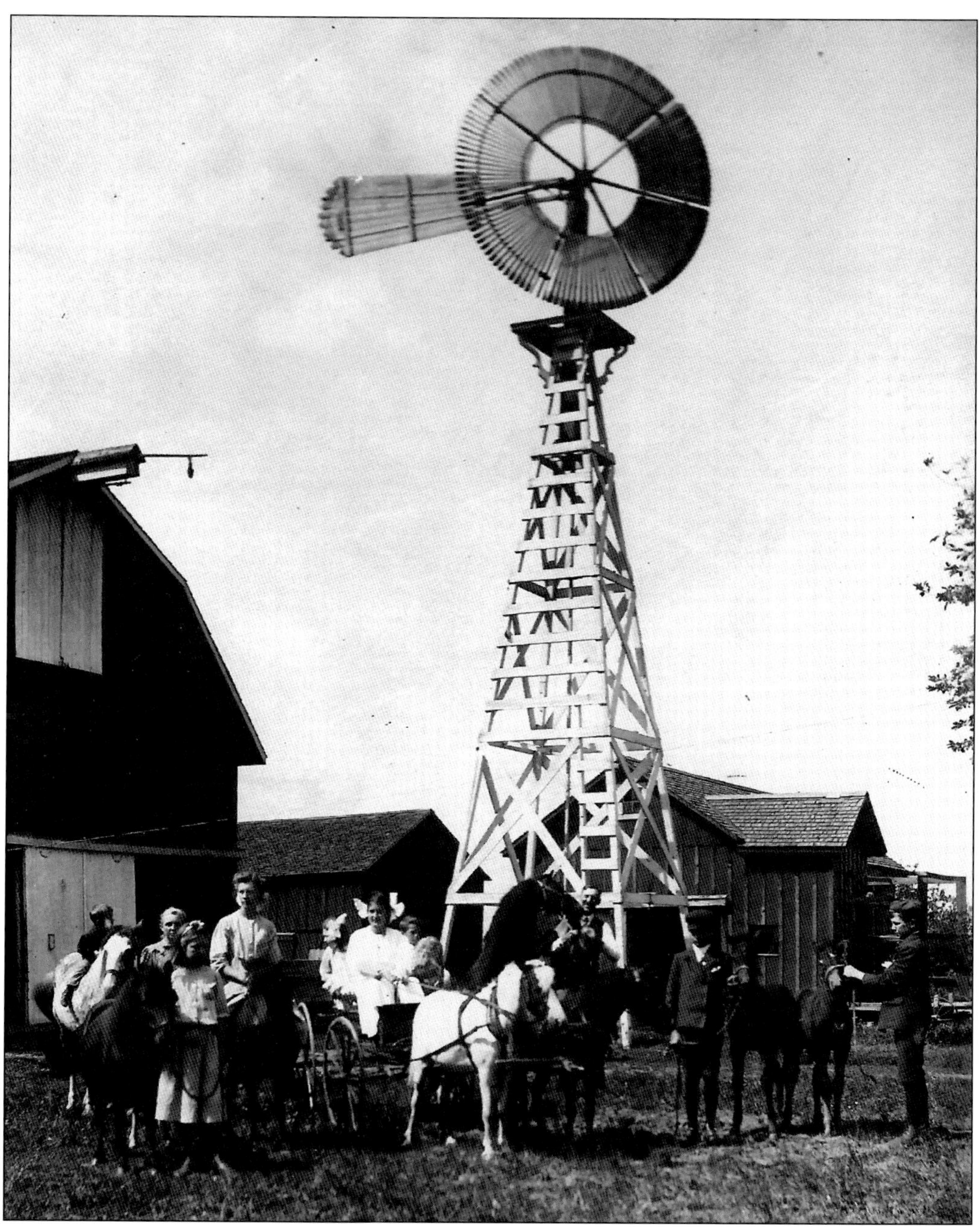

Family Fun. The Olin Miller family members pose with their ponies. Windmills were an important factor in power for water supply. Olin was nicknamed "Pony Miller" because he always had ponies. The farm is on Oak Orchard Road near the Carlton-Gaines town line. Garland Miller is seen second from the right in this photograph. (Courtesy of Garland Miller.)

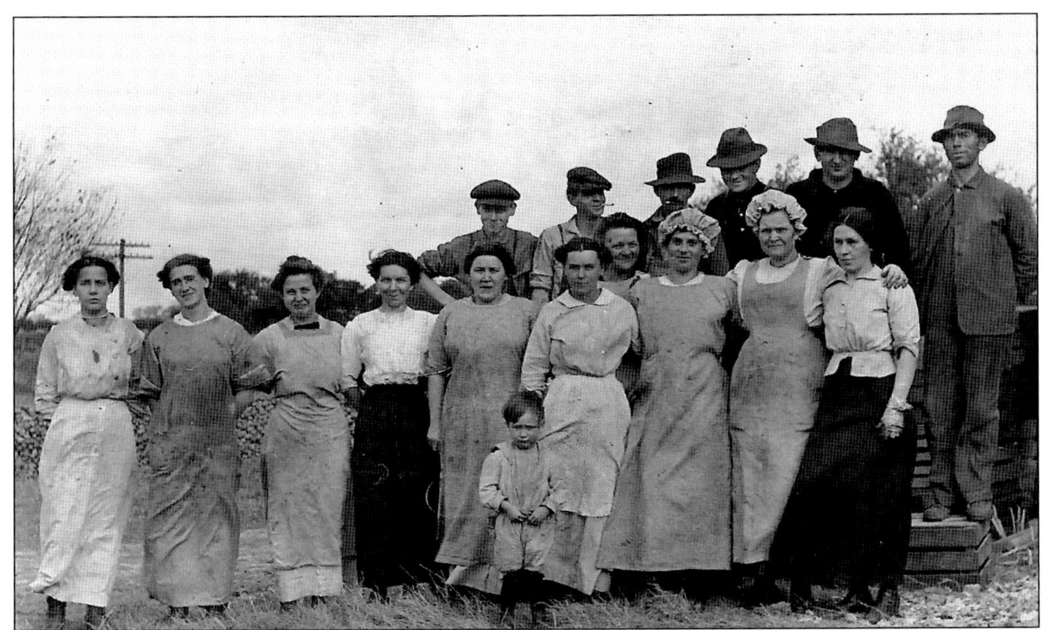

Kenyonville Dry House Workers. All are unidentified except Esther Simmons Boyce, the woman in the first row, fourth from the right, with her hand behind the small boy. (Courtesy of Sandy Tombari Freeman.)

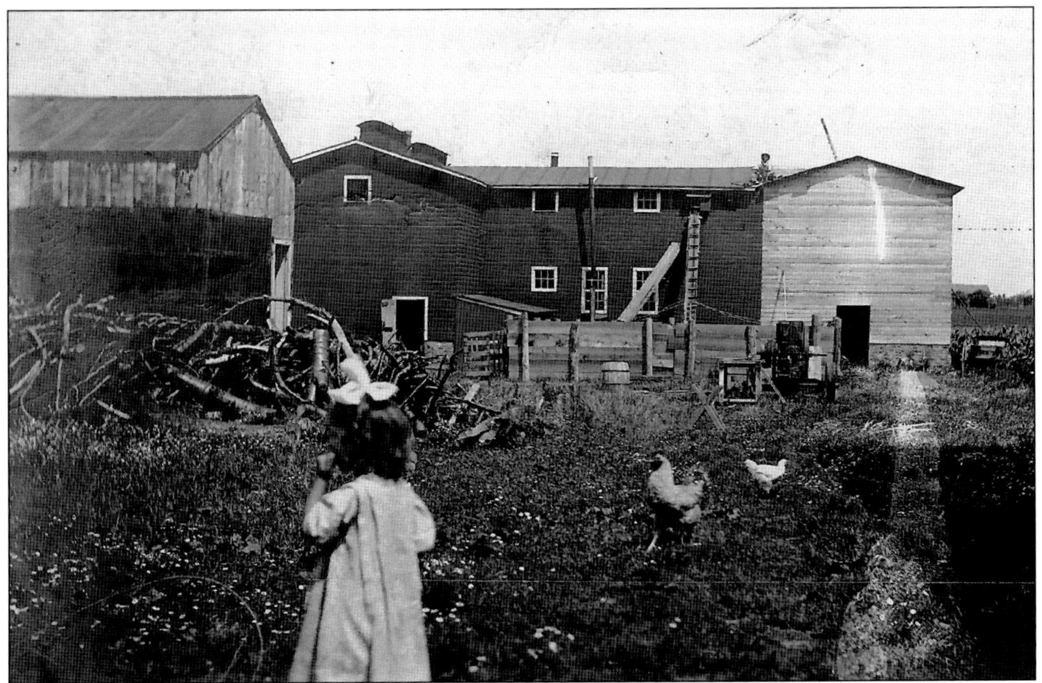

Beardsley's Dry House. Little Thelma Beardsley was visiting her grandparents the George Ballards at their dry house at Carlton Station around 1910. (Courtesy of Orleans County Department of History.)

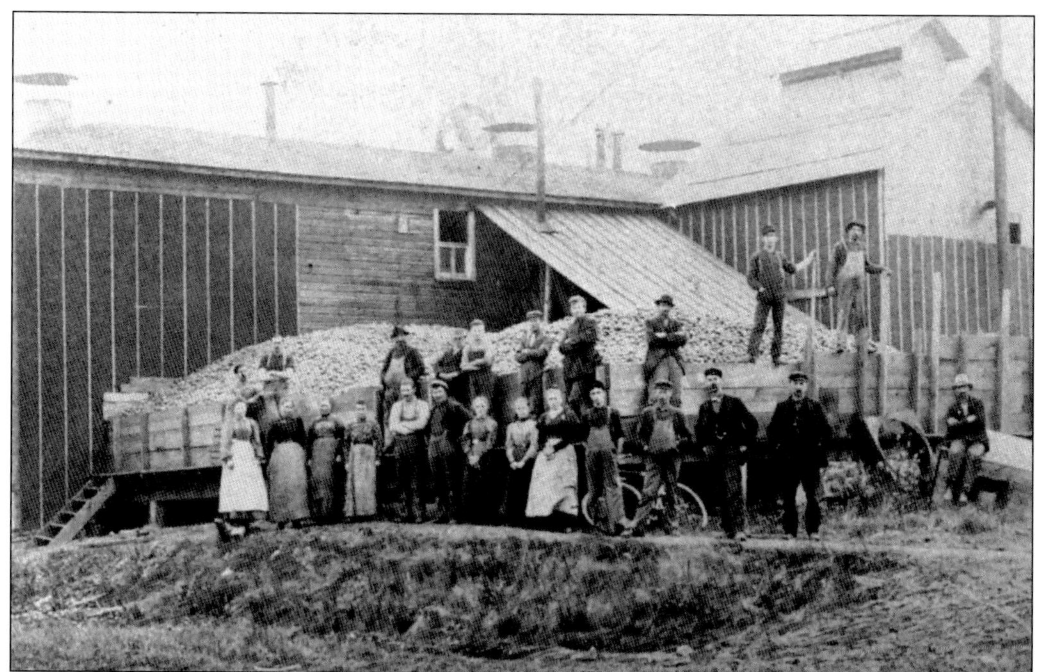

CARLTON DRY HOUSE. This unidentified group of folks are working at the dry house and cider mill behind the depot in Carlton in 1905. The huge pile of apples will be turned into cool, sparkling cider. (Courtesy of David Kelsey.)

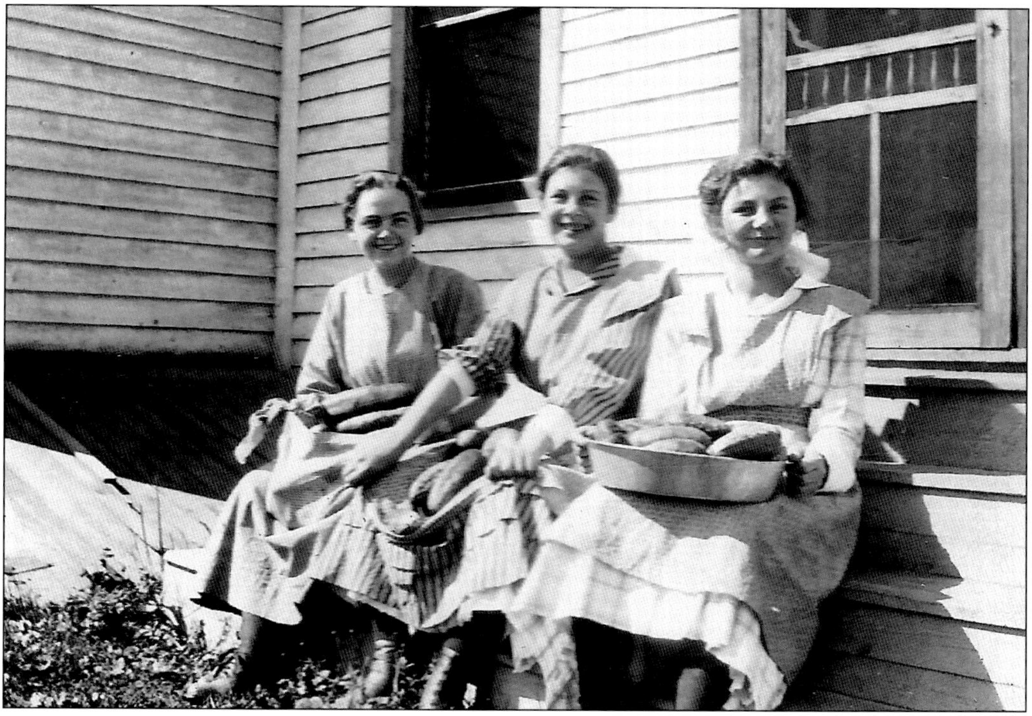

PICKING CUCUMBERS. These women from the Broadwell Farm pose after picking some large cucumbers, possibly for making some pickles. (Courtesy of Pauline Kast Broadwell.)

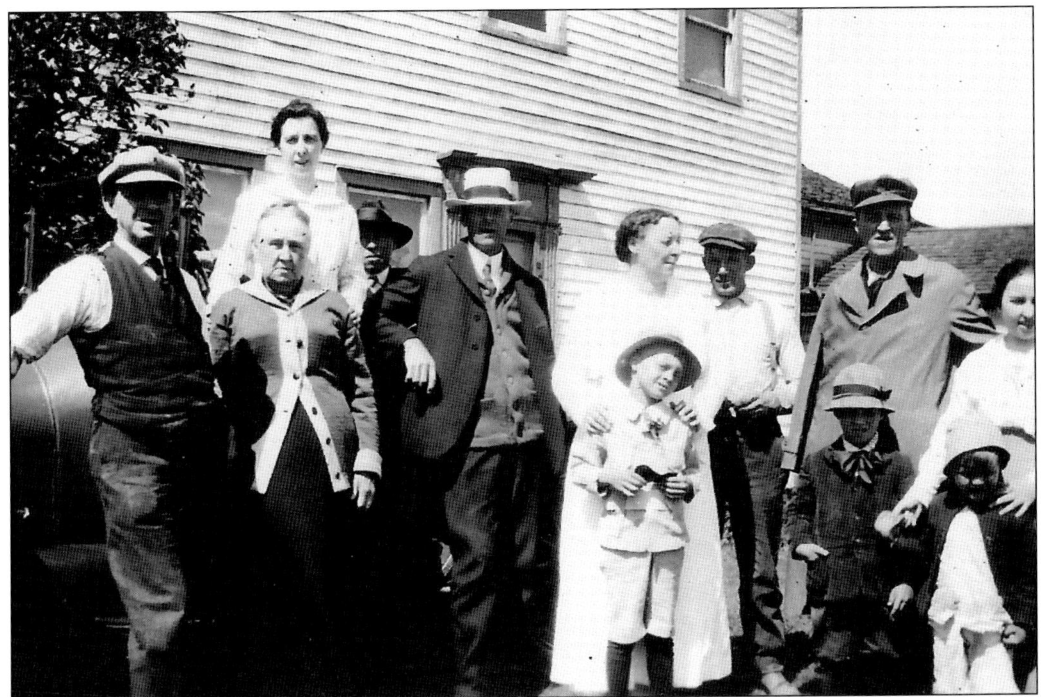

THE IVES FAMILY, 1917. Members of the Ives family pose outside their home. Unfortunately, no names are available. (Courtesy of Jessica Matson.)

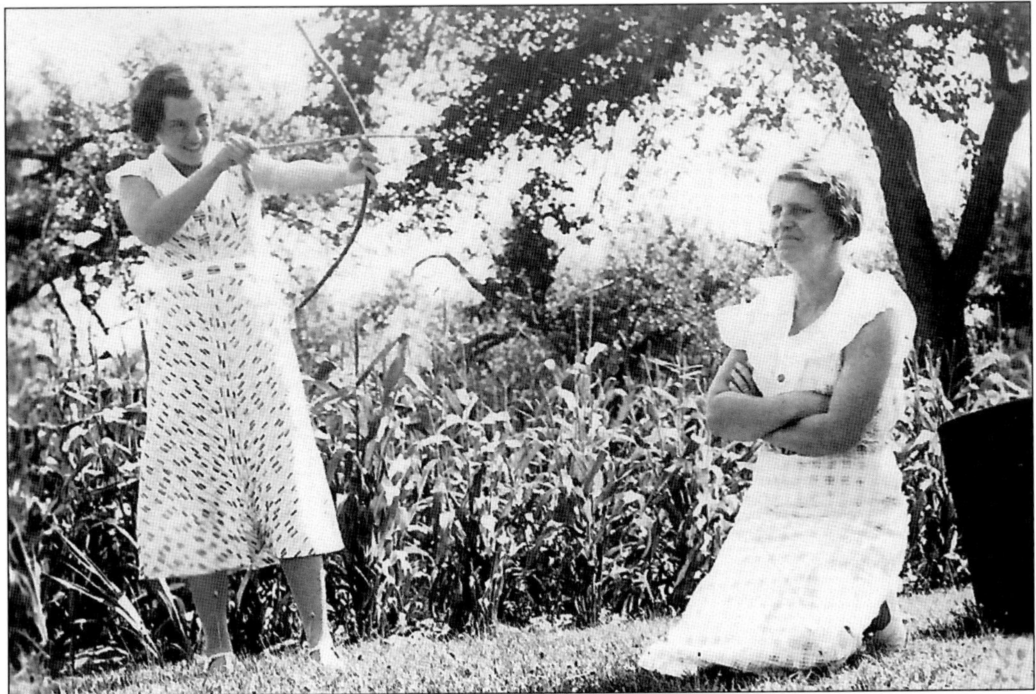

STRAIGHT AS AN ARROW. From left to right, Margaret Rath and Eva Kelsey enjoy a day in the sunshine around 1940, posing for the photographer in a humorous fashion. (Courtesy of David Kelsey.)

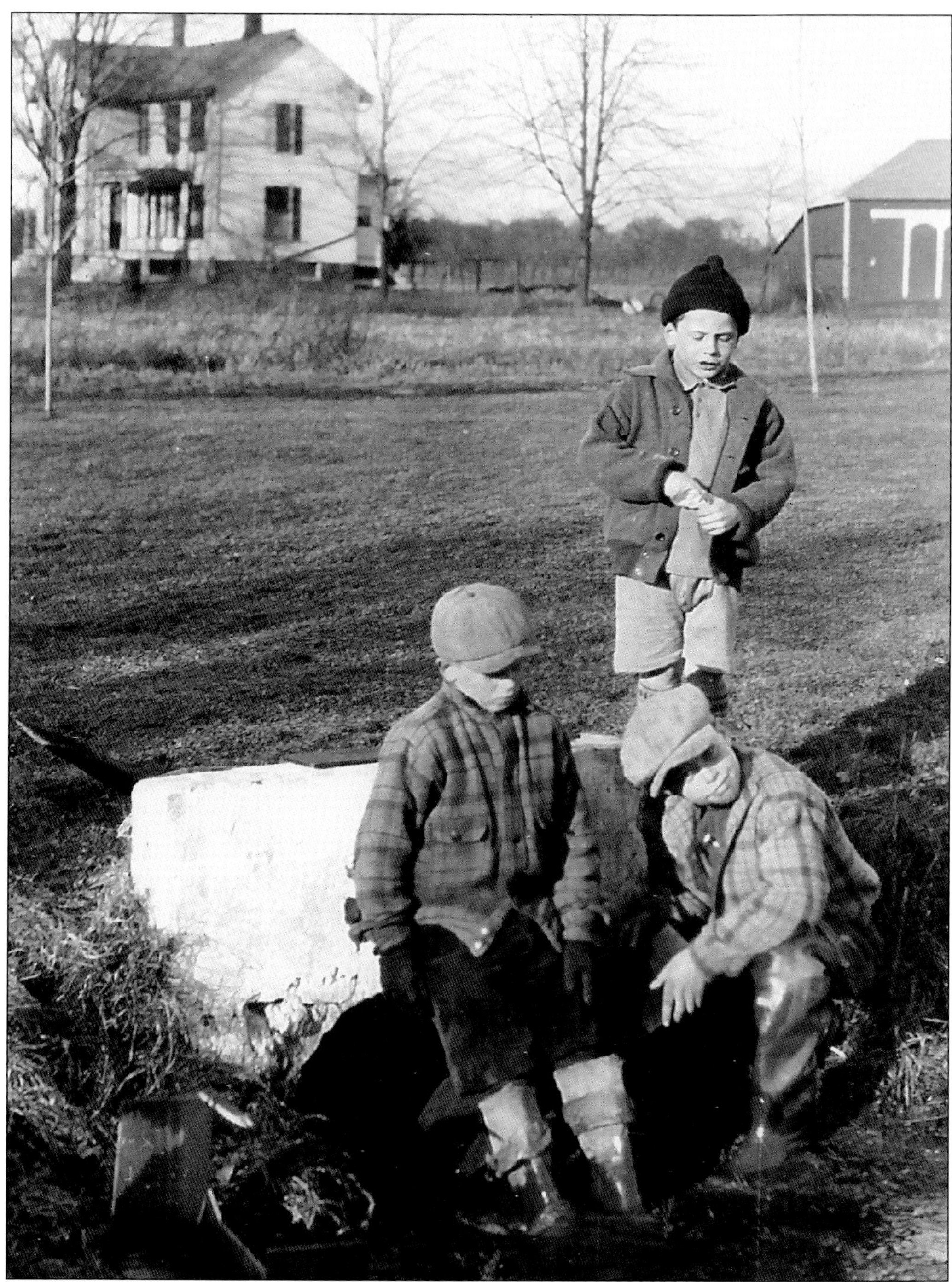

The Family Farm. The Kelsey and Callard children, like children of all eras, enjoy playing in water in the ditch on Oak Orchard Road. The home in view is now the Hauer home. (Courtesy of Garland Miller.)

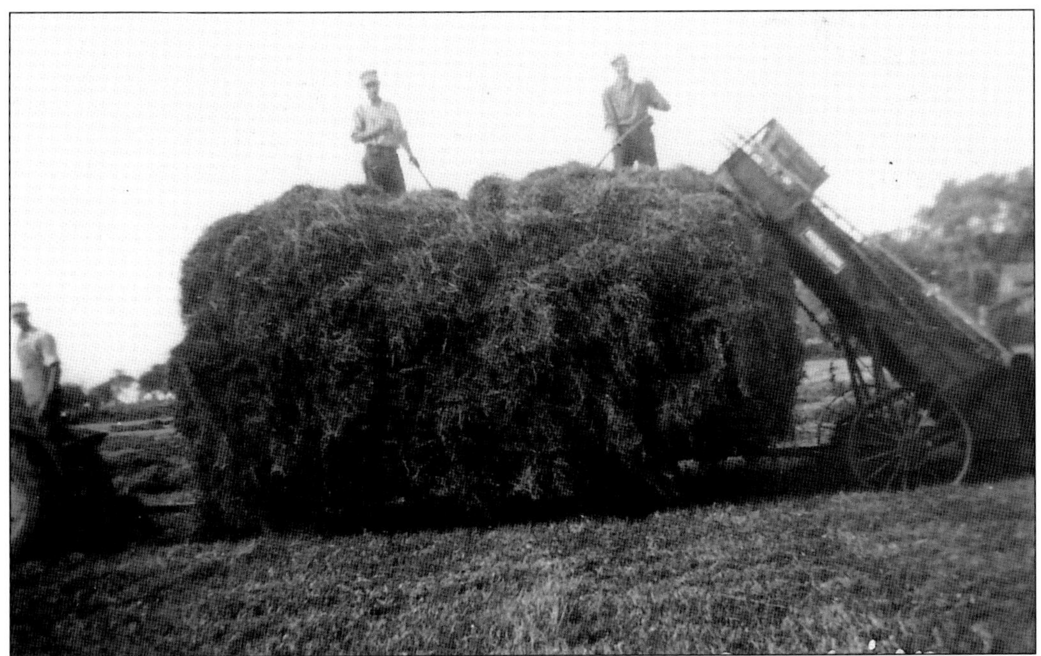

SECOND CUTTING. Most hay is cut in June or July, and if the weather is right, a second cutting can be obtained. This was cut in September 1947, so it must have been a good year for hay. From left to right, Gerald Miller, Reed Miller, and Clayton Thiel pose at Meadow Brook Farm. (Courtesy of David Kelsey.)

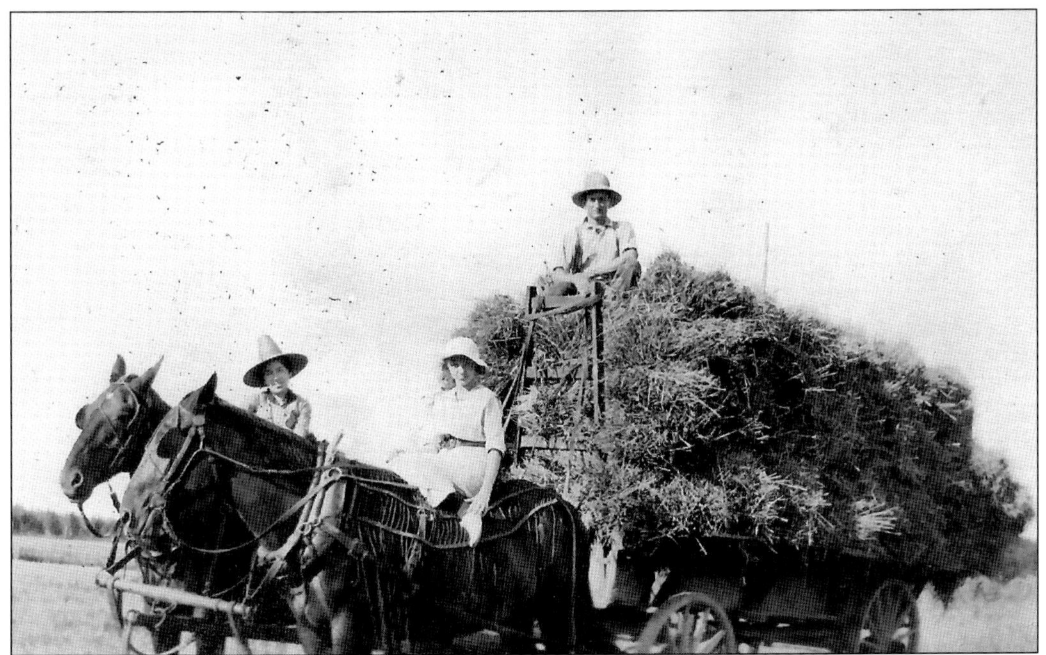

GETTING THE HAY. Friends and family of the Ives clan wisely sport hats for protection from the sun while gathering a wagonload of hay around 1930. (Courtesy of Jessica Matson.)

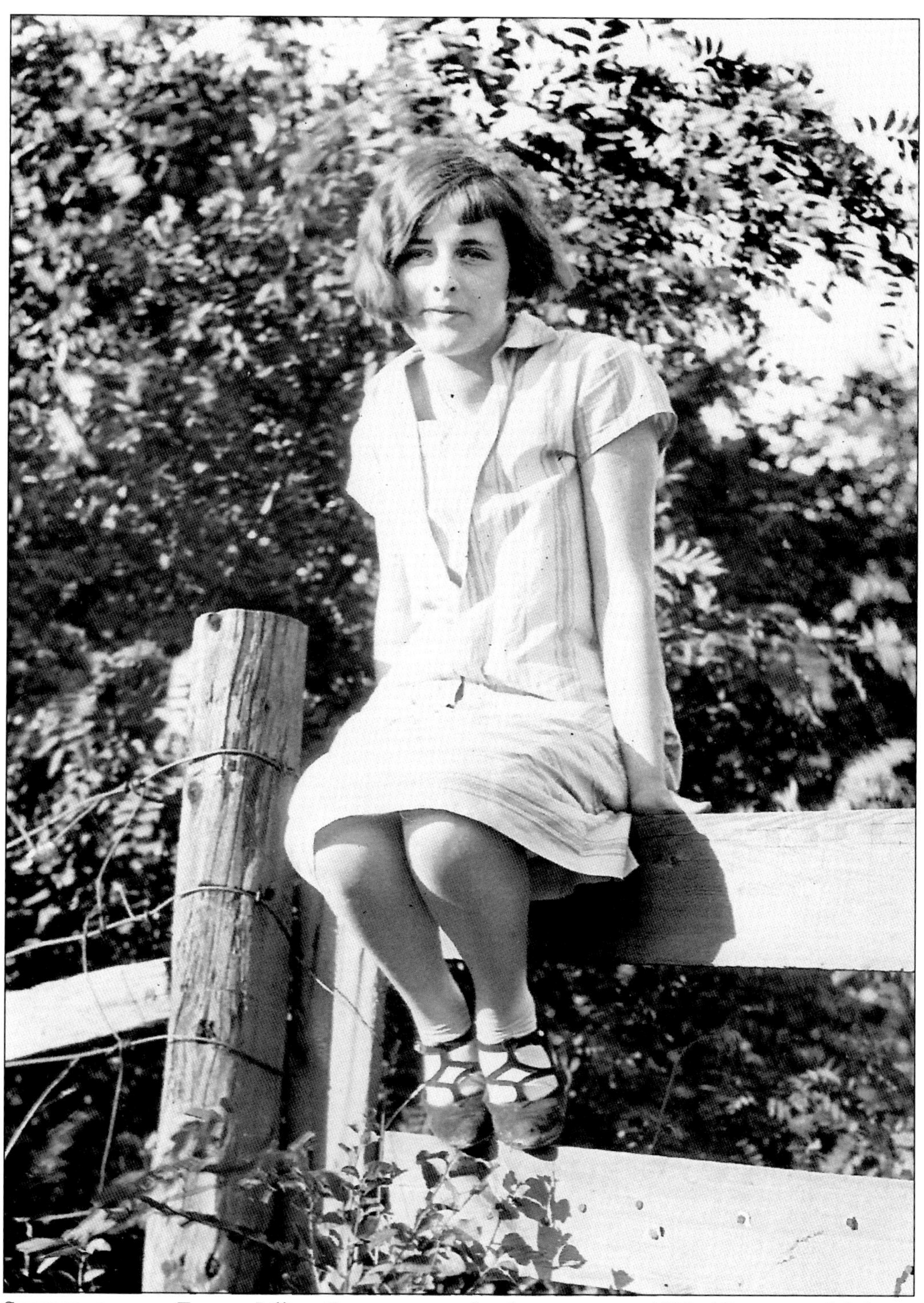

SITTING ON THE FENCE. Lillian Sargent poses for the camera in 1925. (Courtesy of Orleans County Department of History.)

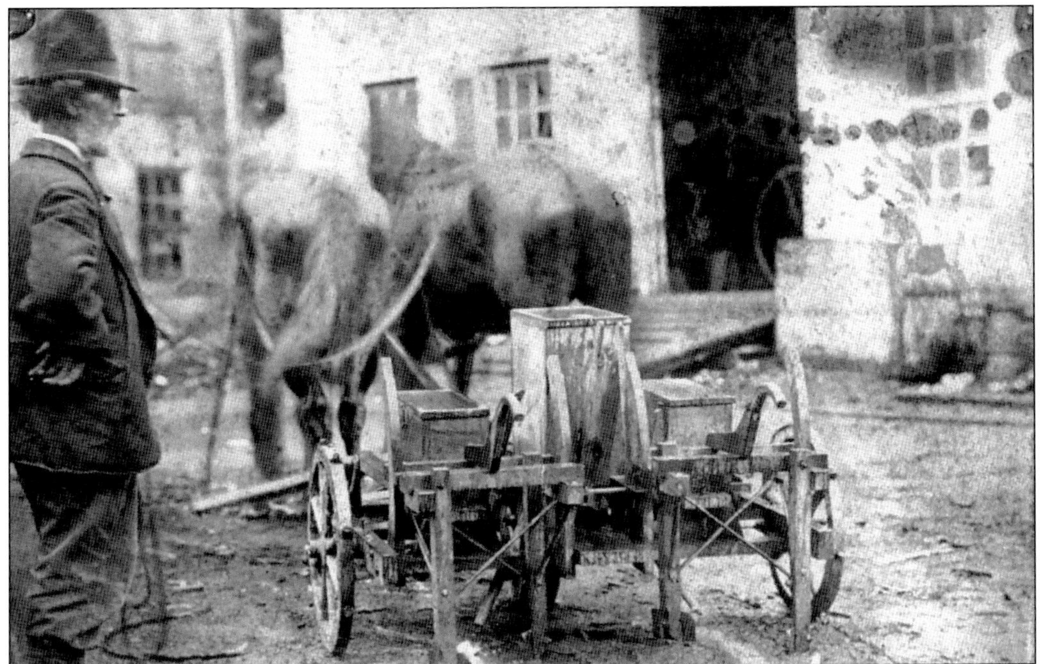

INVENTIVE BEAN MAN. Henry Clement poses with the horse-drawn bean planter he invented. He built three of these planters, and they were the first machines ever used to plant beans. He owned a sawmill on Marsh Creek, northeast of Sawyer Road. When this photograph was taken, he advised the photographer to blur the horses so just he and his machine were clear, a remarkable feat for the late 1800s. (Courtesy of Orleans County Department of History.)

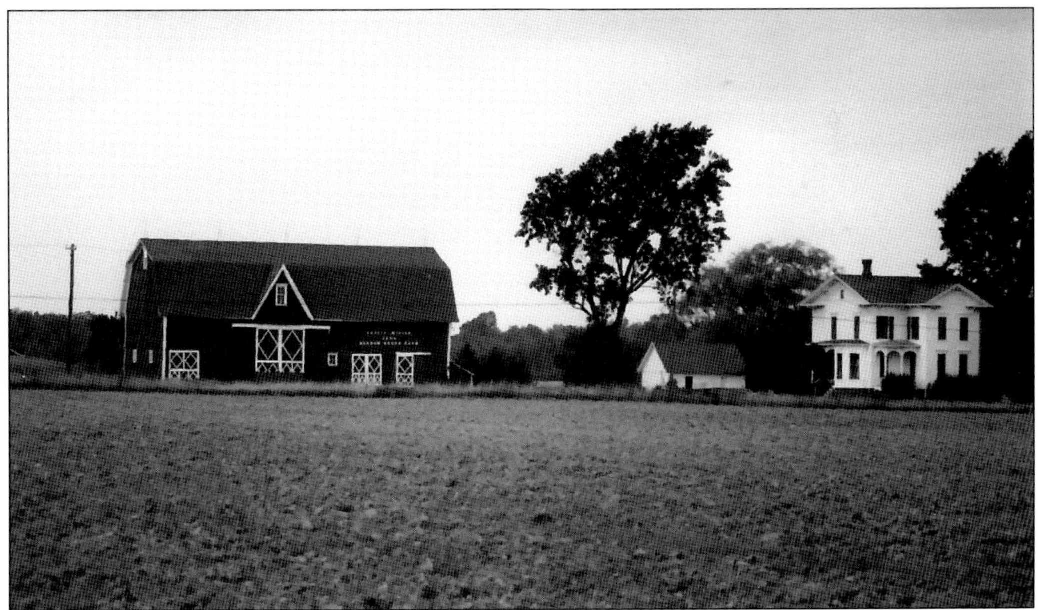

MEADOW BROOK FARM. Like many in the area, the barn was lost to a fire. This home is located on Oak Orchard Road, just north of the town line, in Carlton, and is occupied by the fourth generation of the Miller family now. (Courtesy of Garland Miller.)

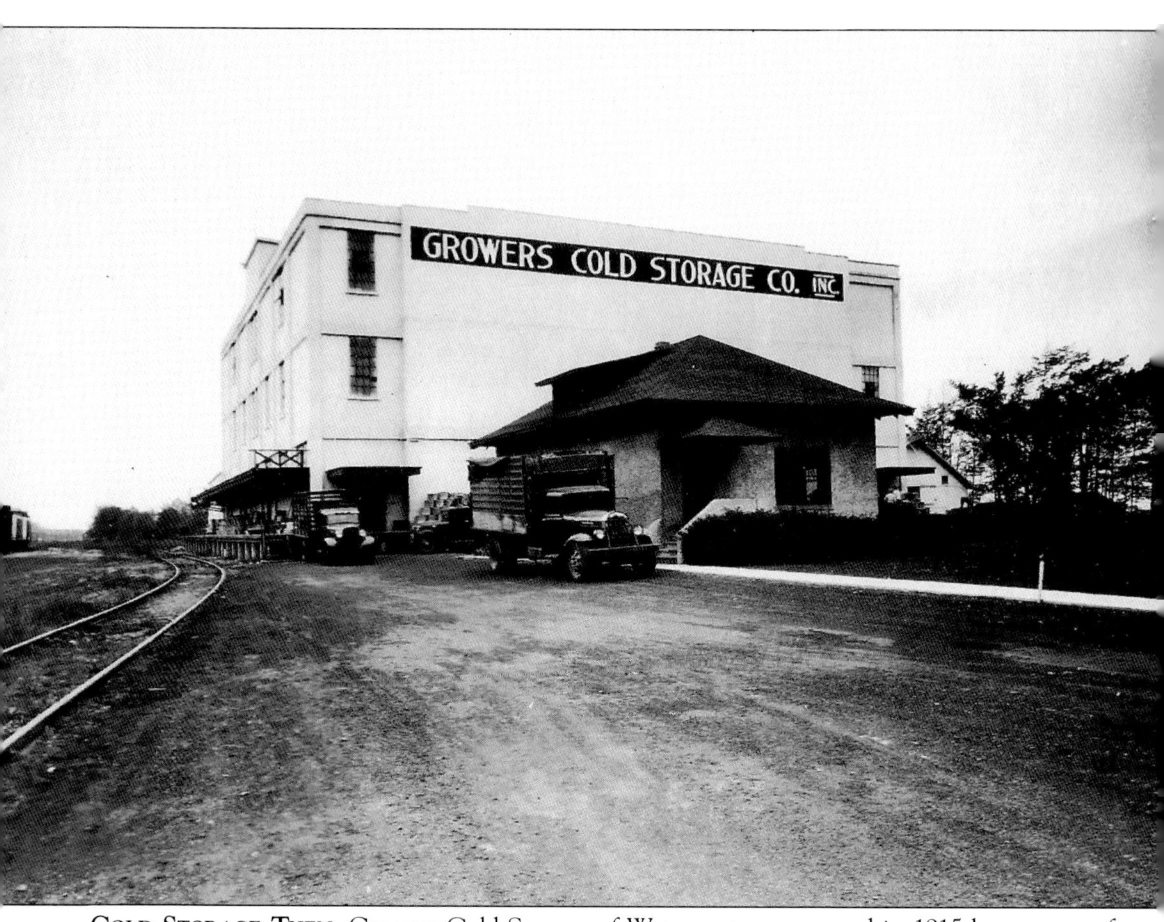

COLD STORAGE THEN. Growers Cold Storage of Waterport was opened in 1915 by a group of fruit growers. The storage plant played an important role in World War I, moving food supplies to Europe, including locally grown frozen food products. (Courtesy of John Sawyer.)

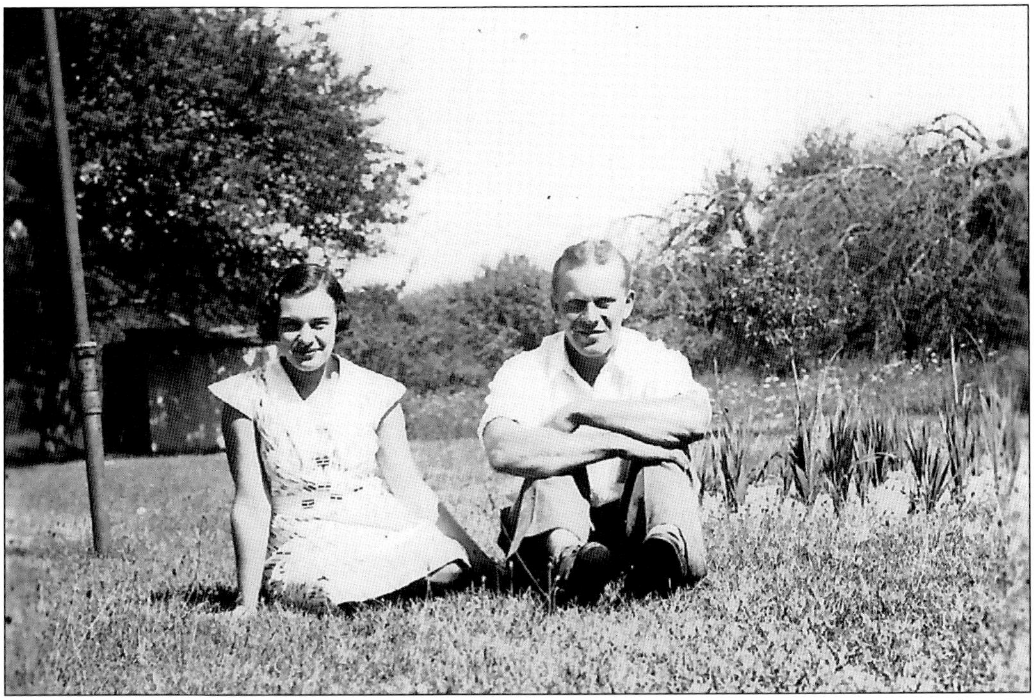

ENJOYING THE SUNSHINE. Bill and Margaret Kelsey enjoy a day in the sun around 1950. (Courtesy of David Kelsey.)

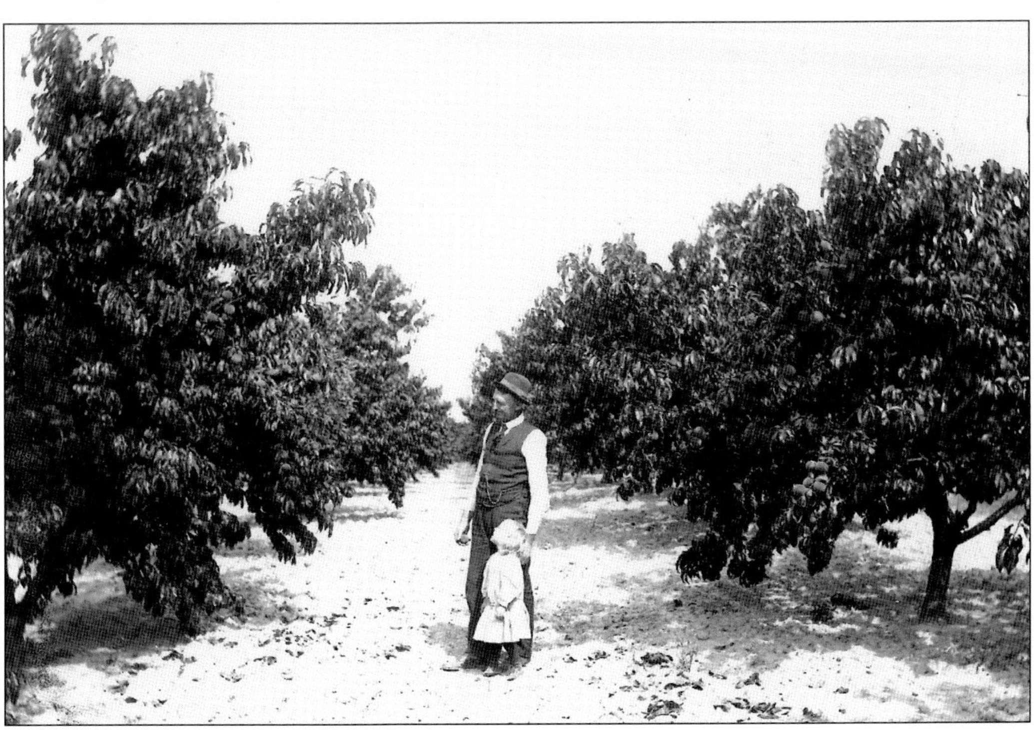

IN THE ORCHARD. This unidentified man checks out his orchards with a young girl, possibly his granddaughter. (Courtesy of Orleans County Department of History.)

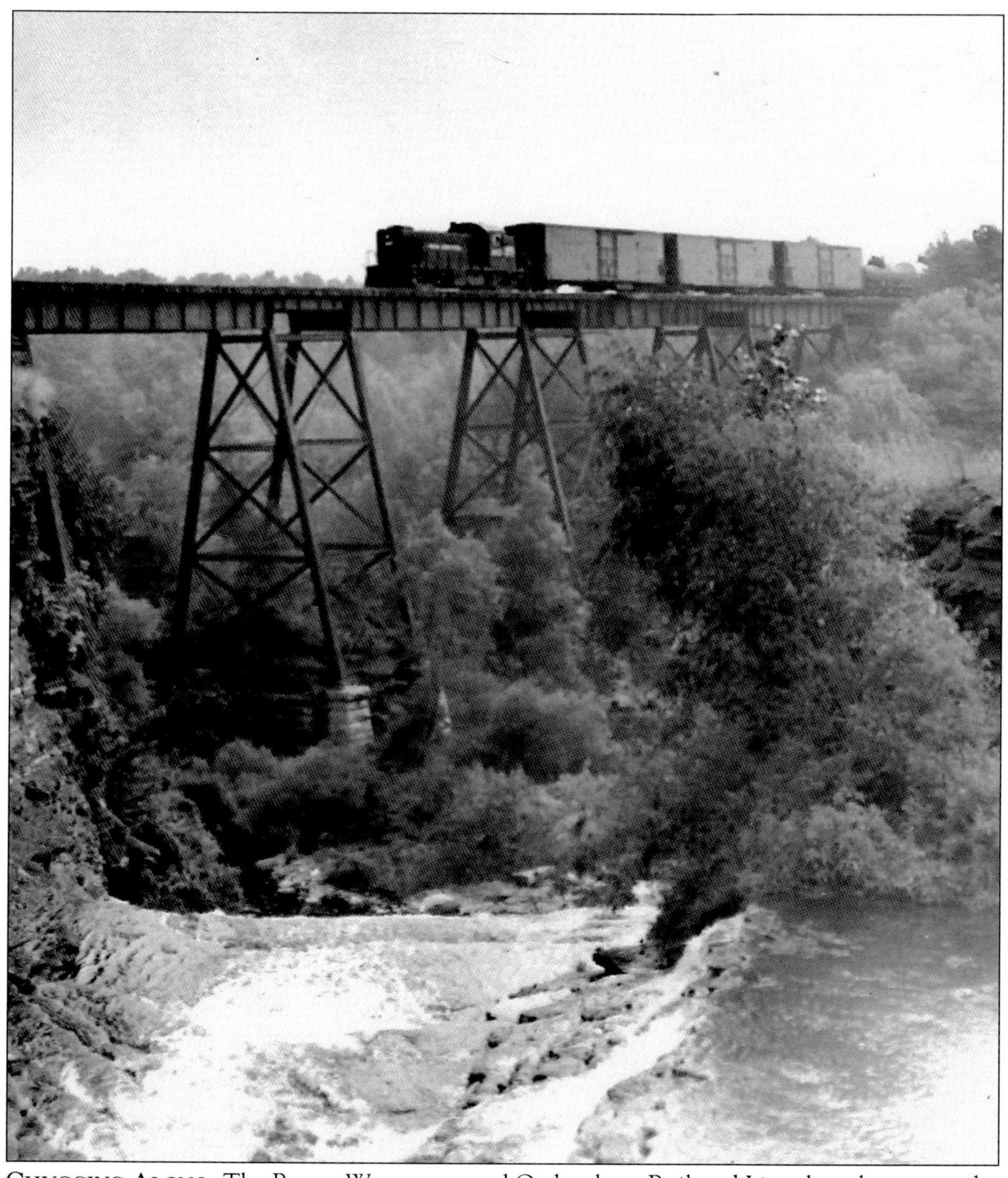

Chugging Along. The Rome, Watertown and Ogdensburg Railroad Line, later known as the Hojack Line, ran more than nine and a half miles through Kent, Carlton Station, Waterport, and Ashwood in the town of Carlton. This photograph is said to be the final train crossing the trestle, in 1978. (Courtesy of Garland Miller.)

Five

Four Stops on the Hojack Line

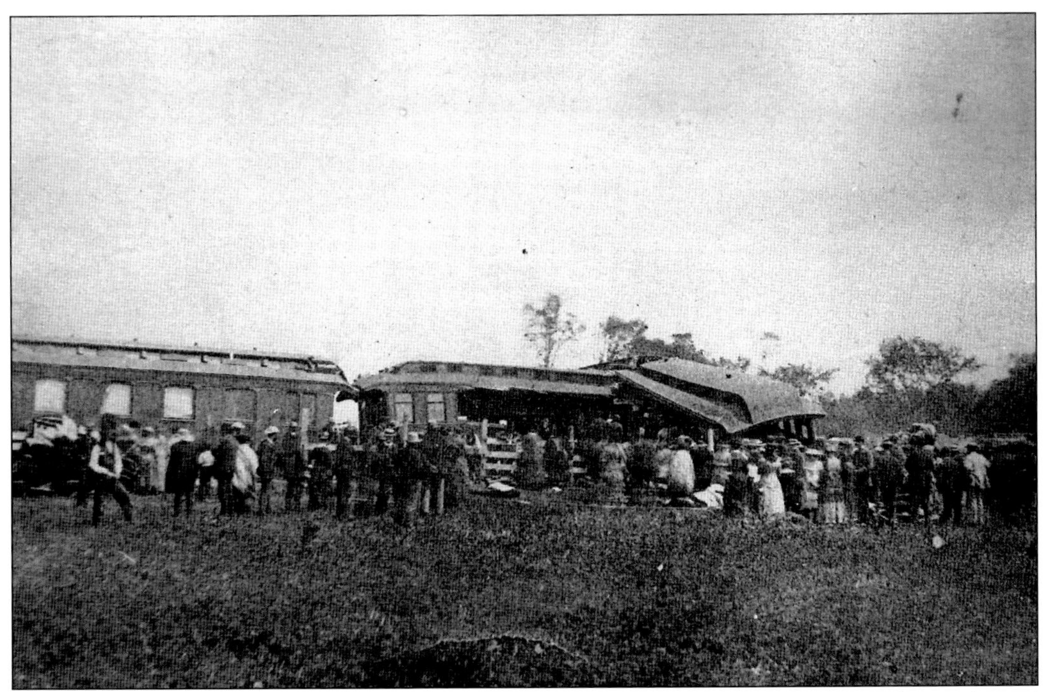

Ashwood Train Wreck. On July 27, 1883, a train struck a boxcar sitting idle on the tracks and derailed at Ashwood, killing 17 people and injuring 25. Crowds gathered to see the wreckage. Most of the dead and injured were from Ashtabula, Ohio, though one person from Ashwood was a casualty. Survivors begged locals to take them back to Ohio by horse and buggy. (Courtesy of Orleans County Department of History.)

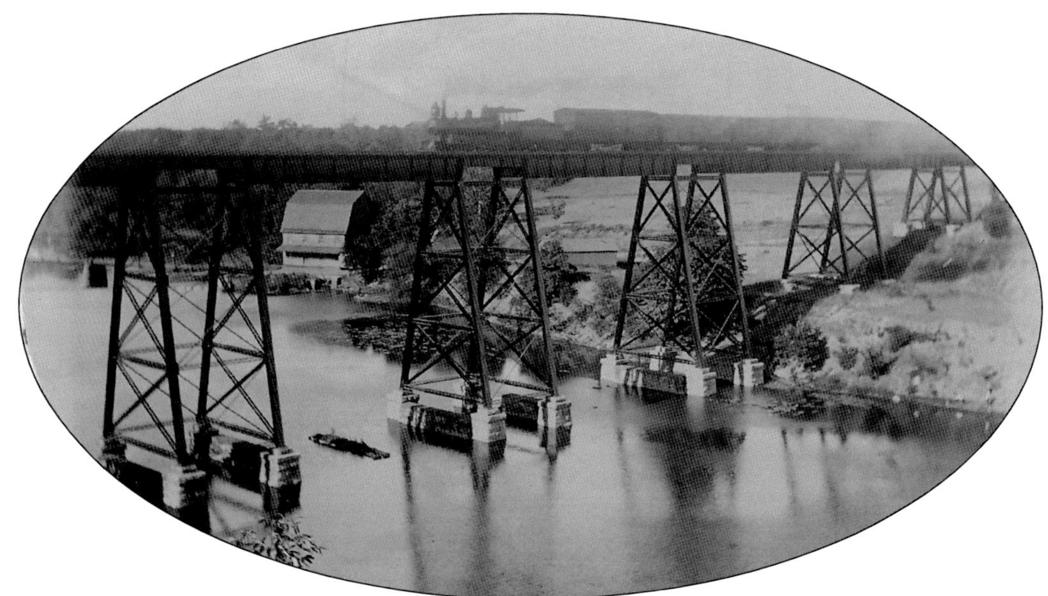

COMING THROUGH THE FOG. A train makes its way through the fog over Clark's Mills around 1900. (Courtesy of Orleans County Department of History.)

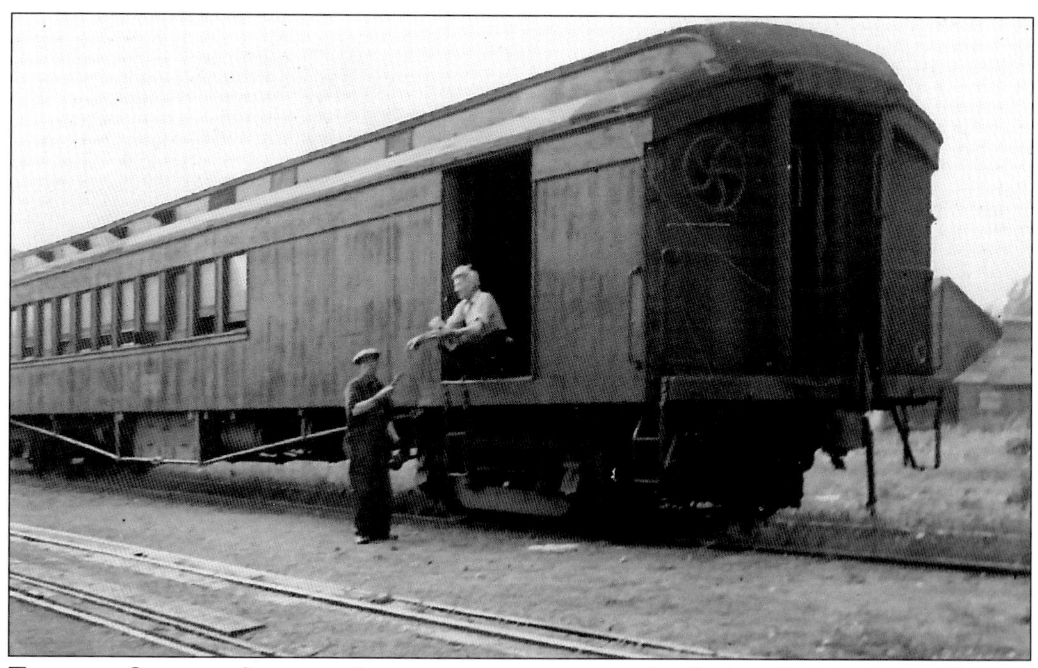

TRAIN AT CARLTON STATION. A passenger train waits at the Carlton Station depot. The two men are unidentified. (Courtesy of David Kelsey.)

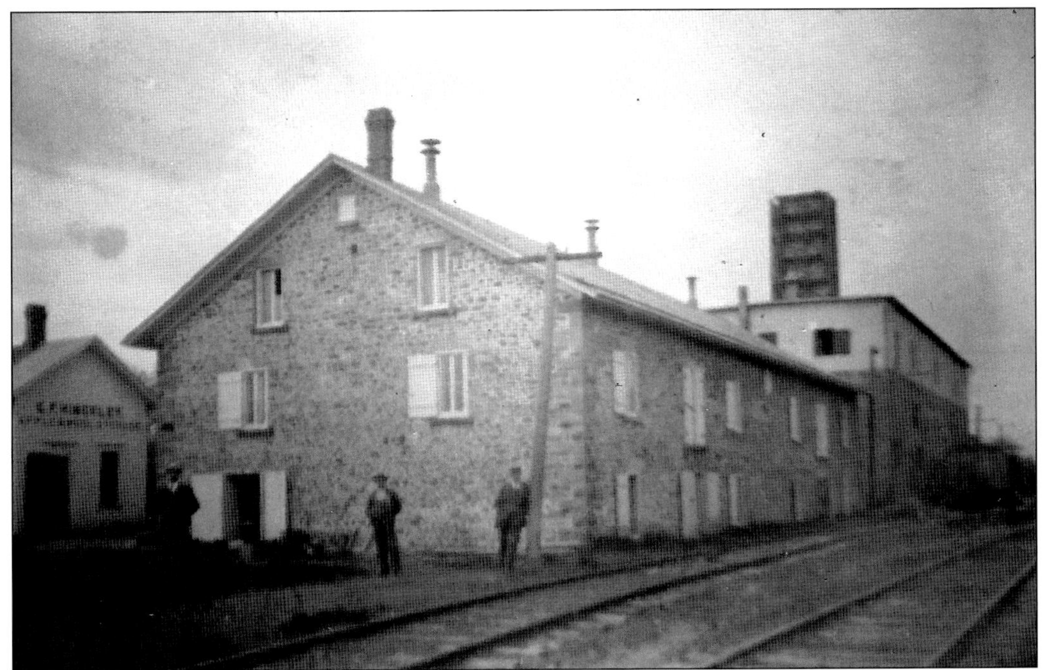

CARLTON STATION COLD STORAGE. This was the cold storage at Carlton Station. It handled passengers from the late 1800s through the 1930s. (Courtesy of Garland Miller.)

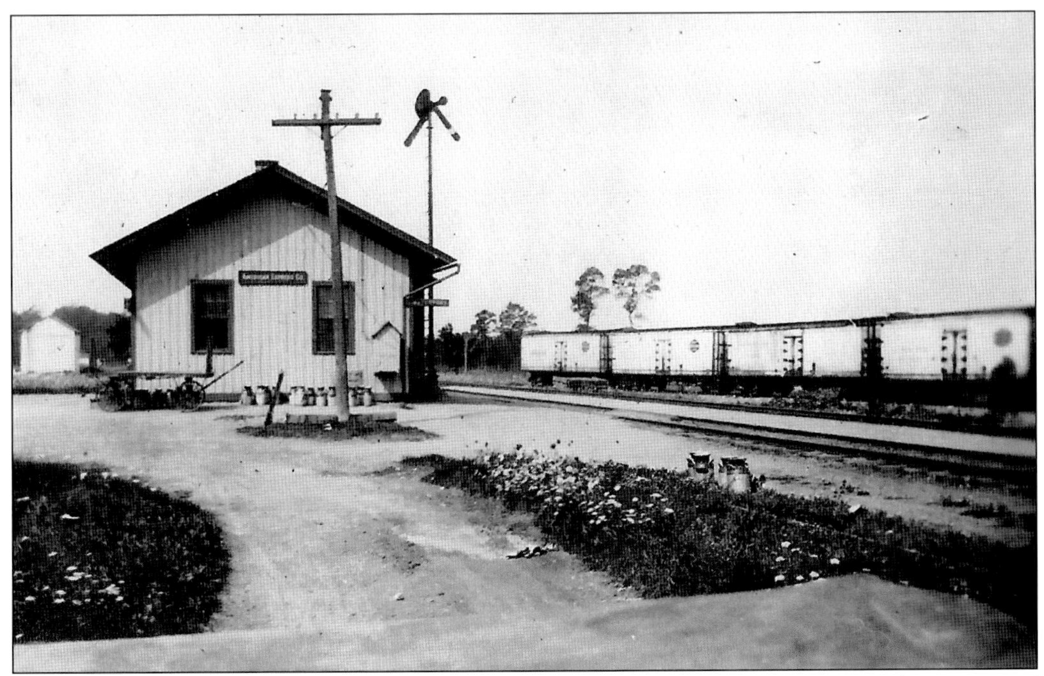

AMERICAN EXPRESS BUILDING. This was the depot at Waterport Station. (Courtesy of Jessica Matson.)

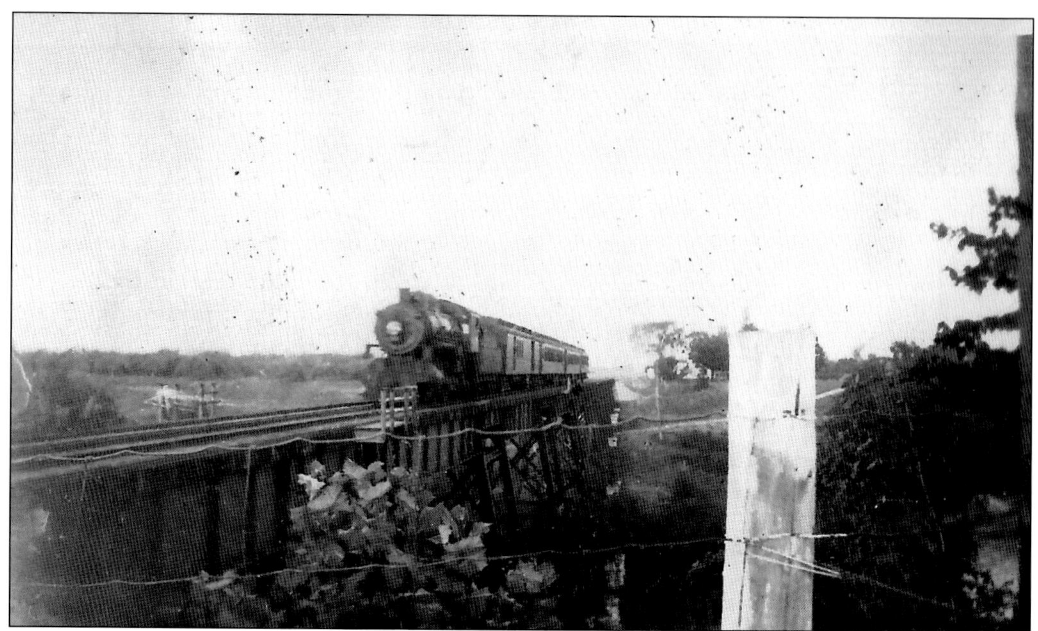

COMING ACROSS THE TRESTLE. The photographer stood very close to the edge of the cliff when taking this picture of the Hojack Line coming across the trestle around 1920. (Courtesy of Jessica Matson.)

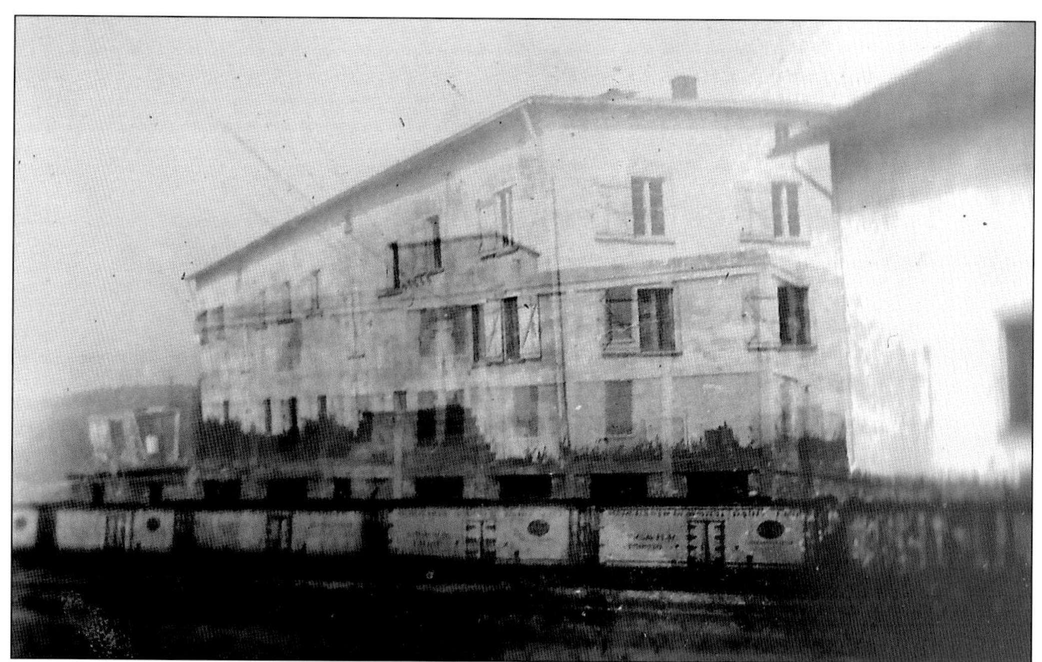

DOUBLE EXPOSURE? This photograph appears to be a double exposure but was kept by the Matson family because it shows a long train traveling through Waterport, with the buildings in the background almost looking like a city. (Courtesy of Jessica Matson.)

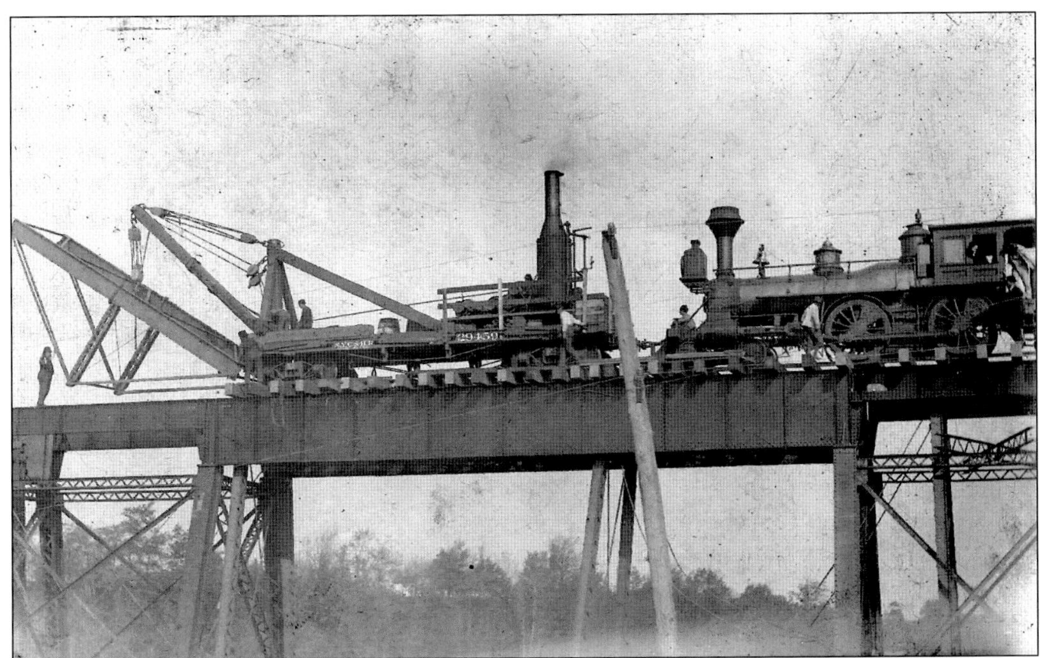

Working Train. A train helps do the work as the new trestle is created at Waterport around 1892. The train helps push the piece of steam-powered equipment down the track and lower the metal beams into place that will hold the railroad ties. (Courtesy of Orleans County Department of History.)

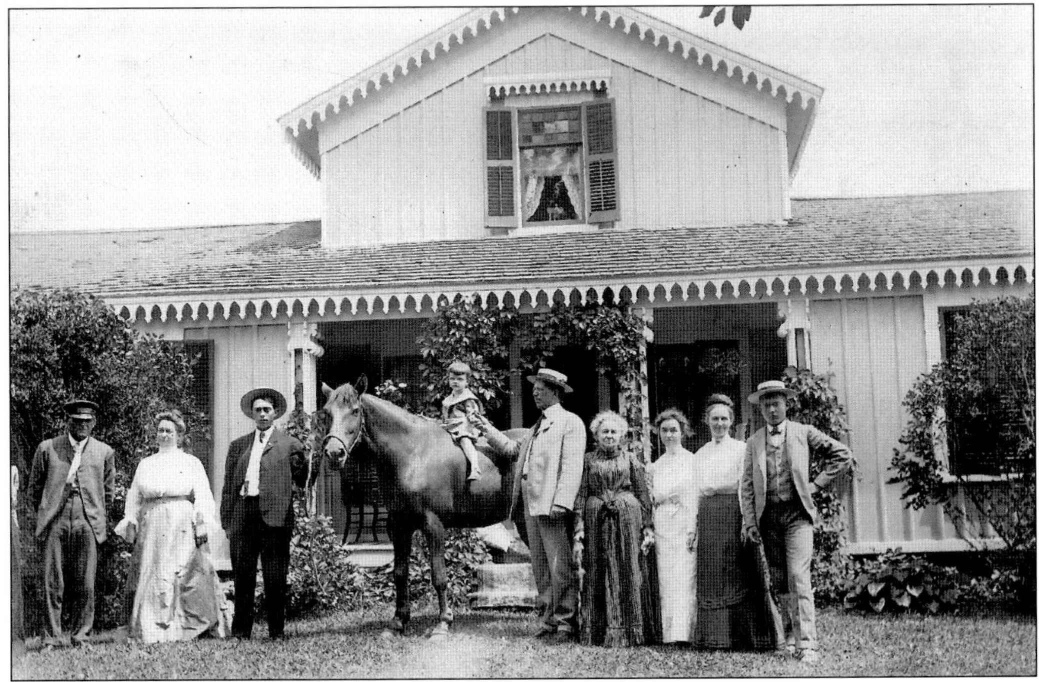

Baker House at Carlton Station. At right are Harry Lattin and Mrs. Baker. The Baker house is still there, on the corner of Baker Road (named for them) and Oak Orchard Road. (Courtesy of Garland Miller.)

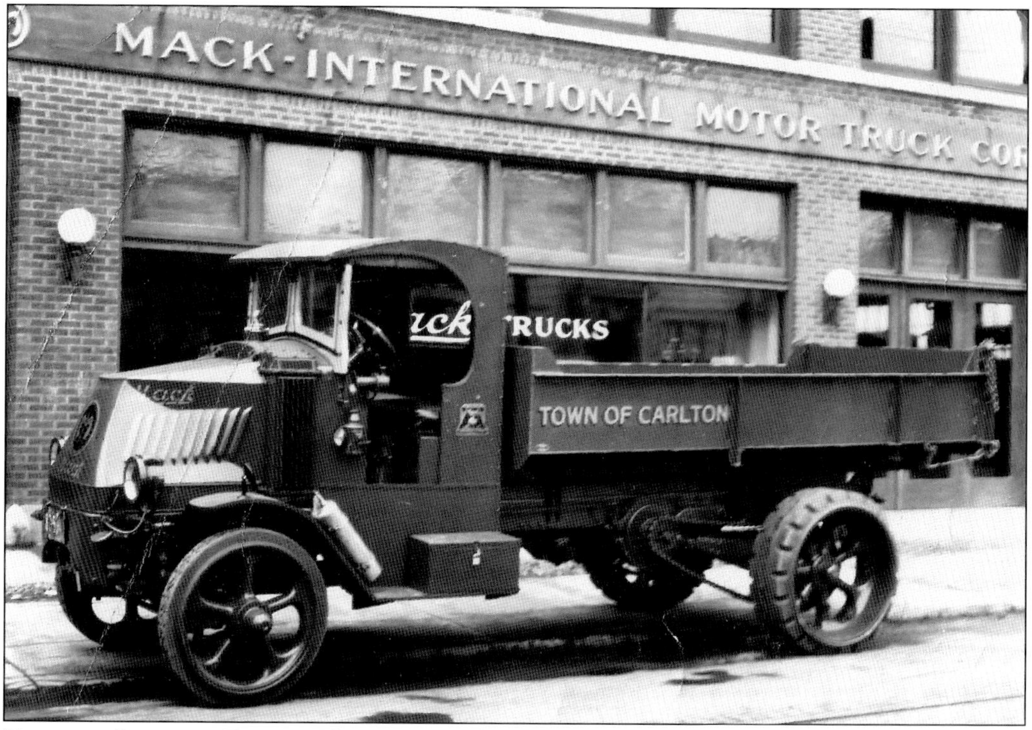

TOWN OF CARLTON TRUCK. This was one of the first town trucks used by the Town of Carlton. Its photograph still hangs in the town hall offices on Waterport-Carlton Road. (Courtesy of Leo Spohr, town of Carlton assessor.)

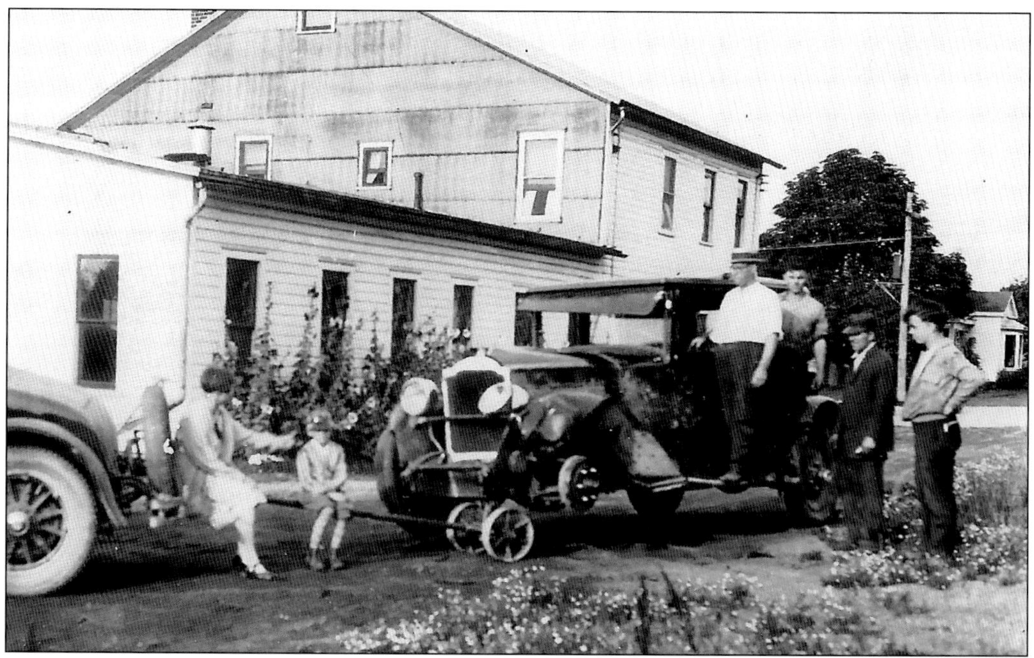

FENDER BENDER. Folks called this the "Big Wreck of Carlton" back in 1925. Although they remembered the wreck, no one remembered who was involved. (Courtesy of David Kelsey.)

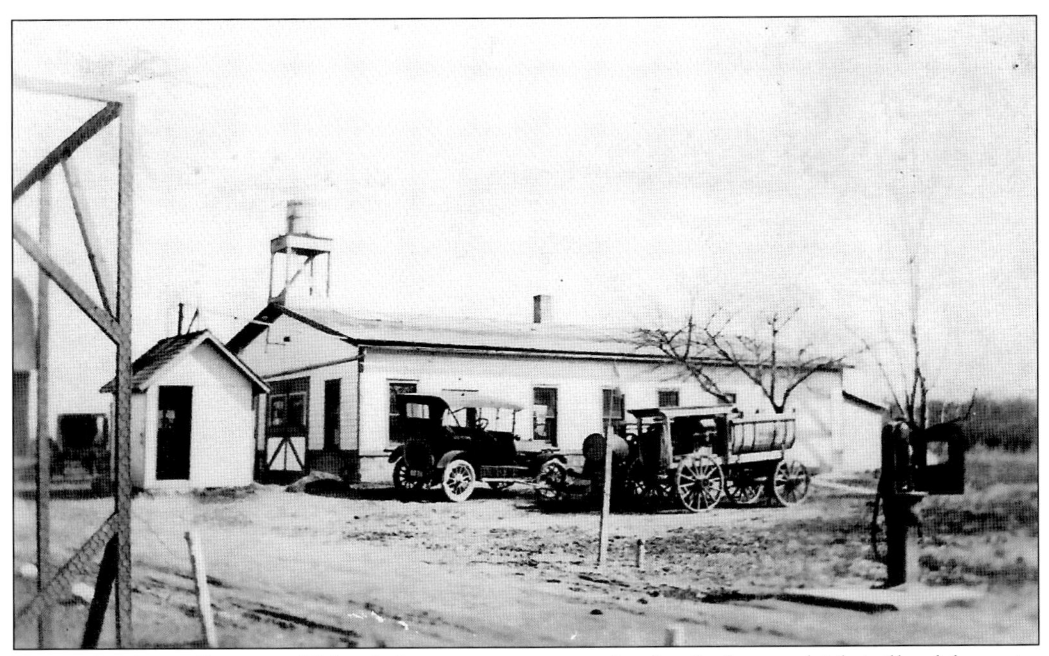

Kelsey's First Garage. Kelsey's first garage was on the family farm, which will celebrate its 170th anniversary in 2006. (Courtesy of David Kelsey.)

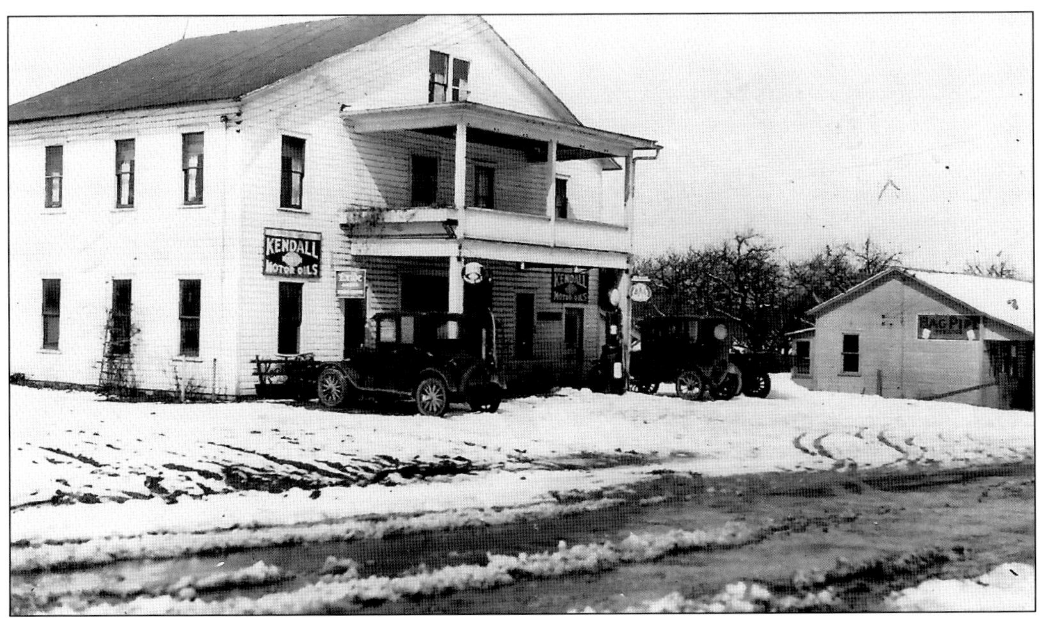

Gas and Motor Oil. Built, owned, and operated originally by Leland Kelsey, the tire and repair shop has served the community for nearly 90 years under different owners. The current owner is Brian Catlin. (Courtesy of David Kelsey.)

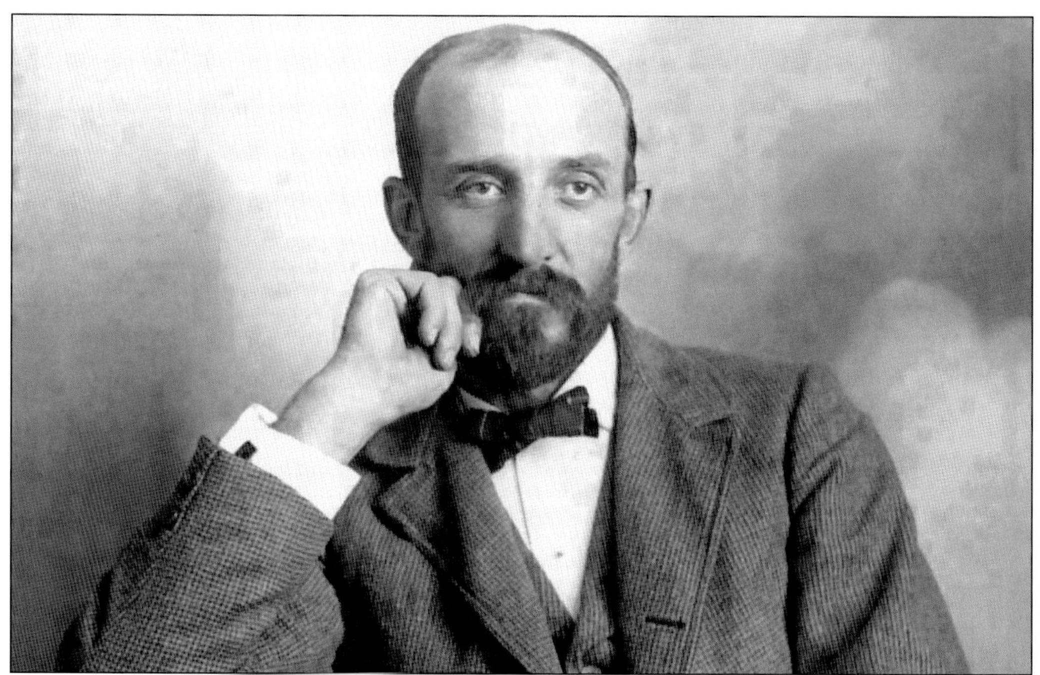

Doc Howes. Dr. Benjamin Howes (1858–1946) was famous in Orleans County for his love of life and passion for his horse, Sandy. He taught school for two years before furthering his education in Toronto to become a veterinarian. He practiced for 55 years. (Courtesy of Mark Rustay.)

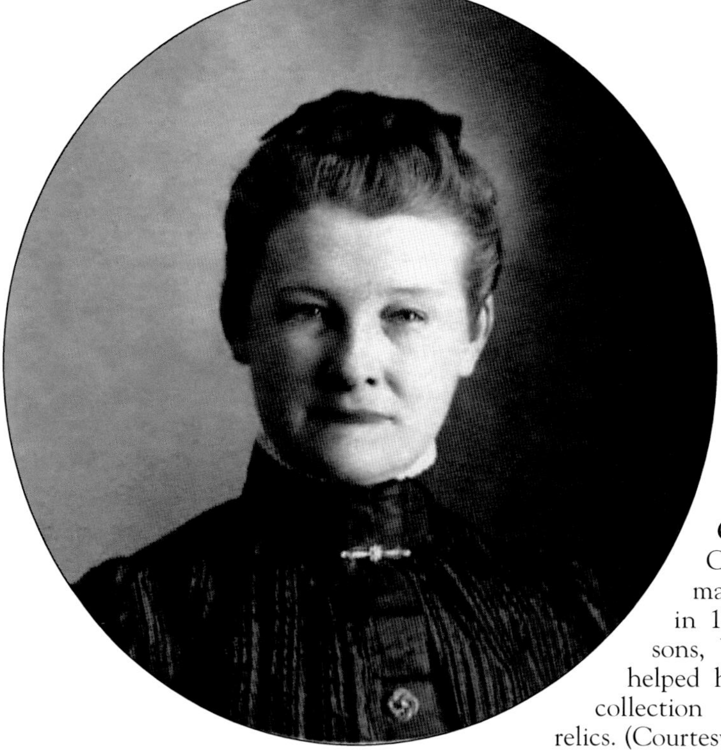

Clara VanCamp Howes. Clara VanCamp (1862–1934) married Dr. Benjamin Howes in 1884. They couple had two sons, Whitney and Murray. She helped her husband amass a large collection of antique primitive farm relics. (Courtesy of Mark Rustay.)

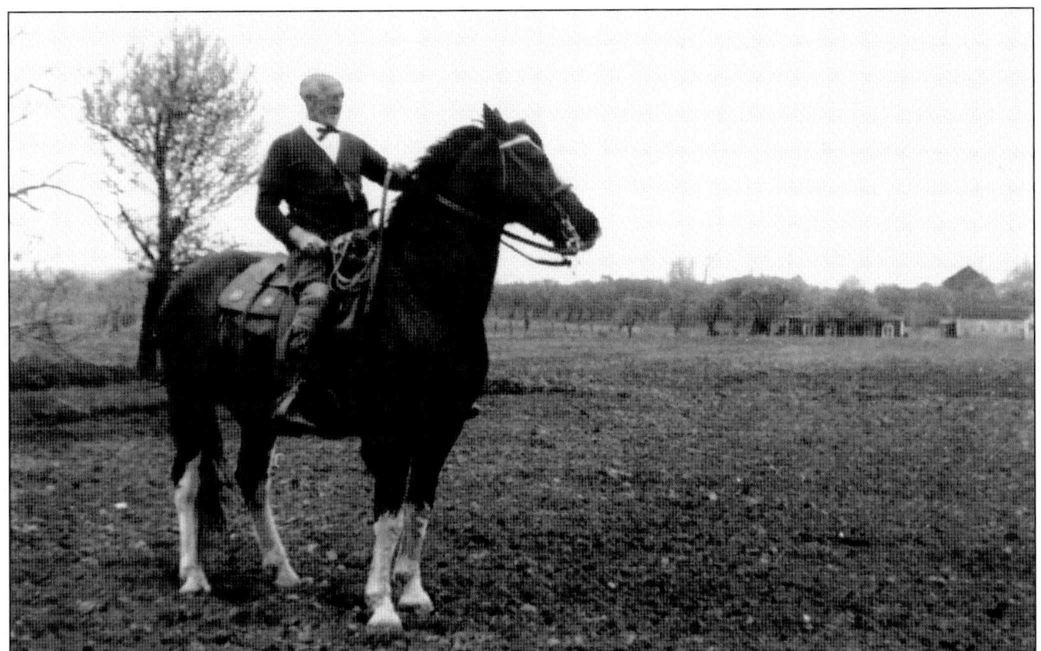

DR. HOWES ON SANDY. Dr. Howes, an expert horseman, belonged to the Orleans County Boots and Saddle Club, and he trained the chestnut-colored Sandy to do many tricks, including rearing up on command. The pair were featured in every parade, and Sandy reared up on cue for the onlookers. (Courtesy of Mark Rustay.)

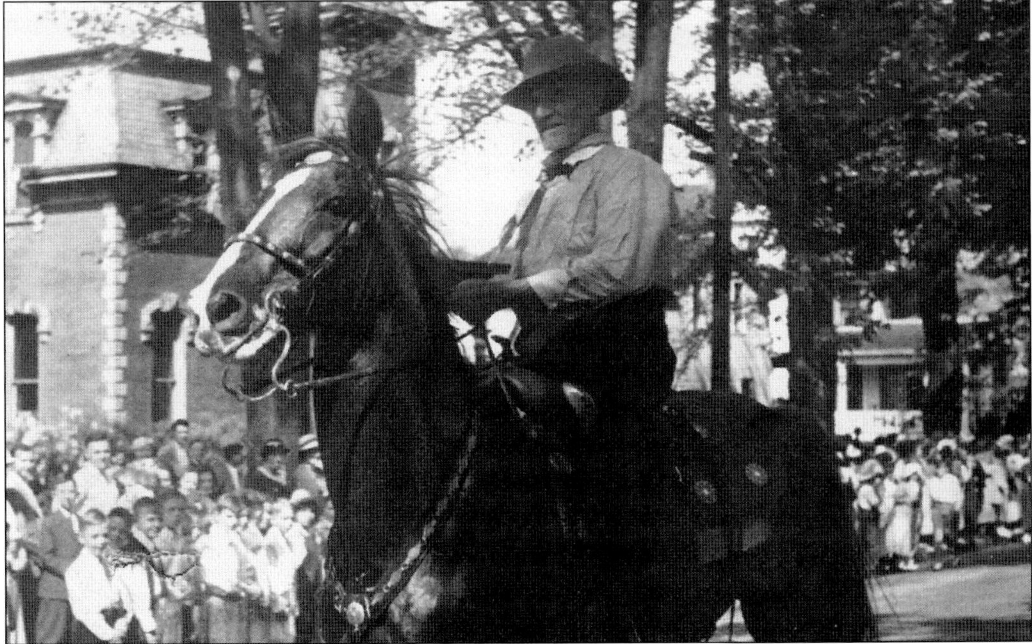

SANDY'S LAST PARADE. On August 18, 1937, Dr. Howes and Sandy appeared at a parade dedicating the new bridge over Oak Orchard Creek. Sandy reared up and had a stroke, collapsing in front of shocked onlookers. He was shot by a state policeman. It was the end of Dr. Howe's rides. People still talk of it today. (Courtesy of Orleans County Department of History.)

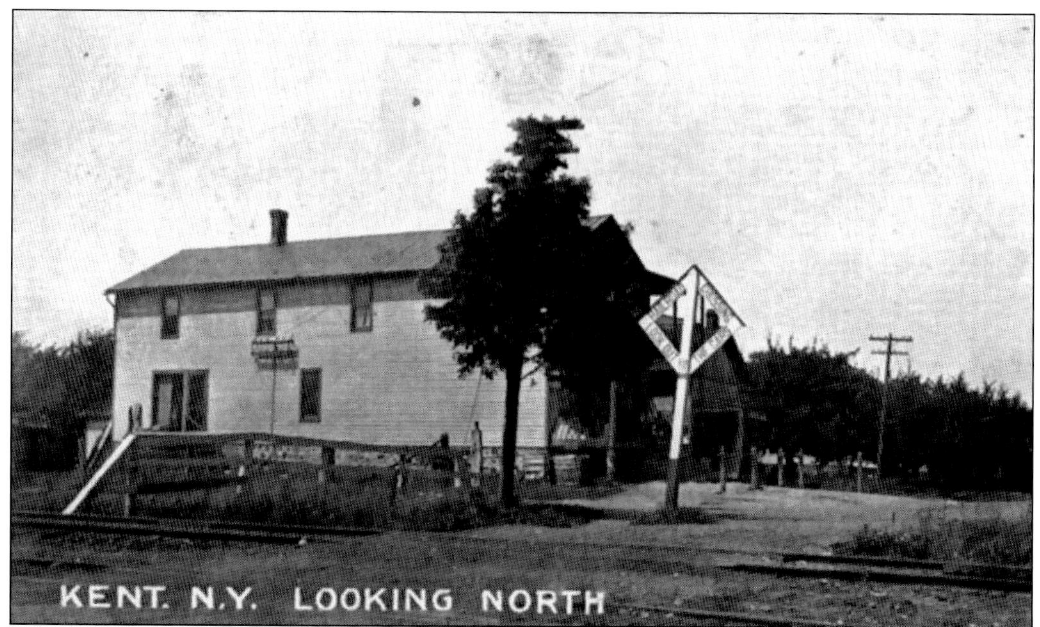

THE CROSSING AT KENT. This is a view of the tracks and crossing passing over Kent Road at Kent around 1910. The view faces north. (Courtesy of Orleans County Department of History.)

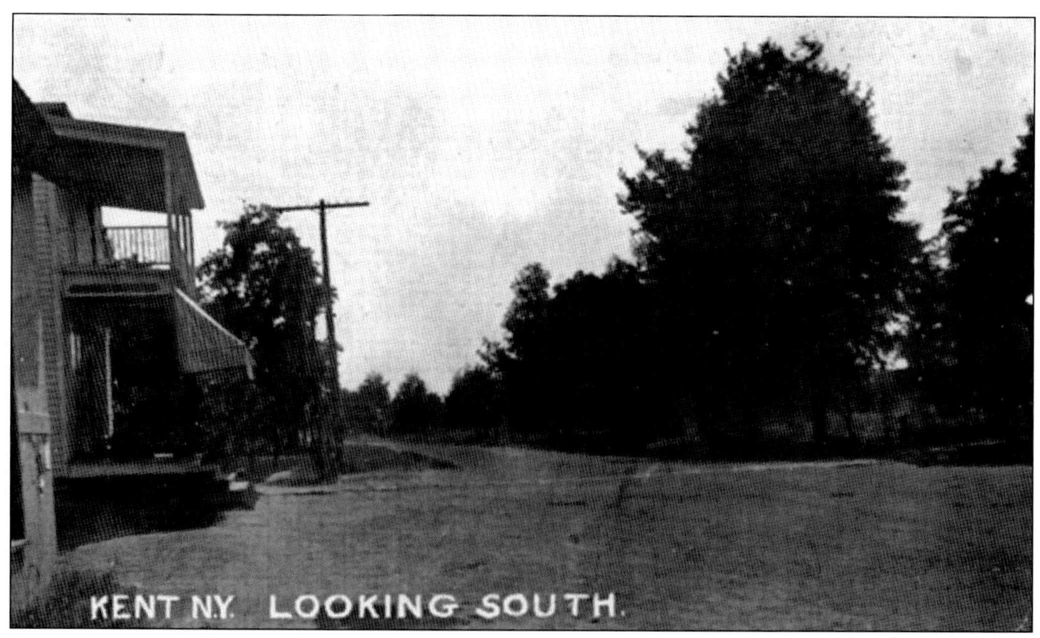

KENT, LOOKING SOUTH. The tracks are almost invisible in this photograph, showing Kent Road, looking in a southerly direction. (Courtesy of Orleans County Department of History.)

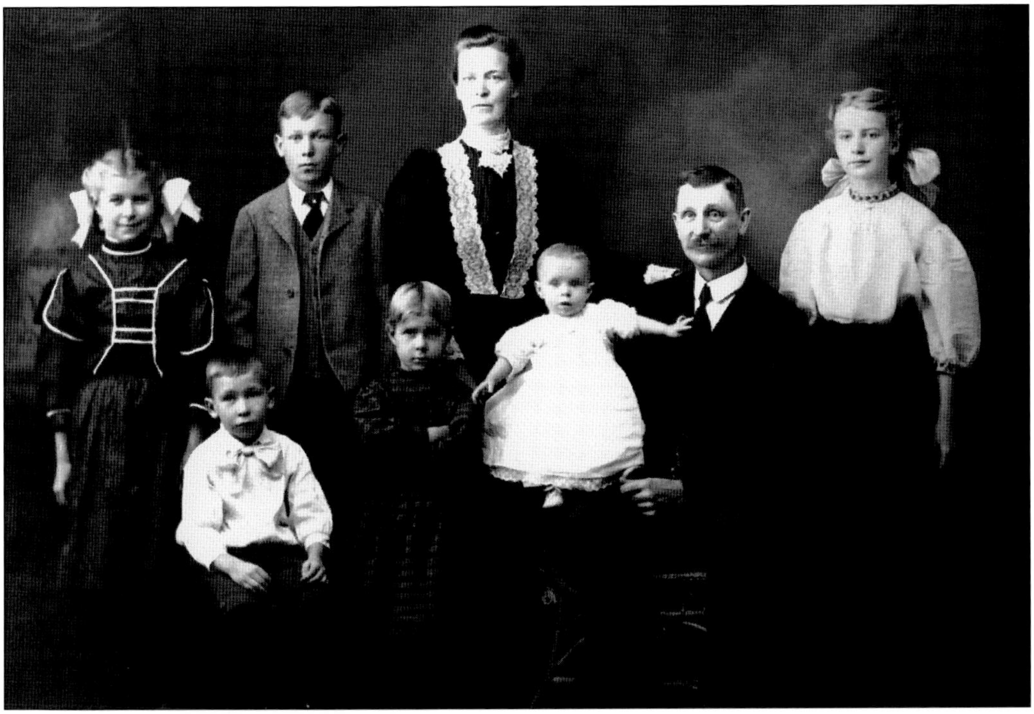

THE BENJAMIN MILLER FAMILY, 1911. Posing for this professional portrait are, from left to right, (first row) Everett, Frances, Hilda, and Benjamin; (second row) Lettie, Charles, Elizabeth Blissett Miller, and Florence. (Courtesy of Mark Rustay.)

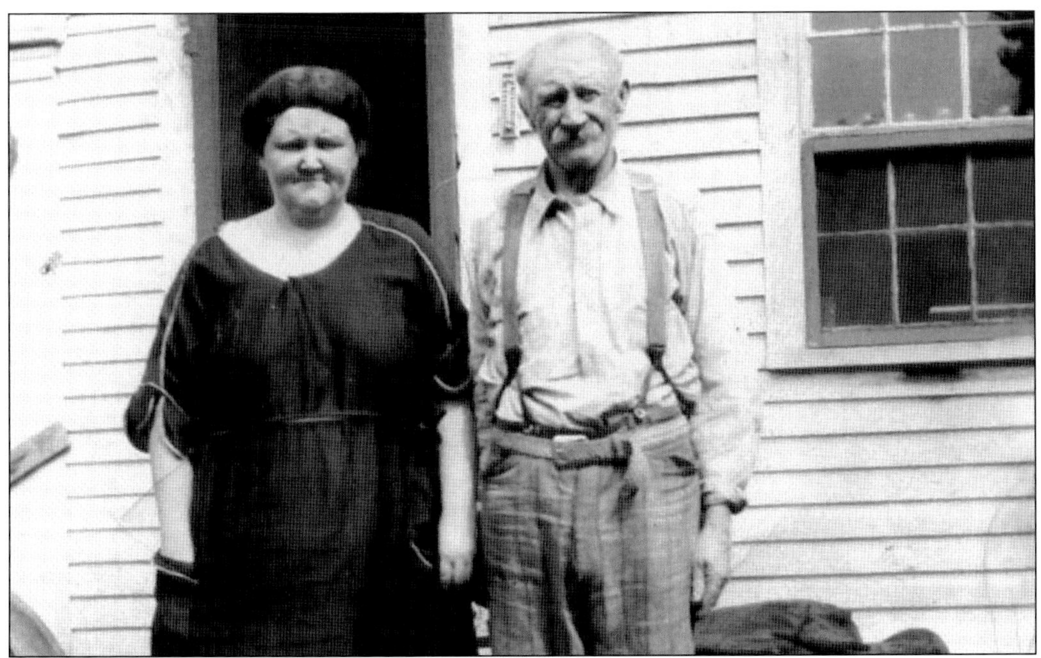

THE CROSSENS. Patrick Crossen poses with his daughter May Rose outside their home in Kent in 1923. The Crossens lived in Kent all their lives. (Courtesy of Mark Rustay.)

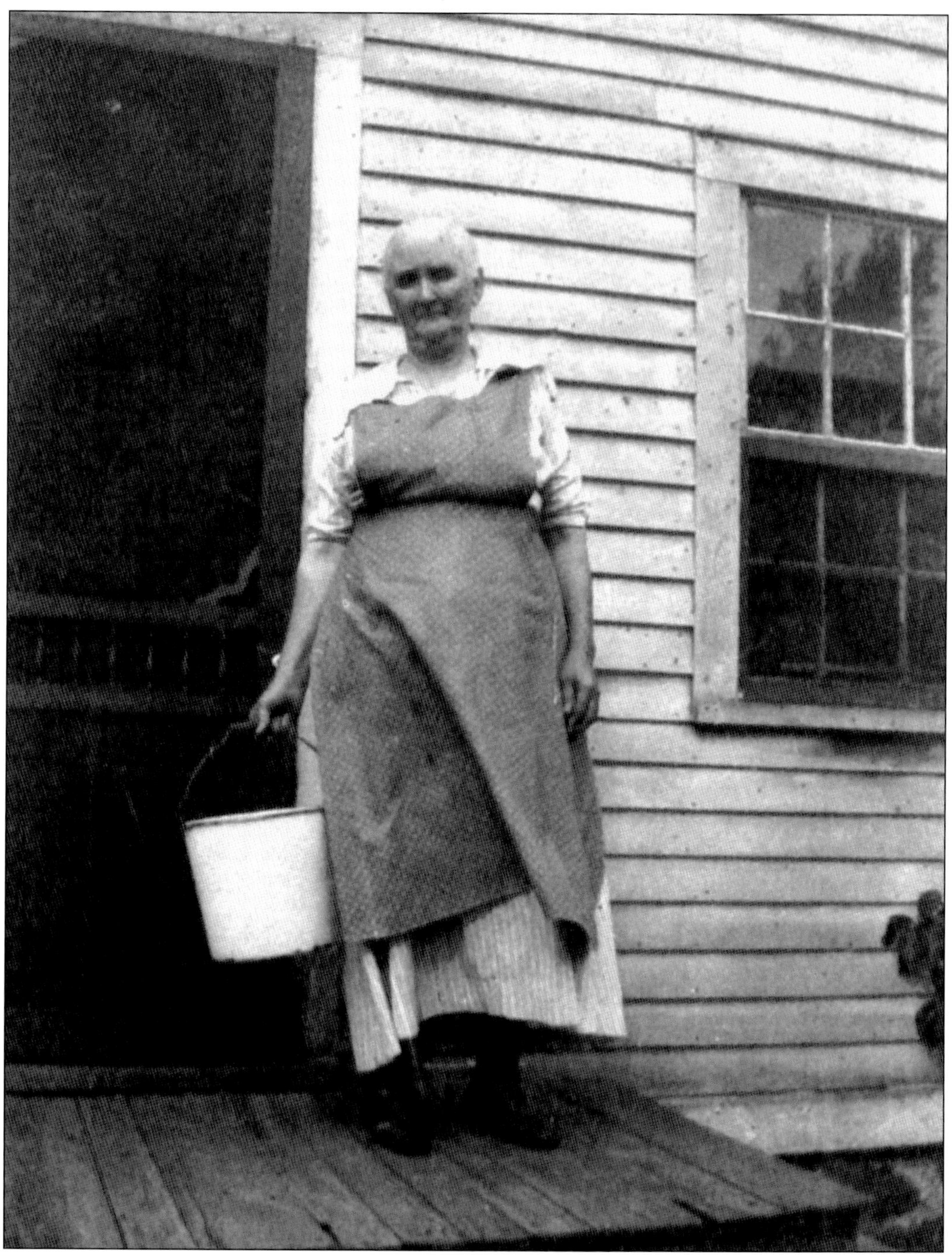

IRISH BLOOD. Anna Kelley's parents crossed the ocean and settled in nearby Newfane. Kelley met her husband, Patrick Crossen, and they spent the rest of their lives on their farm in Kent. (Courtesy of Mark Rustay.)

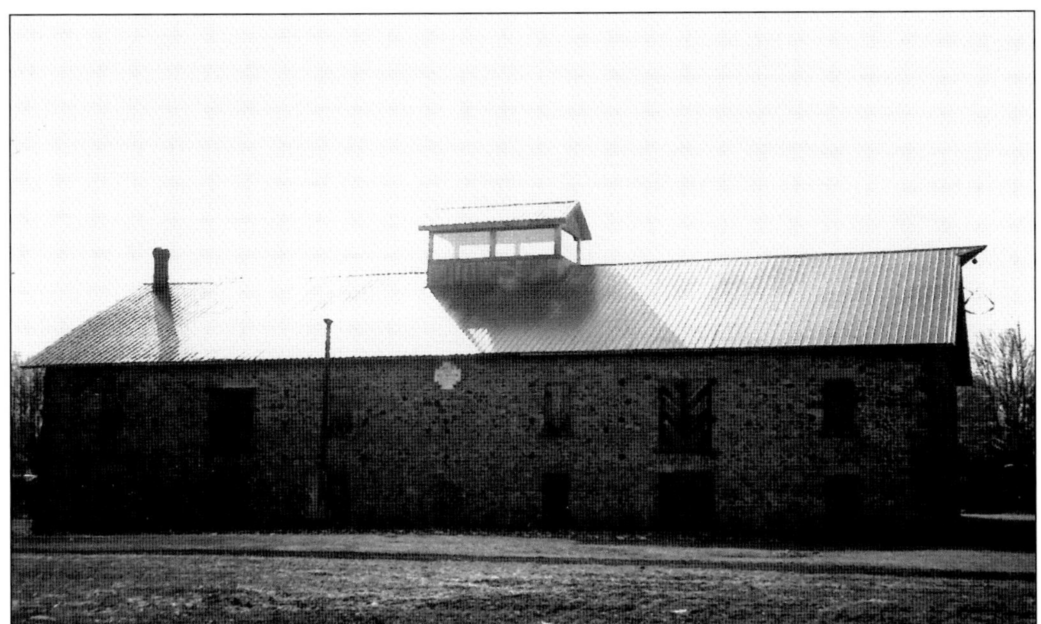

Carlton Station Cold Storage. The cold storage building constructed in 1881 was built by Albert W. Wood, a pioneer in fruit growing. Through his interest and dedication to the propagation of fruit orchards, he developed one of the most outstanding fruit farms in the area. For several yeas, the state used portions of his farm for experimental orchard work involving students from Cornell Agricultural College. (Courtesy of Bud Canham.)

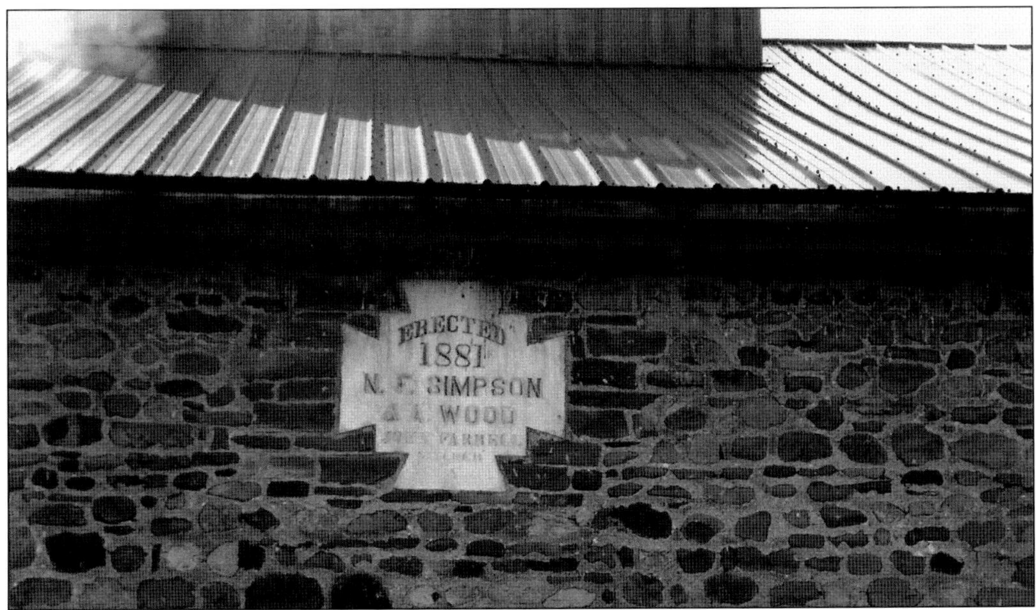

Wood's Marker. When Albert Wood built the cold storage, he made sure his name would live on for as long as the building. It is an eye-catcher, and all who visit the building are drawn to the marker to see what it says. (Courtesy of Bud Canham.)

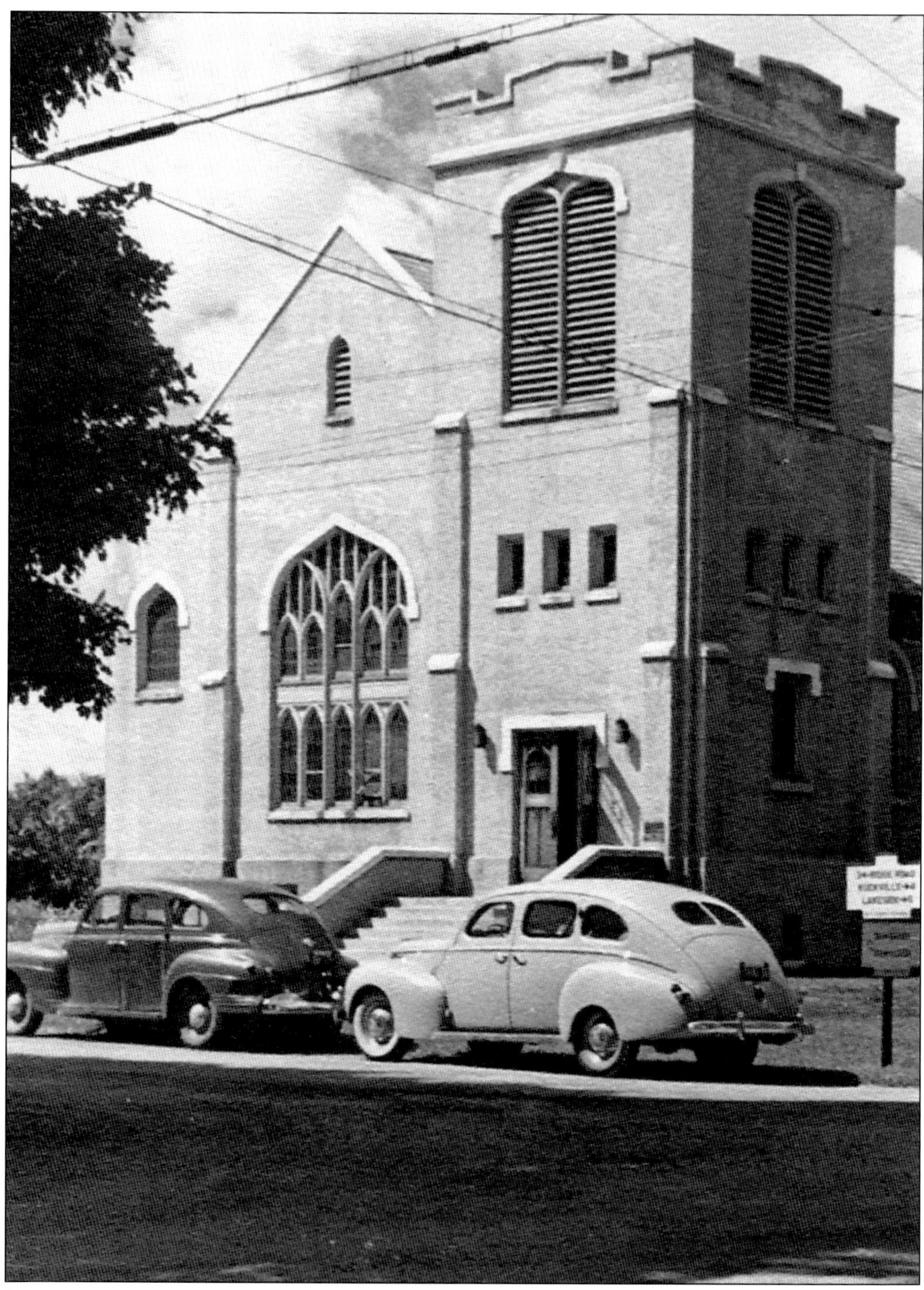

WATERPORT METHODIST. The original Waterport Methodist Church was built before 1890 and burned in 1924, having to be rebuilt. At the time, people believed this fire was set by the Ku Klux Klan, as it was reported in newspapers of the day. The church was rebuilt. This photograph was taken around 1940. (Courtesy of Orleans County Department of History.)

Six

Churches and Schools

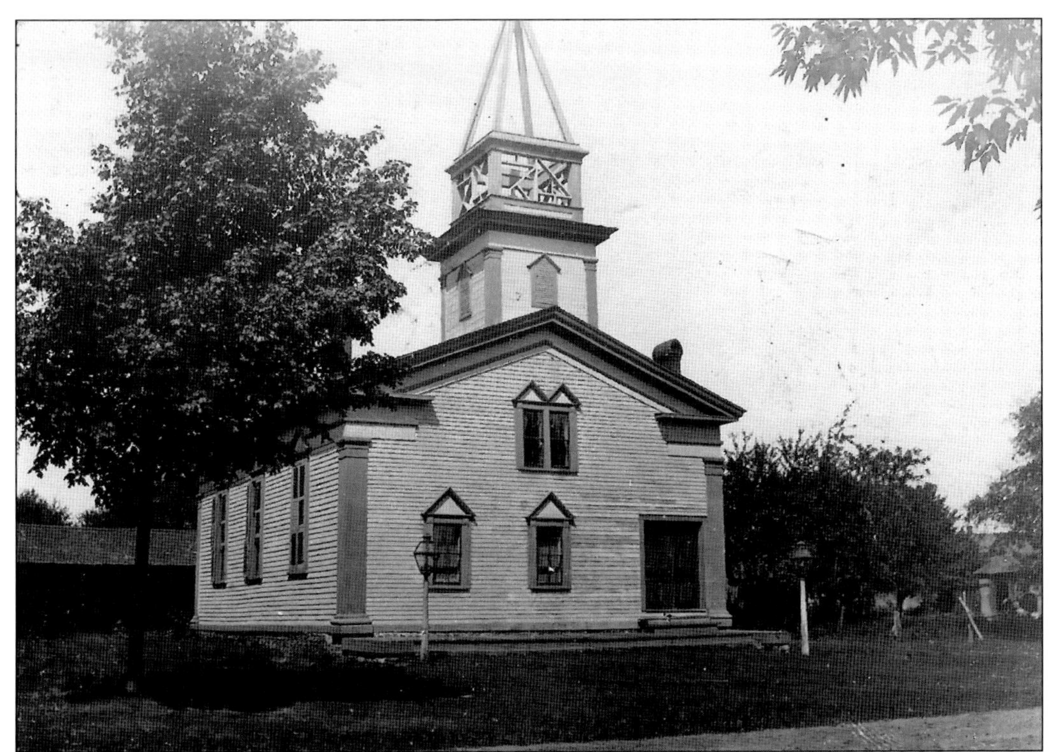

Kenyonville Methodist. This was the Methodist church at Kenyonville, the very first church in Orleans County. (Courtesy of Orleans County Department of History.)

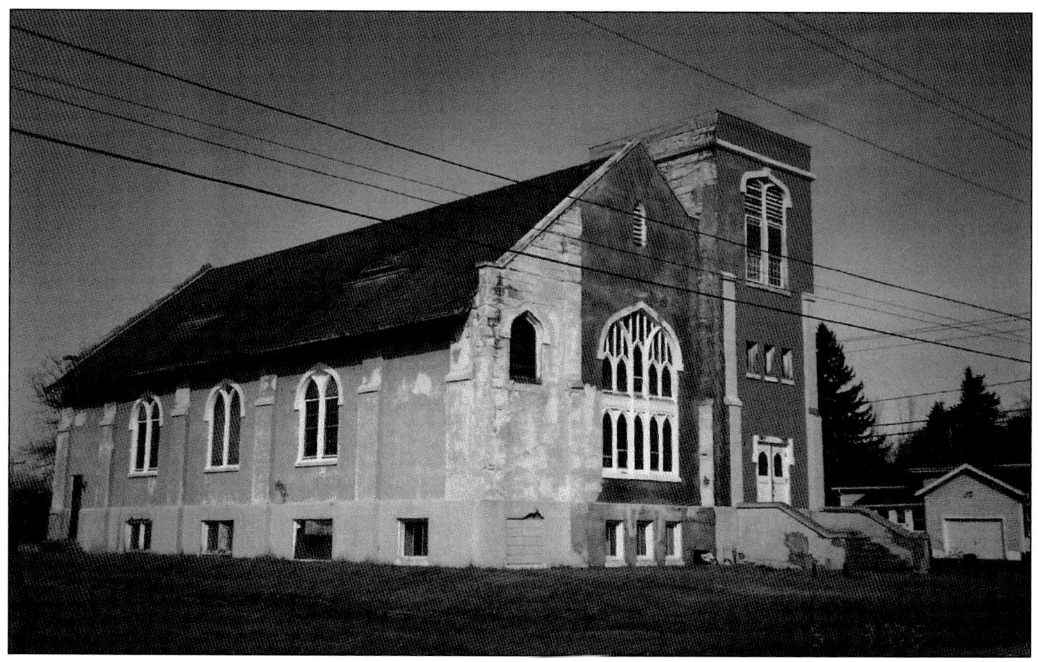

ANOTHER VIEW. This is a full view of the Waterport Methodist Church. (Courtesy of Orleans County Department of History.)

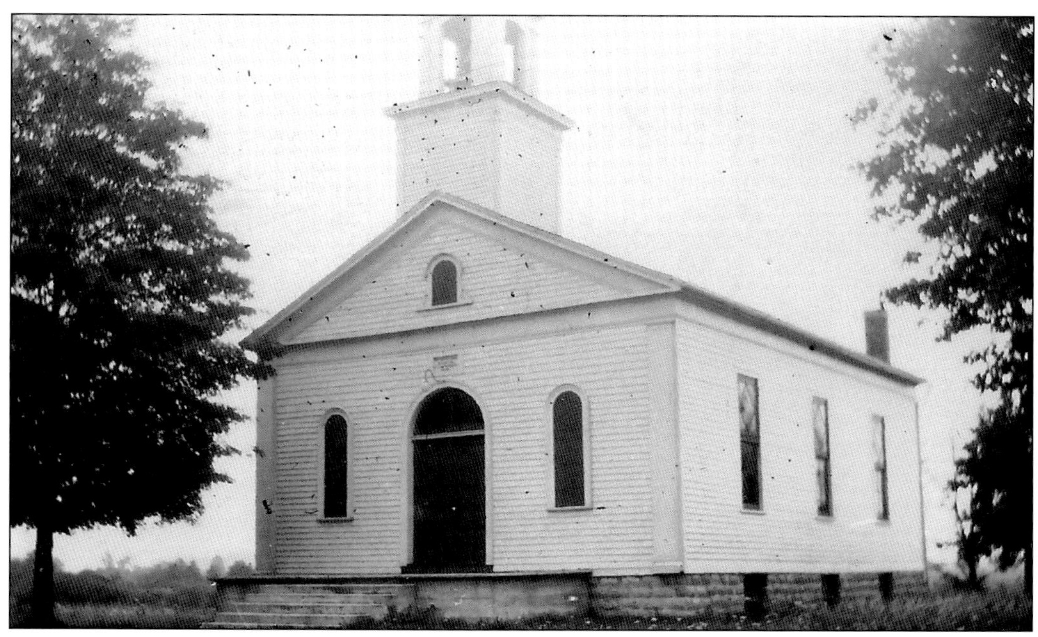

KENT BAPTIST CHURCH. This church was first built in the mid-1800s, then was moved, and it subsequently burned. (Courtesy of Orleans County Department of History.)

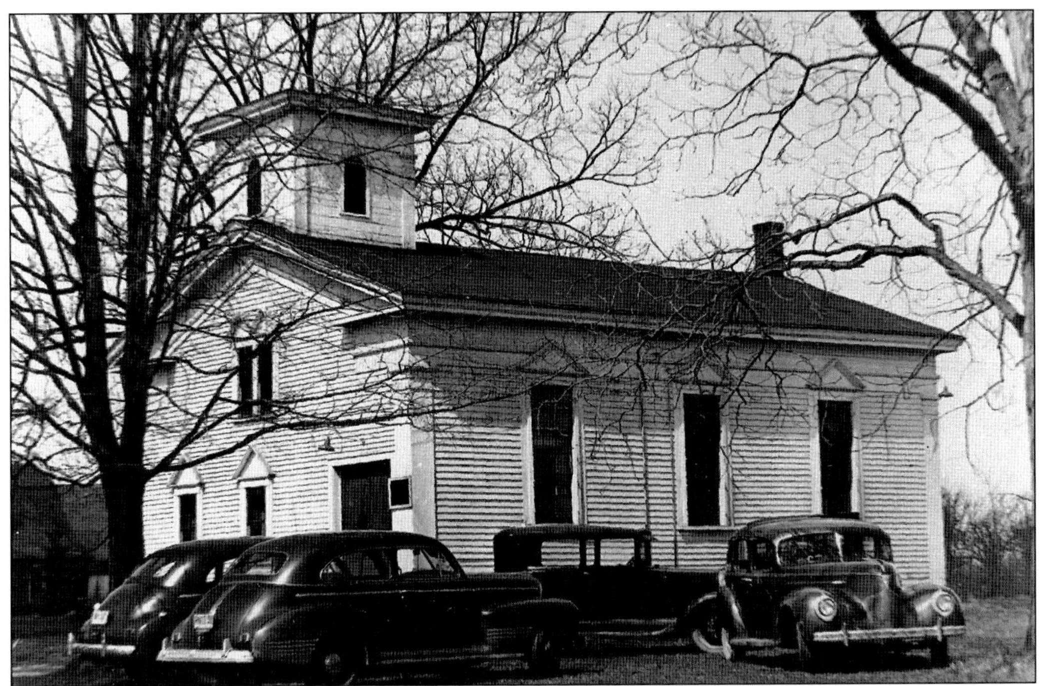

KENYONVILLE METHODIST CHURCH, C. 1940. The church was rebuilt, and instead of horses and buggies bringing people to church, cars now took them. (Courtesy of Mike and Chris Elam.)

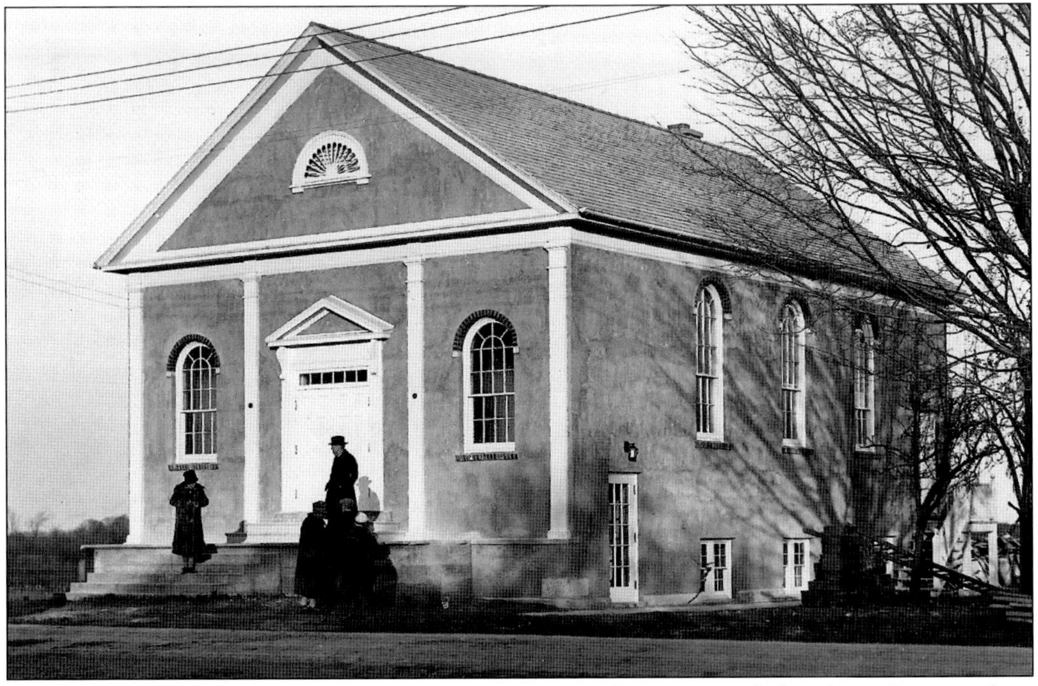

KENT BAPTIST CHURCH, C. 1925. This was a very well-constructed church, and its members were proud of their efforts. In 1935, the three Baptist churches, at the Bridges, Kent, and East Gaines, united to be become the Gaines-Carlton Larger Parish. (Courtesy of Orleans County Department of History.)

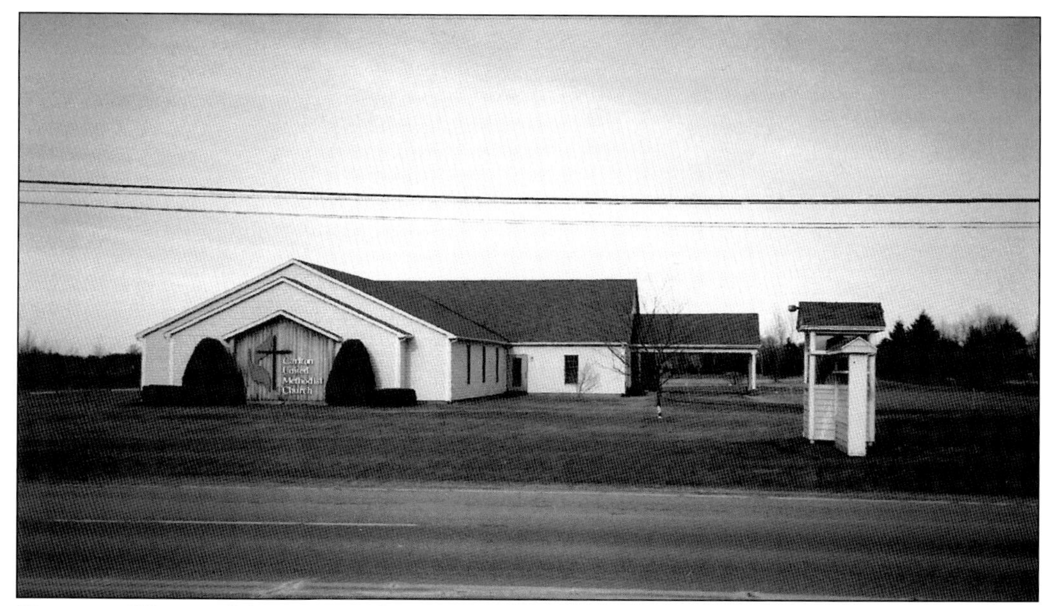

CARLTON UNITED METHODIST CHURCH TODAY. This church, located on Route 18 west of Waterport, has replaced and united all three former Methodist churches of Carlton. (Courtesy of Bud Canham.)

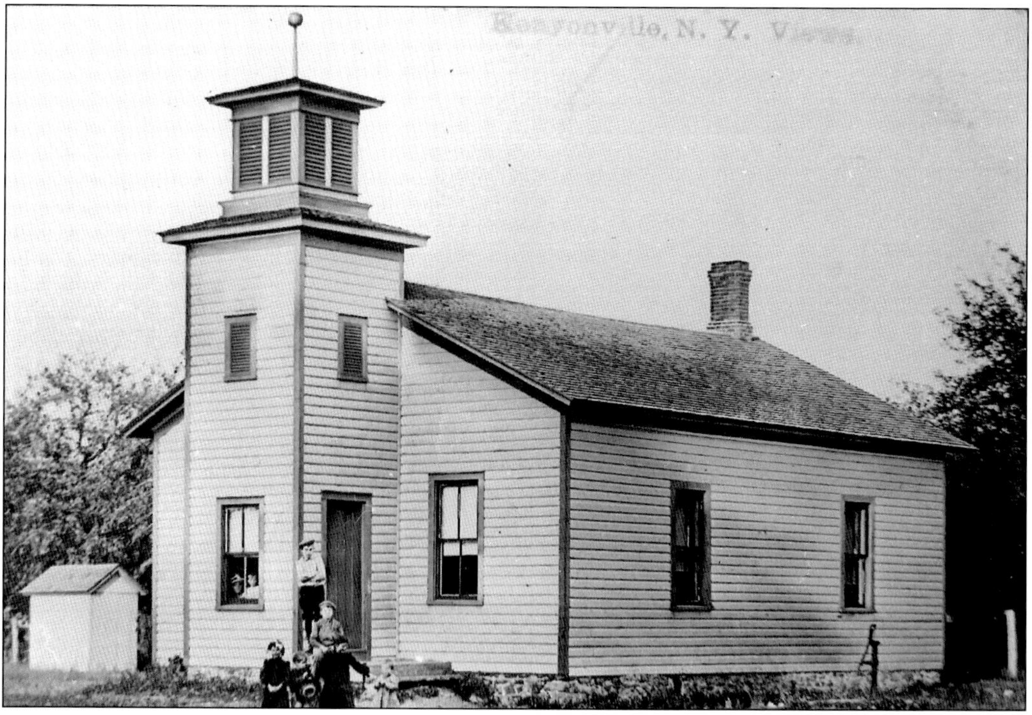

KENYONVILLE SCHOOL, C. 1910. This school was on Harris Road and is now a private residence. (Courtesy of Mike and Chris Elam.)

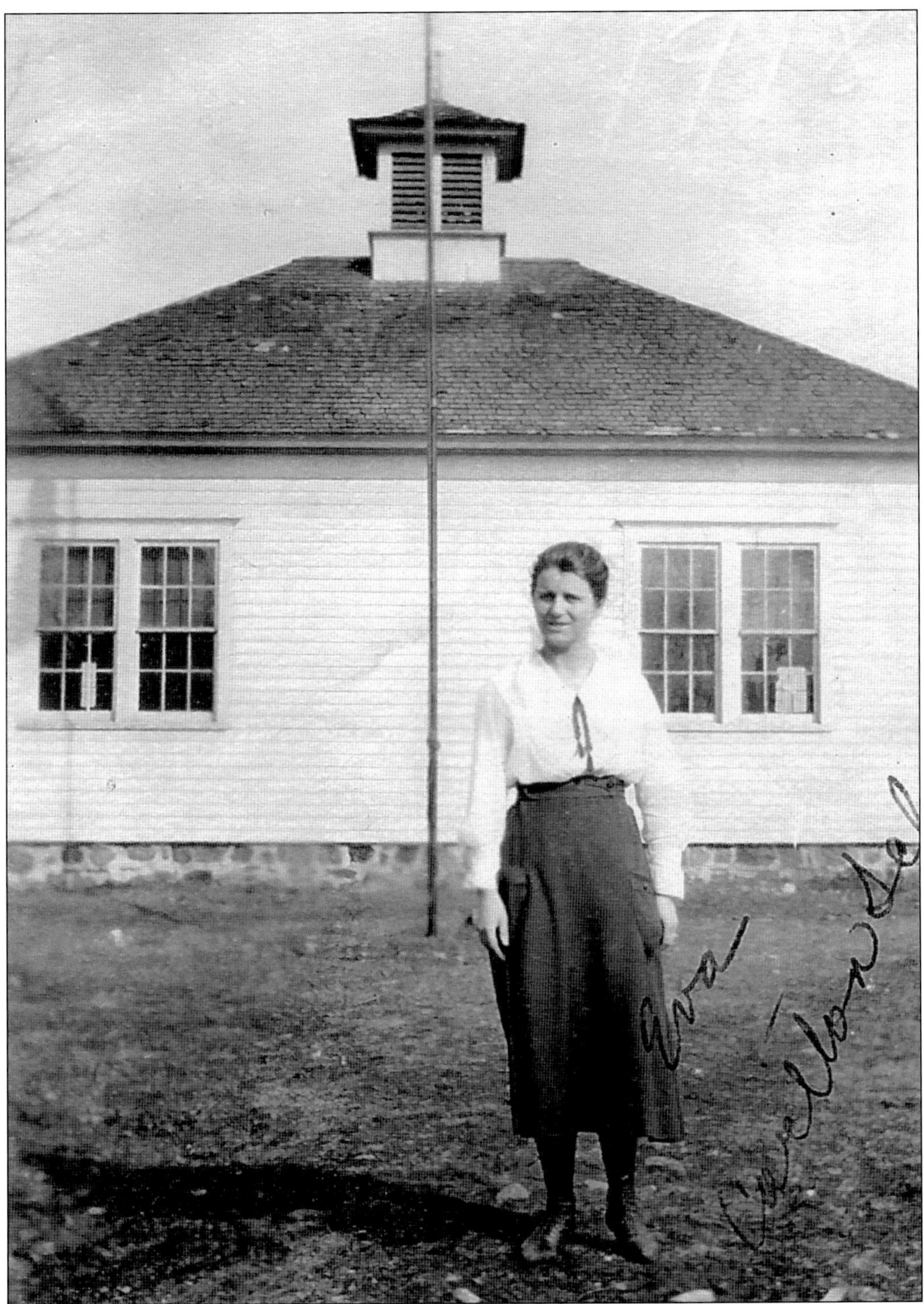

SCHOOL PRIDE. Eva Kelsey, teacher, stands in front of the Carlton School around 1917. The first schoolmaster was Peleg Helms, appointed in 1810. Carlton had the first school in Orleans County. (Courtesy of David Kelsey.)

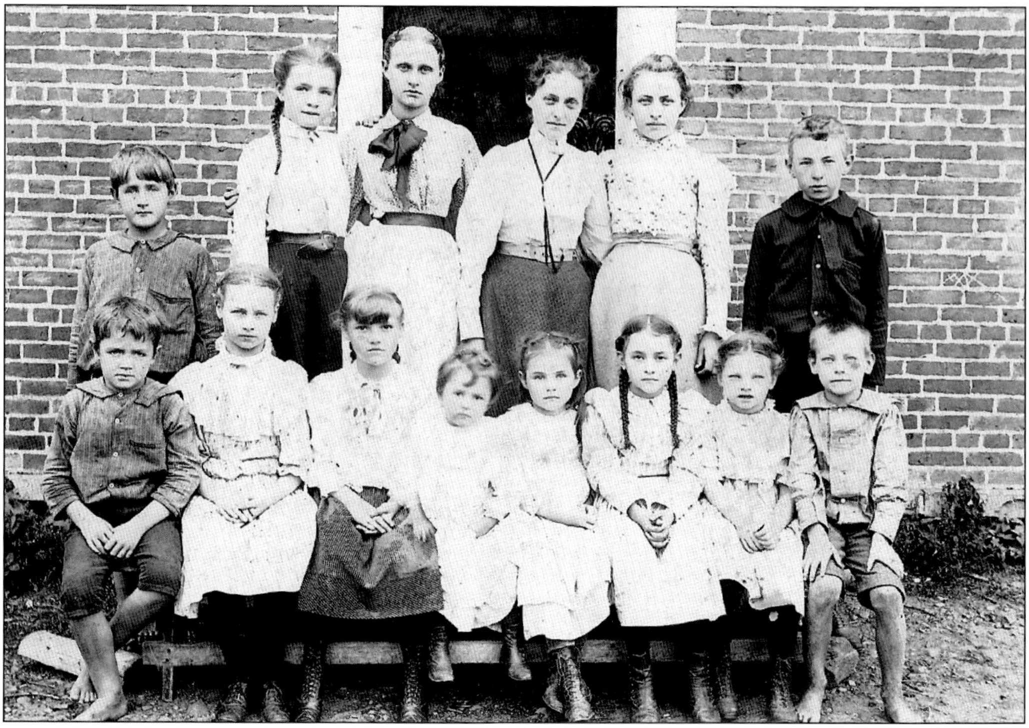

BRICK SCHOOL HOUSE, 1901. Students at the Brick School House in Kent in 1901 are, from left to right, (first row) Charlie Gray, Helen Curtis, Edna Mowers, Bessie Jeffery, Jillian Jeffery, Gertrude Spaulding, Berenice Curtis, and Leon Curtis; (second row) Everett Gray, Jeanette Gray, Rosie Yhanke, teacher Nellie Reed, Katie Banker, and Foster Wilcox. (Courtesy of Garland Miller.)

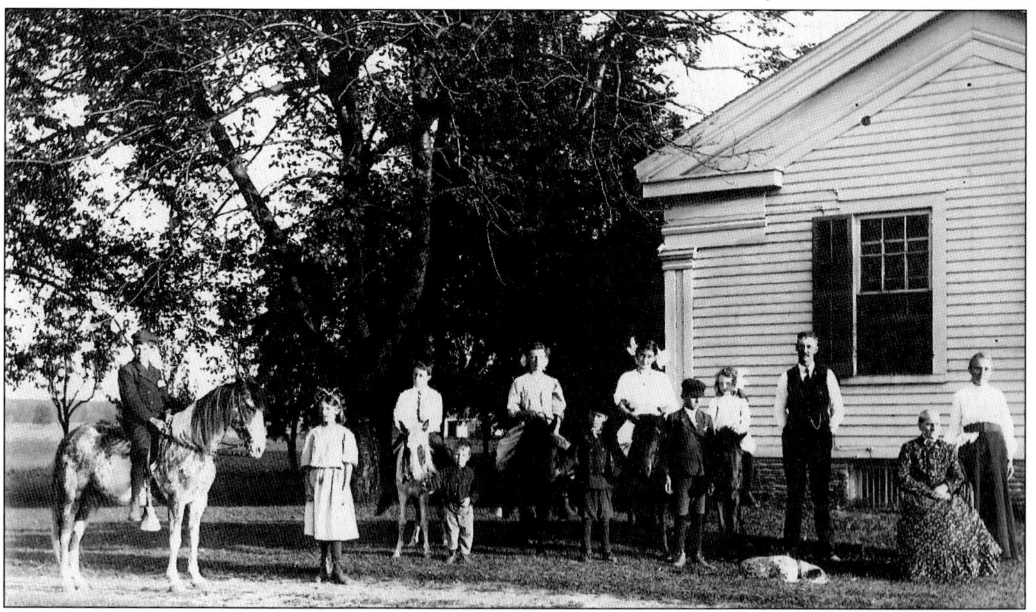

SCHOOLHOUSE, 1908. This school was at the intersection of Baker and Sawyer Roads. From left to right, in the front row, the first two children are Leon and Berenice Curtis. (Courtesy of Garland Miller.)

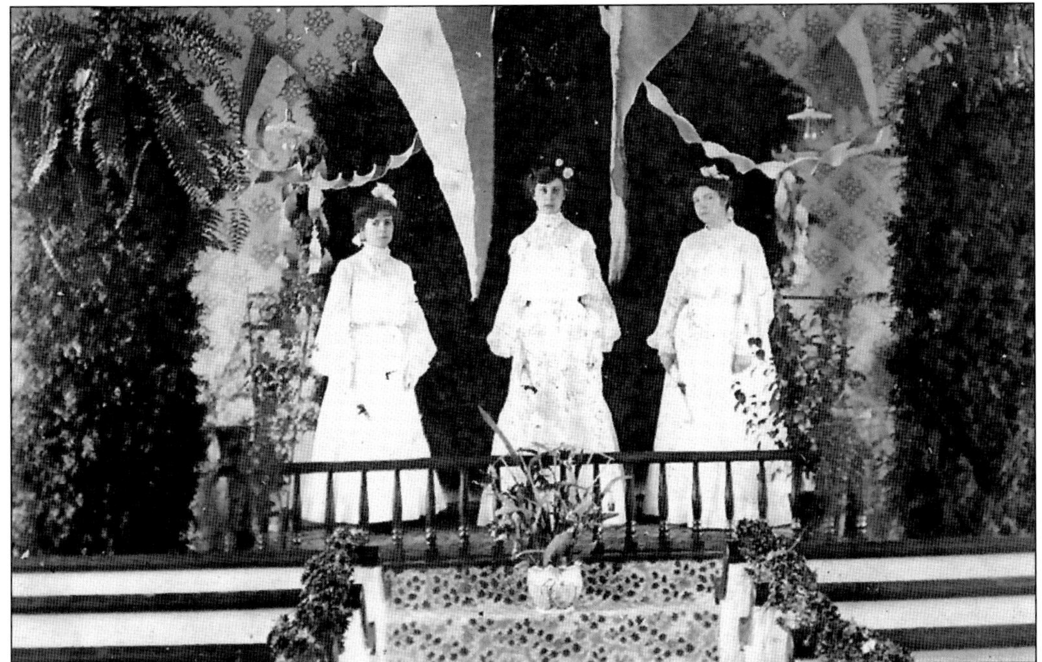

A Class of Three. These three girls made up the entire graduating class of the Waterport Union School in 1903. Graduation was held inside the Waterport Methodist Church. From left to right are Bertha June, Gertrude Plowman, and Susie Sargent. (Courtesy of Beatrice Axtell Young.)

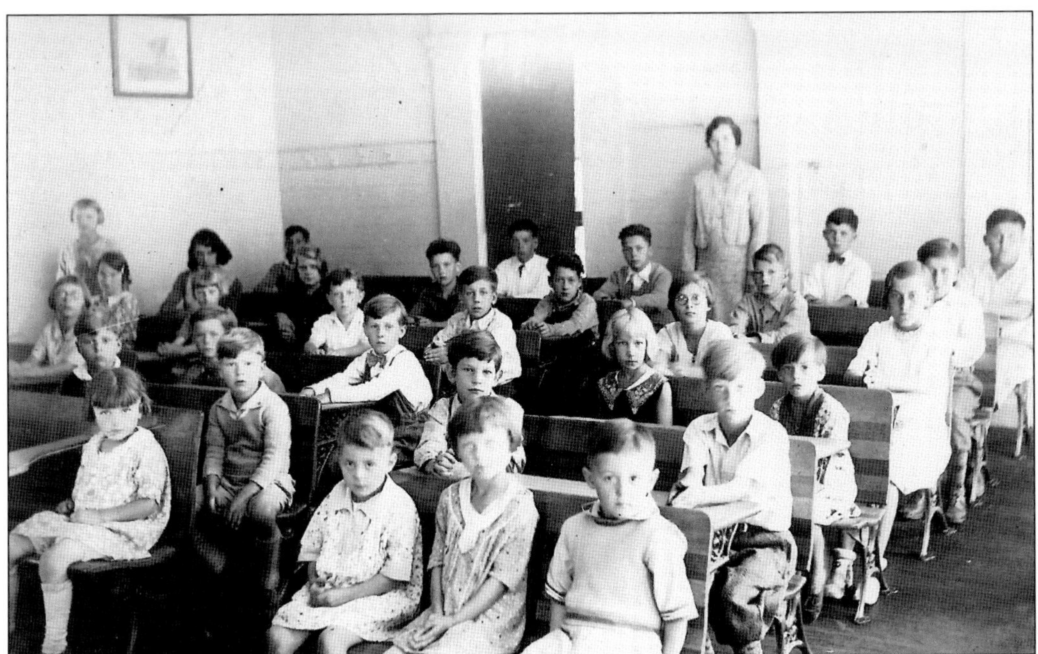

Kenyonville School, 1924. Names are unavailable for many of the children in this classroom, but the teacher at the back of the room is Sylvia Parks. The five children at the front of the photograph are, from left to right, unidentified, Dave Boyce, Julias Marek, Shirley Thompson, and Robert Thompson. (Courtesy of Sandy Tombari Freeman.)

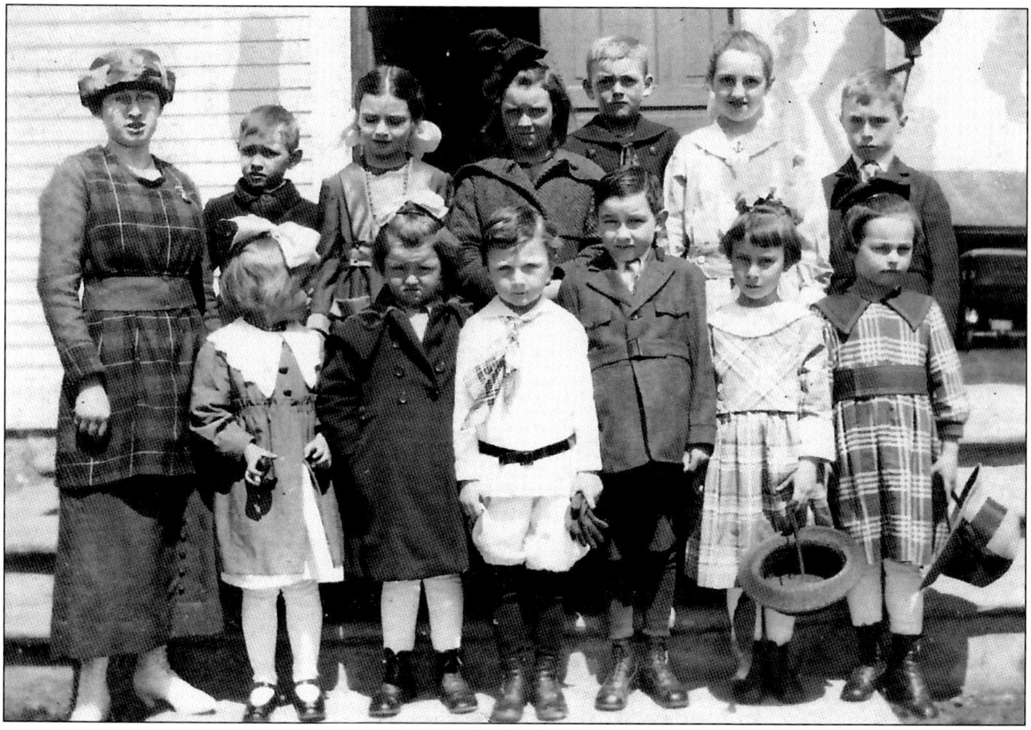

HATS IN THEIR HANDS. Members of Sylvia Parks's class pose for a picture around 1905. The girl standing second from the left in the front row is Gertrude Marvelous Boyce. (Courtesy of Sandy Tombari Freeman.)

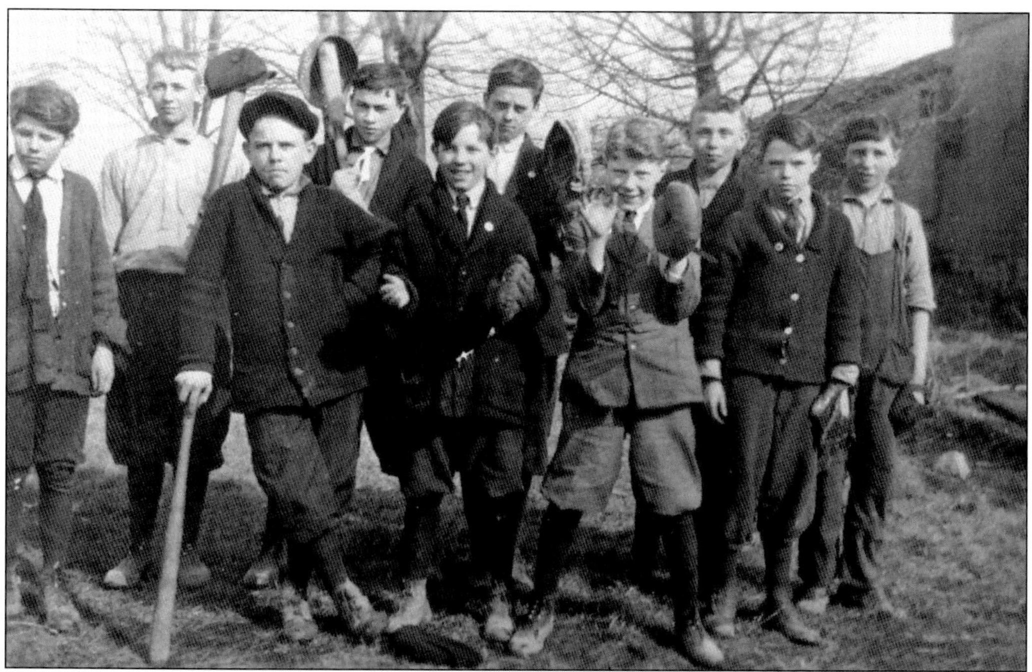

CARLTON DISTRICT NO. 6. Baseball students in Eva Kelsey's class pose for their photograph in 1918. (Courtesy of David Kelsey.)

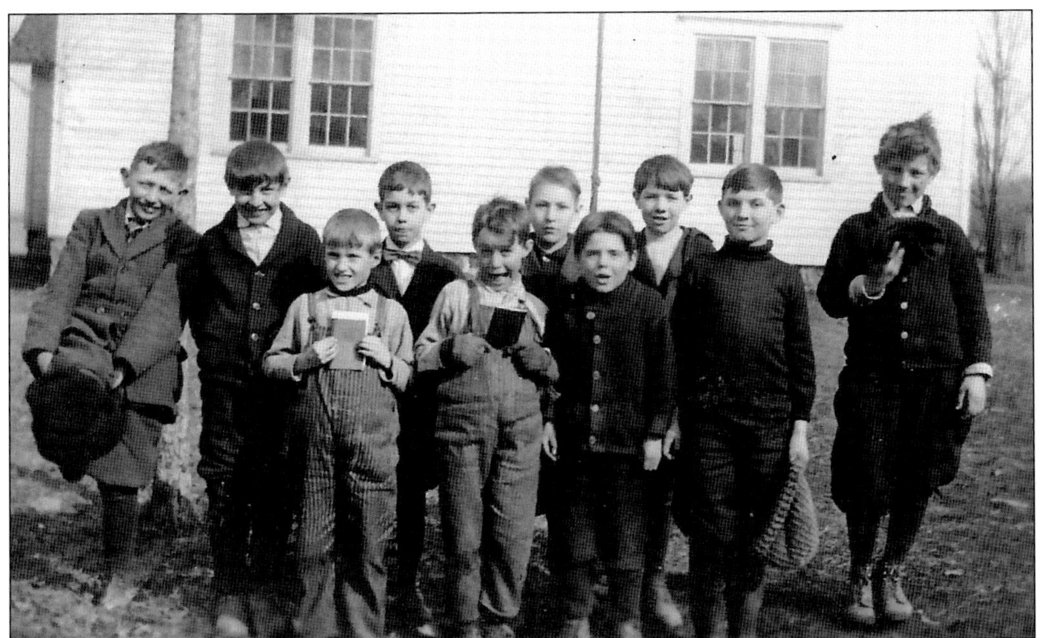

CARLTON STATION YOUNGSTERS, C. 1910. These children were part of the student body that attended class in 17 schoolhouses in Carlton. (Courtesy of David Kelsey.)

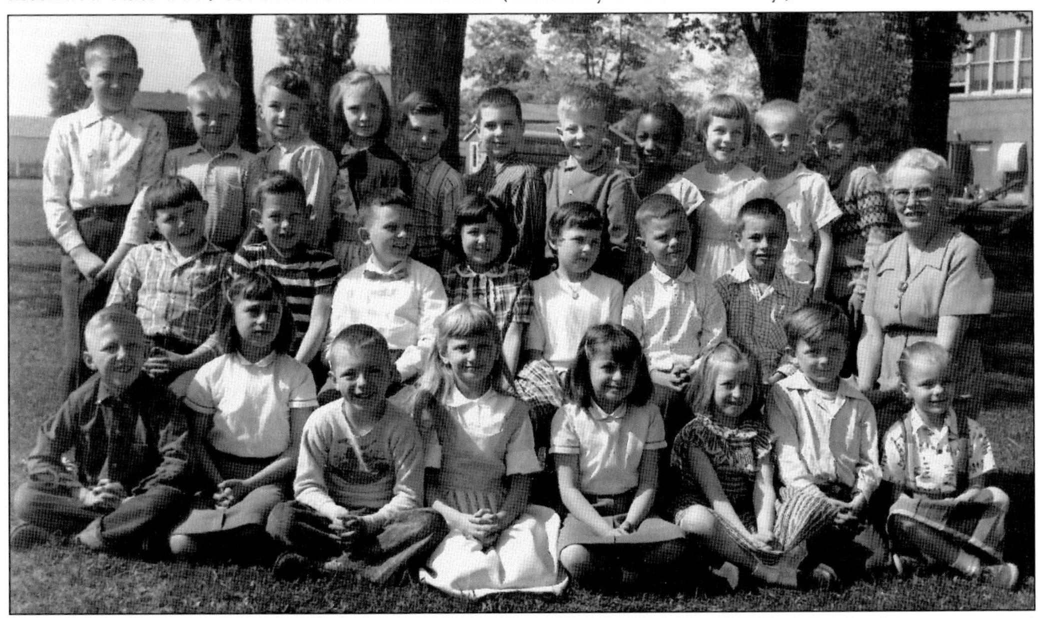

WATERPORT ELEMENTARY SECOND GRADERS, 1958. After 1950, one school building was used in Waterport, but it merged with the Albion district after 1976. From left to right are (first row) Jason Jeffords, Sandra Peruzzini, John Jurs, Kathleen Woolston, Susan Peruzzini, Janet Brown, Kenneth Kuhns, and Linda Garrod; (second row) Robert Canham, Ronald Gursslin, Frank Gould, Karen Van Wycke, Michele Nesbitt, Ronald Marek, and Craig Milliman; (third row) Michael Budynski, Lynn Miller, Thomas Taber, Rosemary Pinson, Michael Kuhns, David Thomas, Curtis Beam, Bertha Walker, Sue Batt, John Mack, and Lynn Gursslin. The teacher is unidentified. (Courtesy of Orleans County Department of History.)

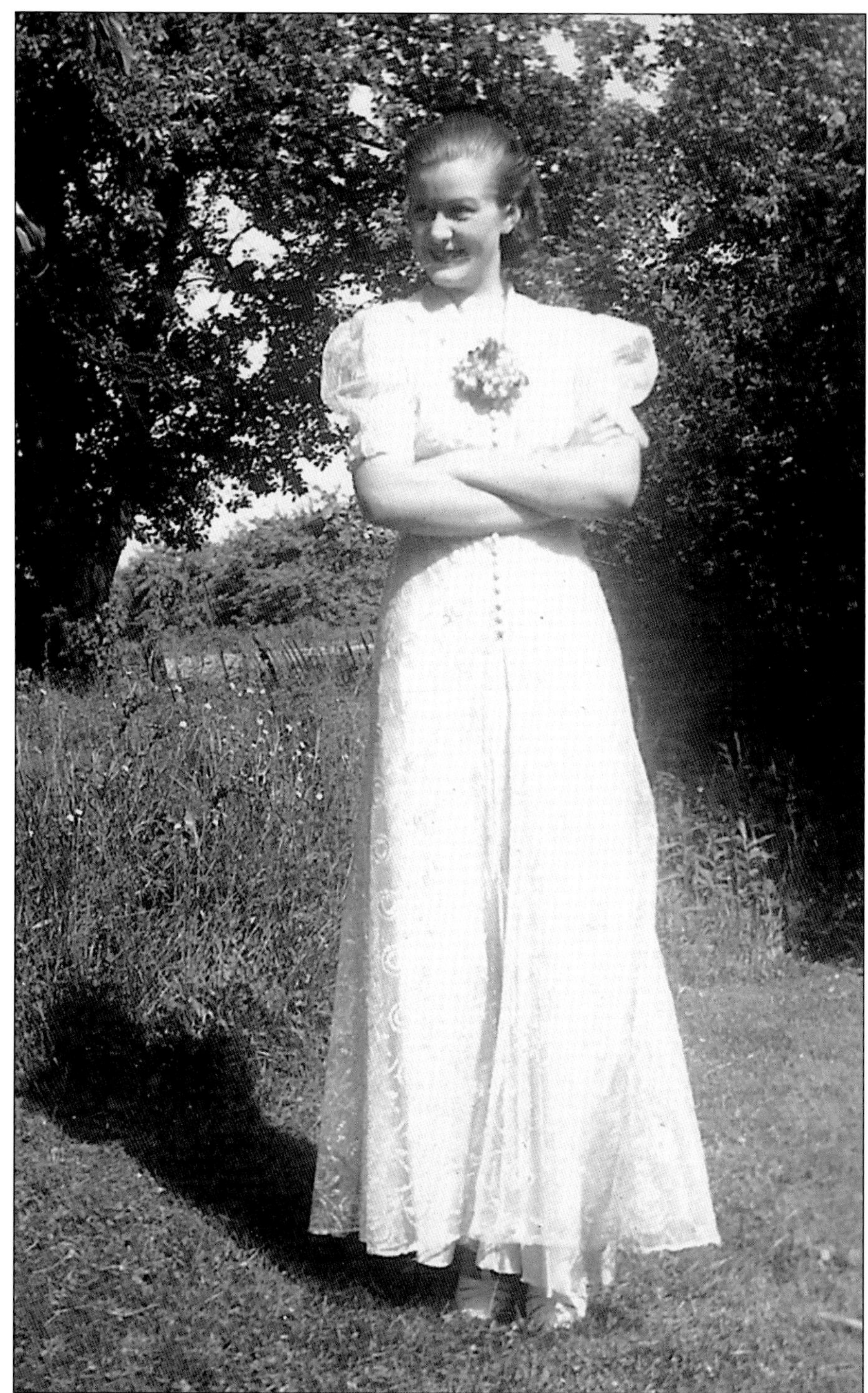

Beautiful Amelia. Born and raised at the Oak Orchard Harbor in 1917, Amelia Hoot Lovewell still reveres the local history passed down by her family. Her grandfather Robert Hoot arrived in this harbor from Sodus, New York, as an eight-year-old boy. Amelia penned one of the dedications on page 4. (Courtesy of the Lovewell family.)

Seven

Post-Depression Memories

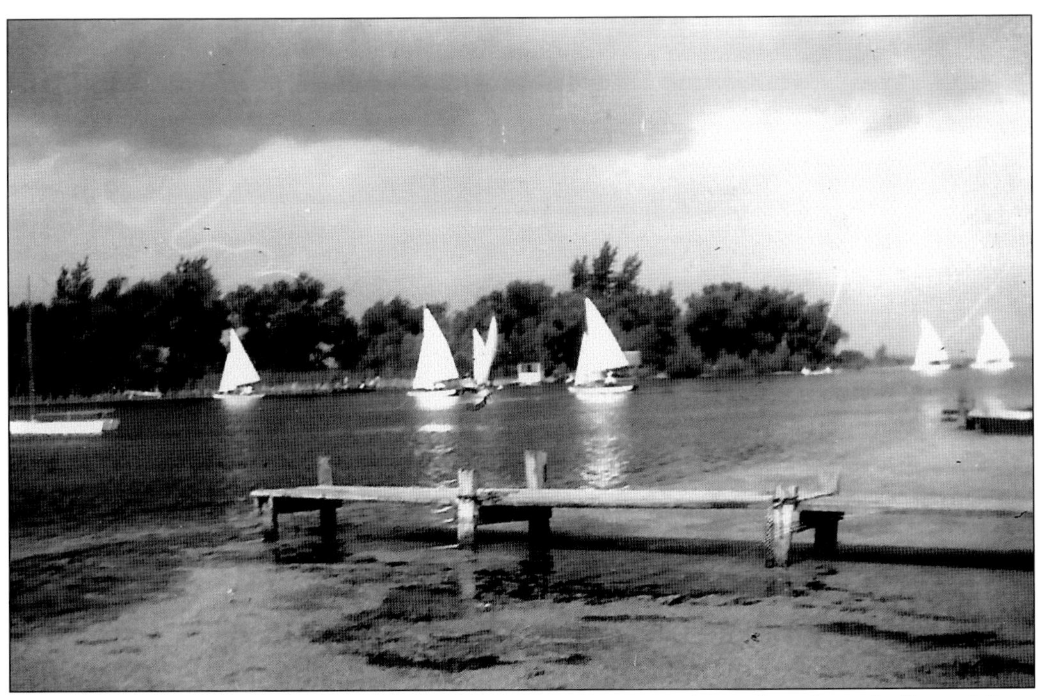

On Oak Orchard Creek. In the late 1940s, a group interested in sailing formed a "snipe" fleet. There were 8 or 10 local snipes. Snipe clubs from western New York came for competition. The various powerboats acted as judges and committee boats. The snipe was a very small sailboat, and it took a good sailor to maneuver it. (Courtesy of Amelia Hoot Lovewell.)

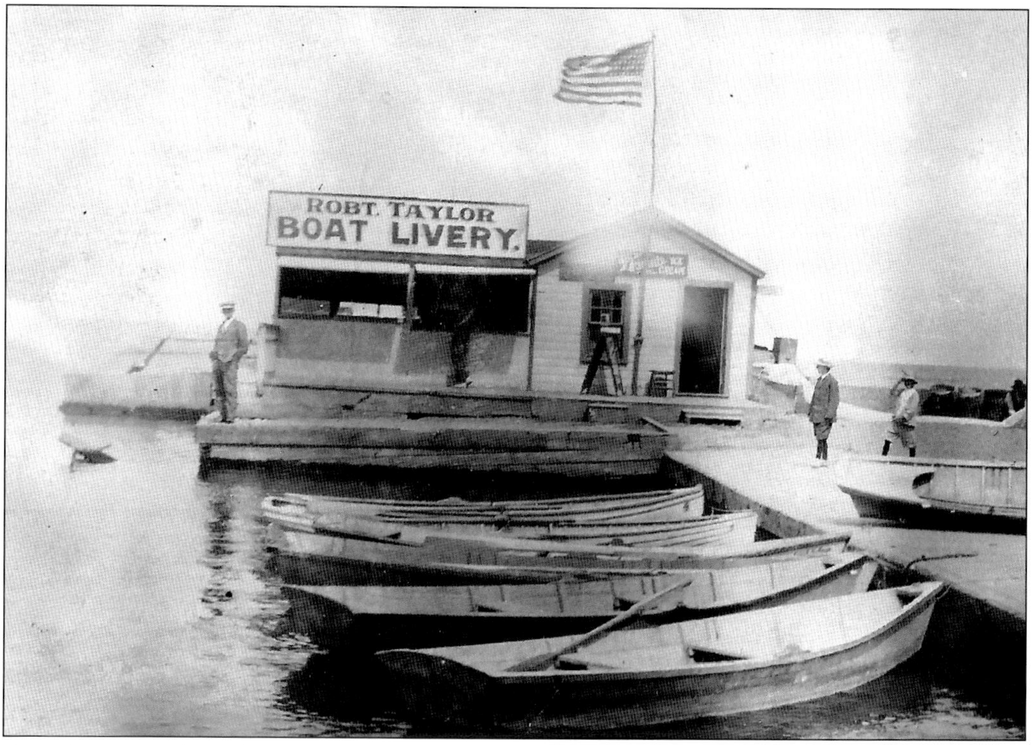

Boat Livery. The Robert Taylor Boat Livery was the place to go in Point Breeze from the early 1900s through the 1950s. Rowboats took fishermen into the harbor for bass fishing. In the early days, people were ferried across the harbor for 5¢ a head. (Courtesy of Mary Sage-Eisvang.)

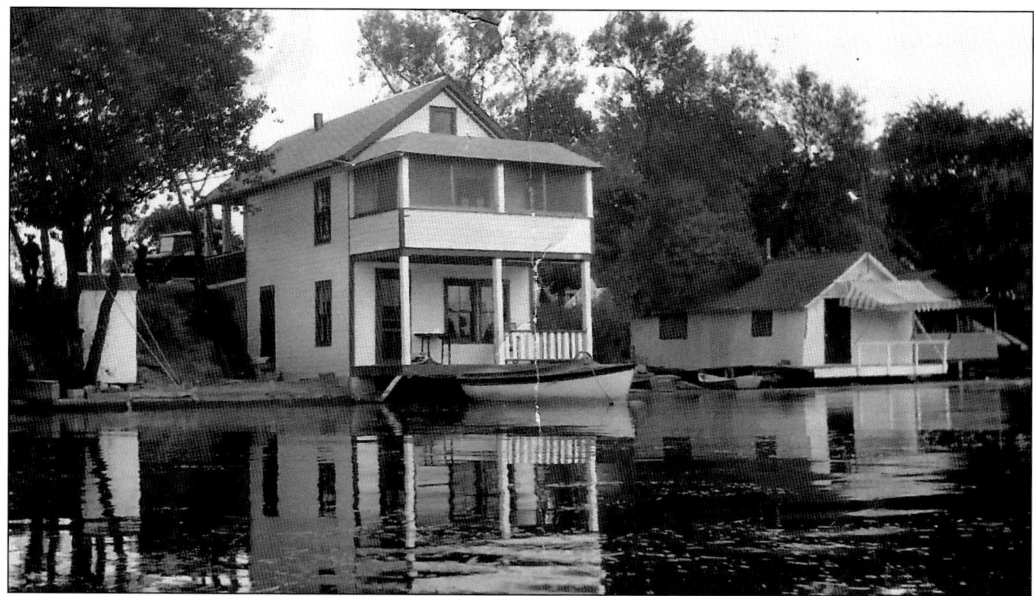

Hoot Cottage. This was the Hoot Cottage on Oak Orchard Creek. Boats sailed through the harbor and out into the lake. (Courtesy of Amelia Hoot Lovewell.)

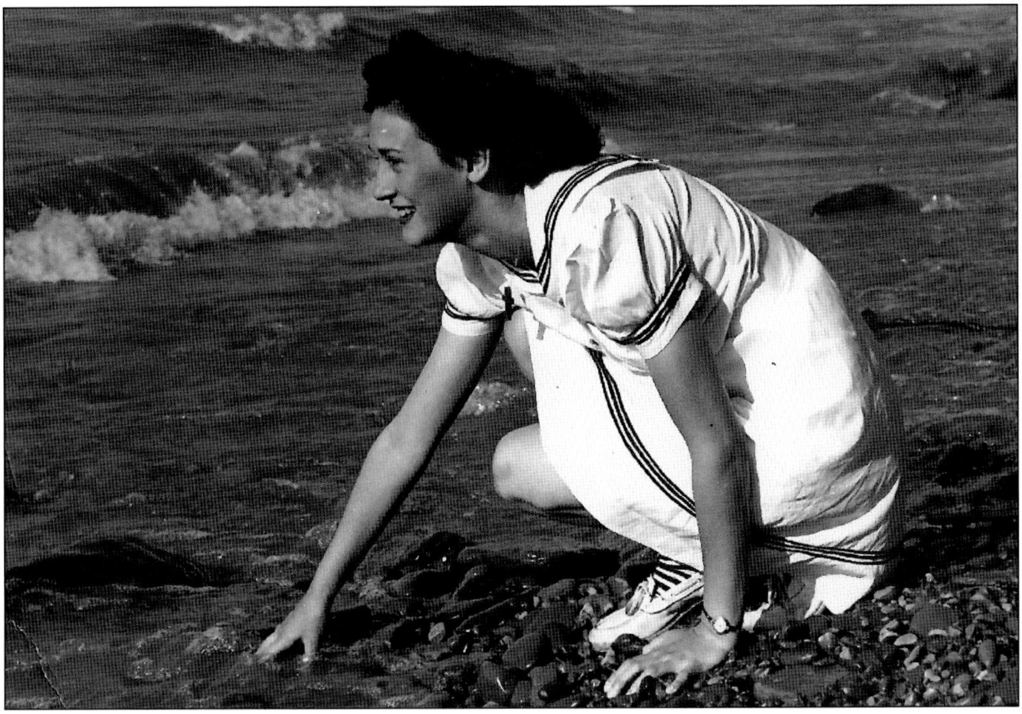

ENJOYING LAKE BREEZES, C. 1939. Marie Mattern looks lovely in her sailor bathing dress as she enjoys the waves and winds over Lake Ontario. Marie contributed to the dedication on page 4. (Courtesy of the Marie Mattern Carlston.)

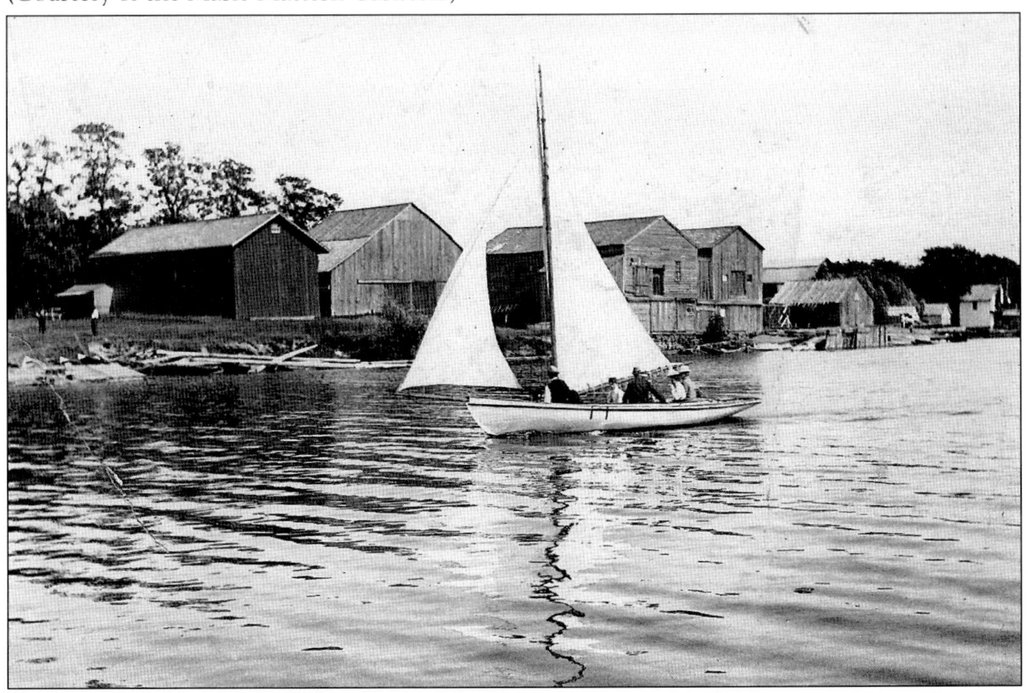

SAILING AT OAK ORCHARD. This sailboat passes a solitary group of barns as people on the shore look on in this 19th-century photograph. (Courtesy of Orleans County Department of History.)

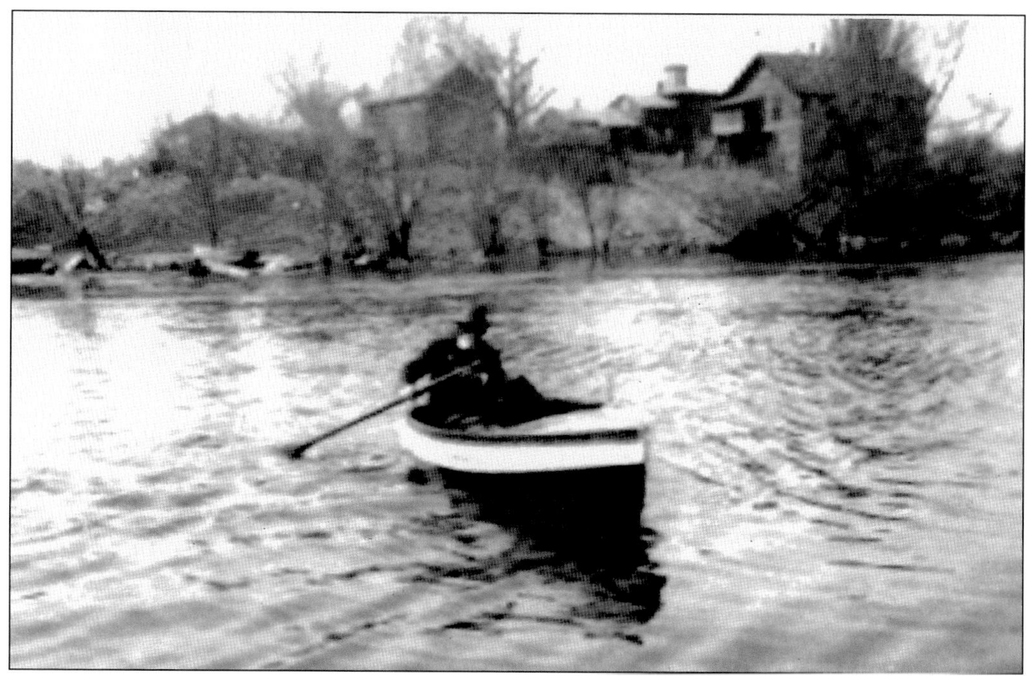

Flooding at the Bridges. Deforest Hatch rows away from the Hatch and Elam boat livery when Oak Orchard River overflowed its banks and flooded the business in 1953. (Courtesy of Mike and Chris Elam.)

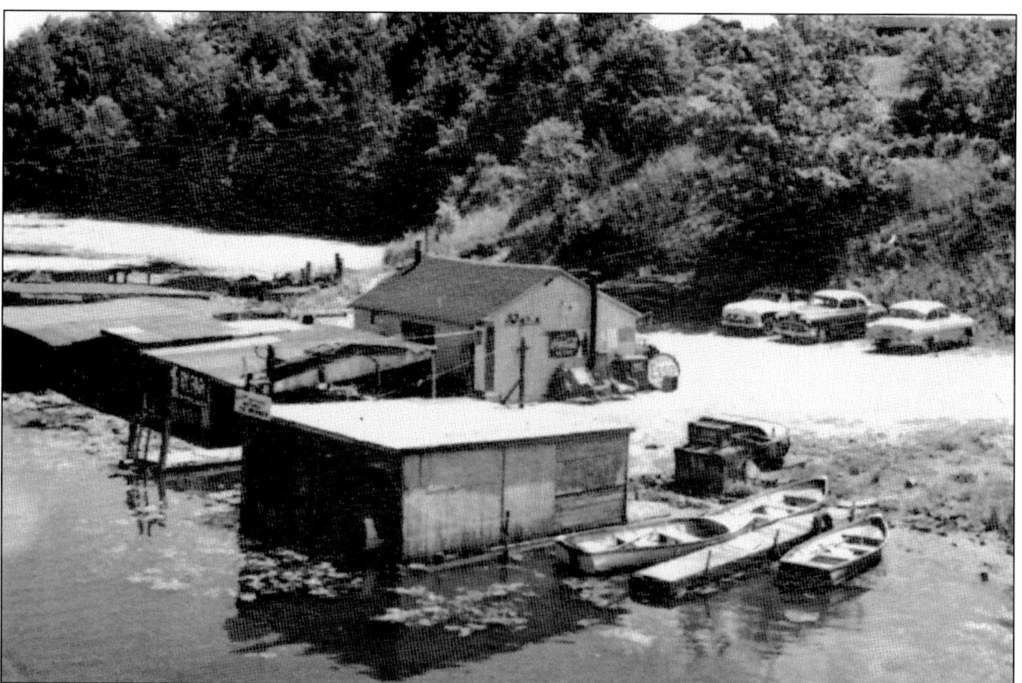

Hatch and Elam. In 1953, water rose higher than usual, and there was general flooding all around the waterfront areas. This flood was at the Hatch and Elam boat livery. (Courtesy of Mike and Chris Elam.)

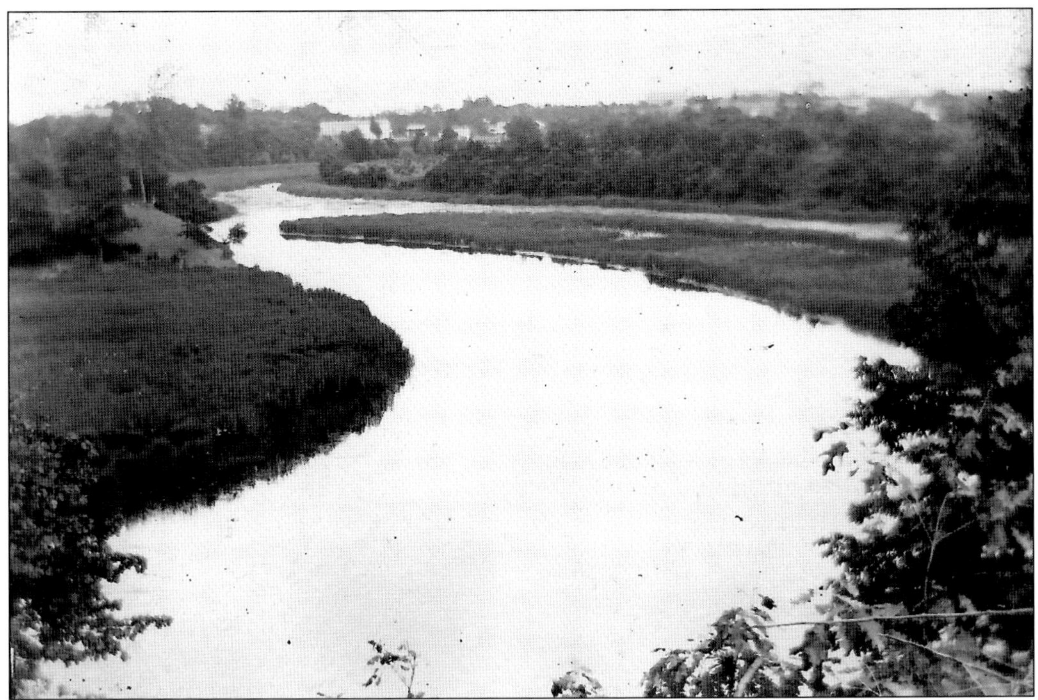

FIDDLER'S ELBOW. This is the area of Oak Orchard Creek north of the Two Bridges area. This photograph was taken on June 16, 1897, but the area does not look much differently today. Good boating skills are required to successfully navigate Fiddler's Elbow. It is very easy to run aground here, and local boaters know to stay well into the channel in this area. (Courtesy of Orleans County Department of History.)

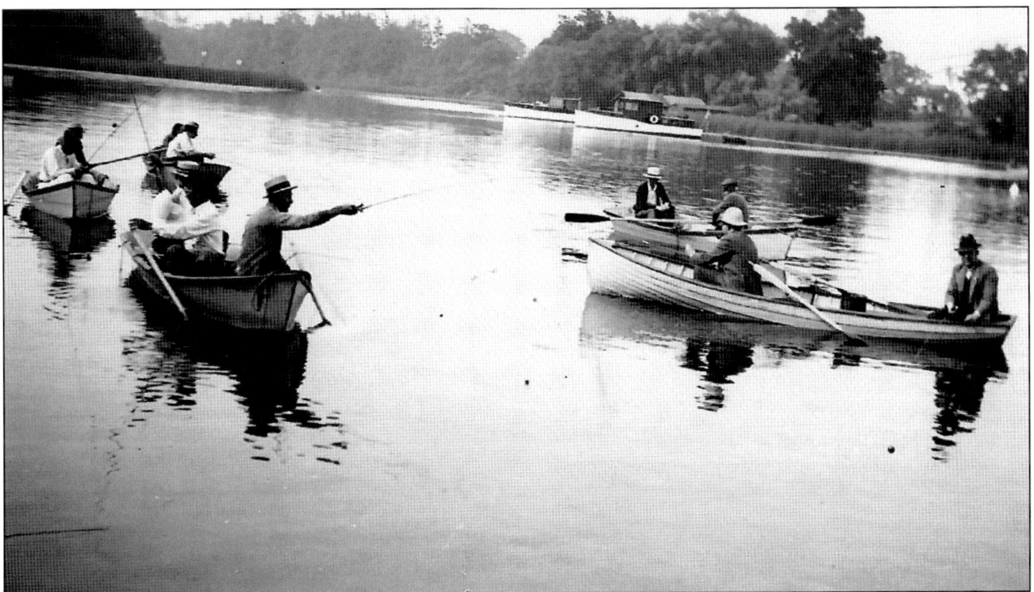

FISHING FOR BASS. This photograph was taken at Point Breeze on the opening day of bass season in 1935. Lake Ontario is known for its tasty bass, but now the big attraction is salmon fishing in the spring and fall. (Courtesy of Amelia Hoot Lovewell.)

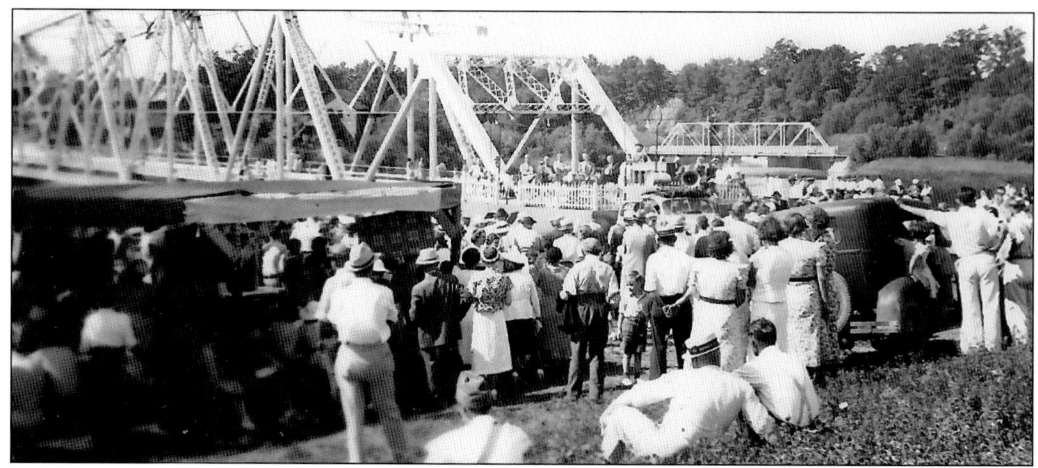

NEW BRIDGE. A large crowd gathers to attend the opening ceremonies of the August 1937 opening of the new bridge over Oak Orchard Creek. Unfortunately, prior to the grand opening, Dr. Benjamin Howes's famous horse, Sandy, died in the parade. (Courtesy of Orleans County Department of History.)

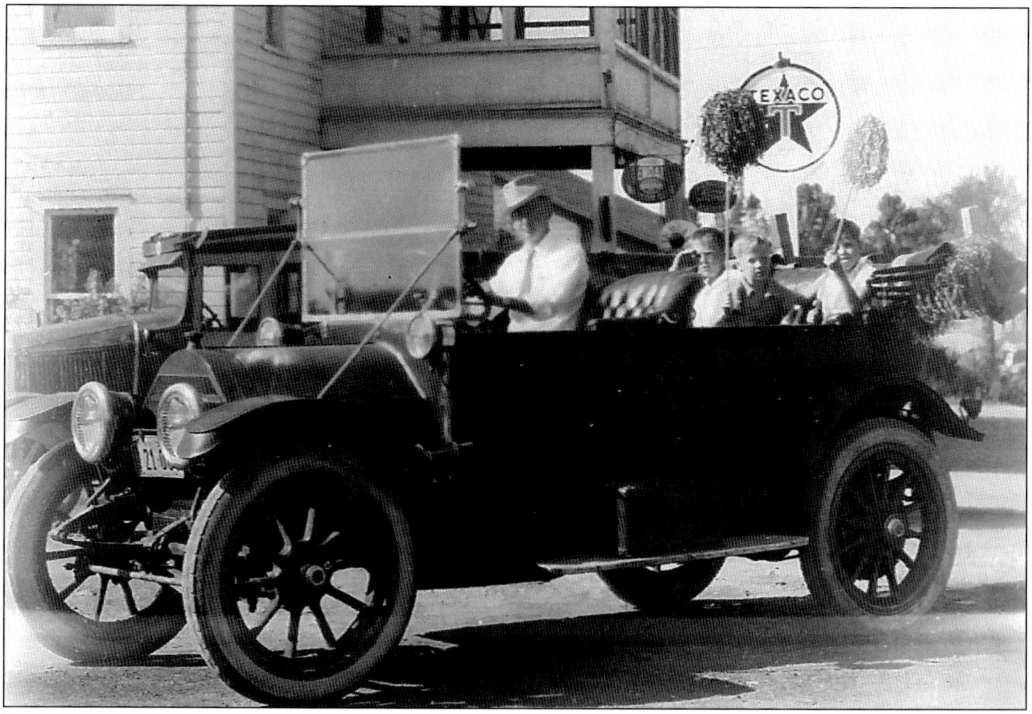

READY FOR THE PARADE. LeLand Kelsey and family prepare for the 1937 opening ceremonies parade. They wait in their car in front of their family business, Carlton Garage, in Carlton Station in 1937. (Courtesy of David Kelsey.)

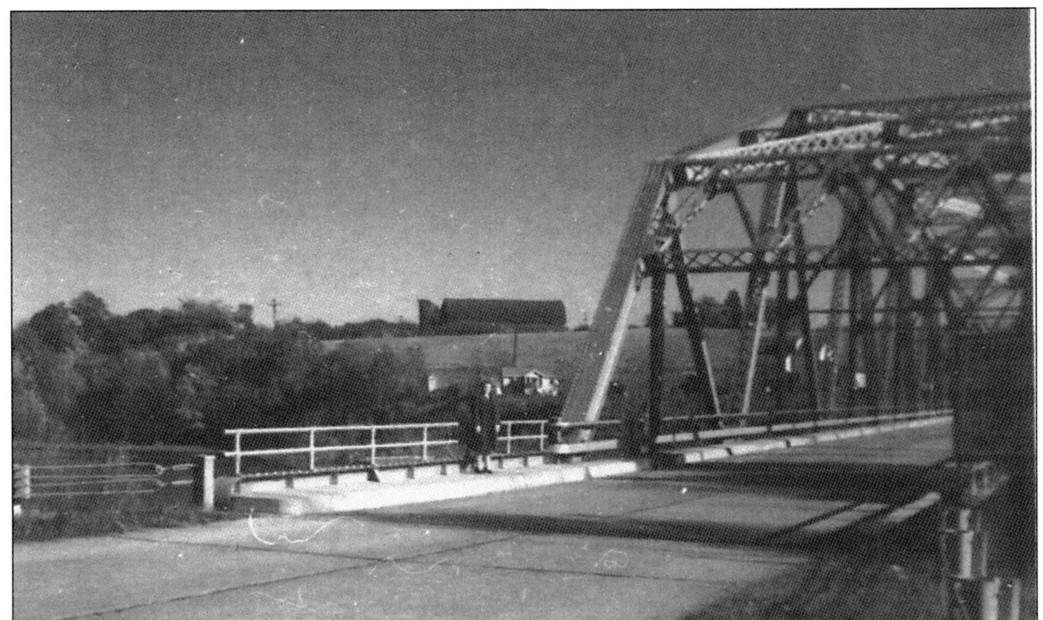

The Iron Bridge. When this bridge was installed, it was the second-largest single-span bridge in western New York. It contains 13,000 steel rivets, 16 carloads of steel, and 1,000 tons of concrete. It is as impressive today as it was in 1937, spanning 40 feet high at the main truss and 100 feet from the top of it to its foundation. (Courtesy of Bud Canham.)

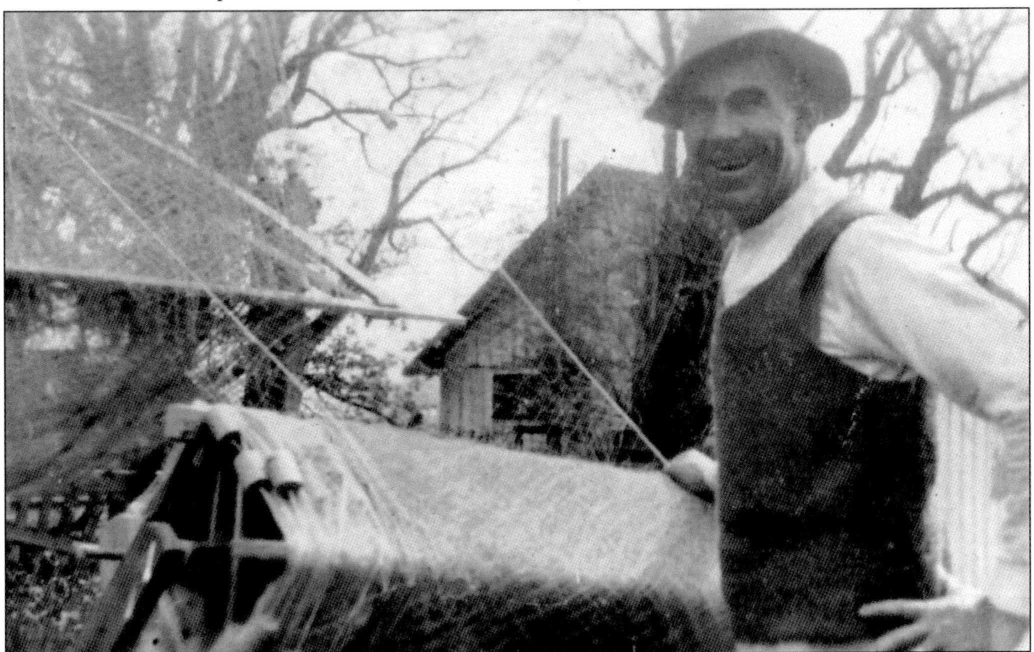

Working the Nets. Winfield "Win" Scott Hoot, born in 1880, is seen putting fishnets on a large reel before going out into Lake Ontario and dropping them for two days. Win would sell the fish to markets, but if he caught suckers, he would use them for bait to catch sturgeon, which provided luxurious caviar. This he packed in ice and shipped to New York City by rail. (Courtesy of Amelia Hoot Lovewell.)

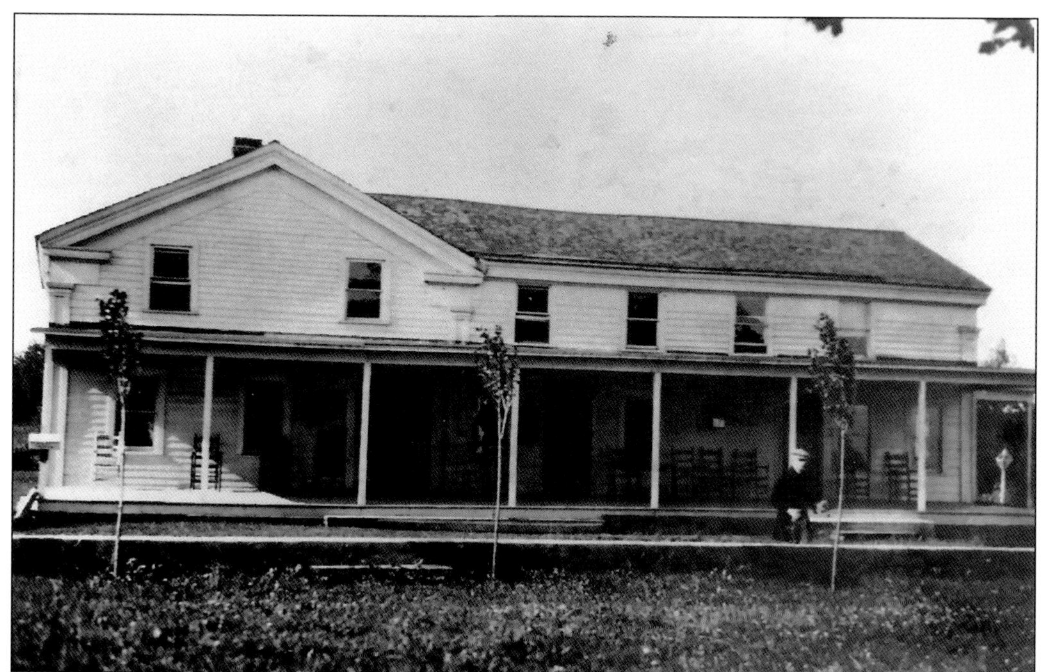

The Black North Inn. The Black North Inn has been a focal point in Point Breeze for over 100 years, and it still is in operation today. The Murray family, shipbuilders, constructed the building. Pioneers coined the term "Black North," referring to lands lying north of Ridge Road dense with heavily timbered forests, making passage during the daylight hours dark as night. (Courtesy of Shirley Bennett Belson.)

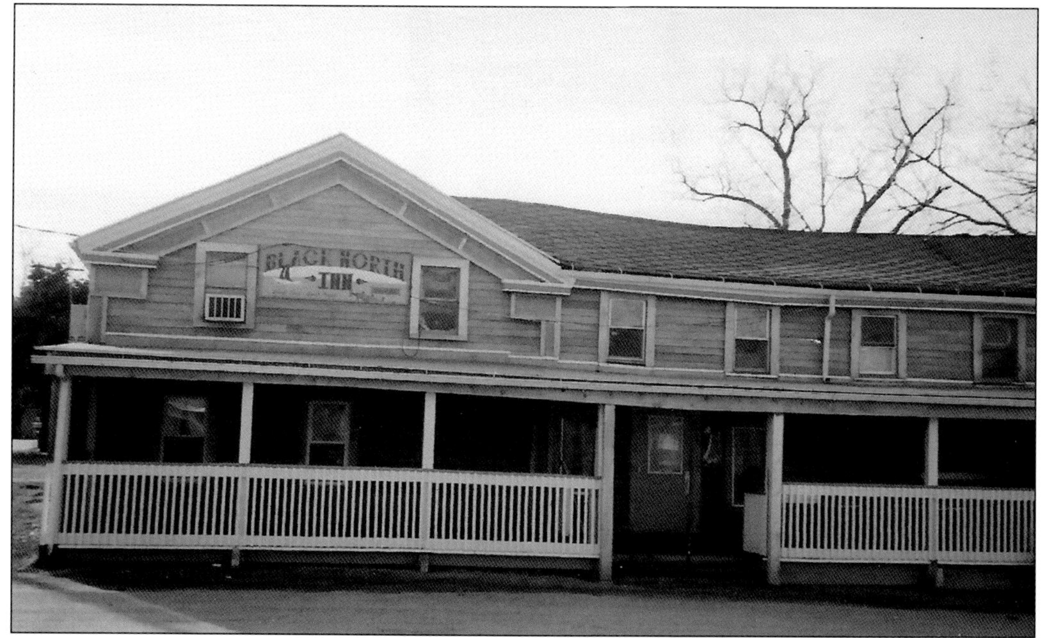

The Black North Today. The restaurant is a popular spot for boaters, fishermen, and summer tourists as they stop at Point Breeze for rest and relaxation. The wooden structure is accented with pink, sea blue, and white. (Courtesy of Avis A. Townsend.)

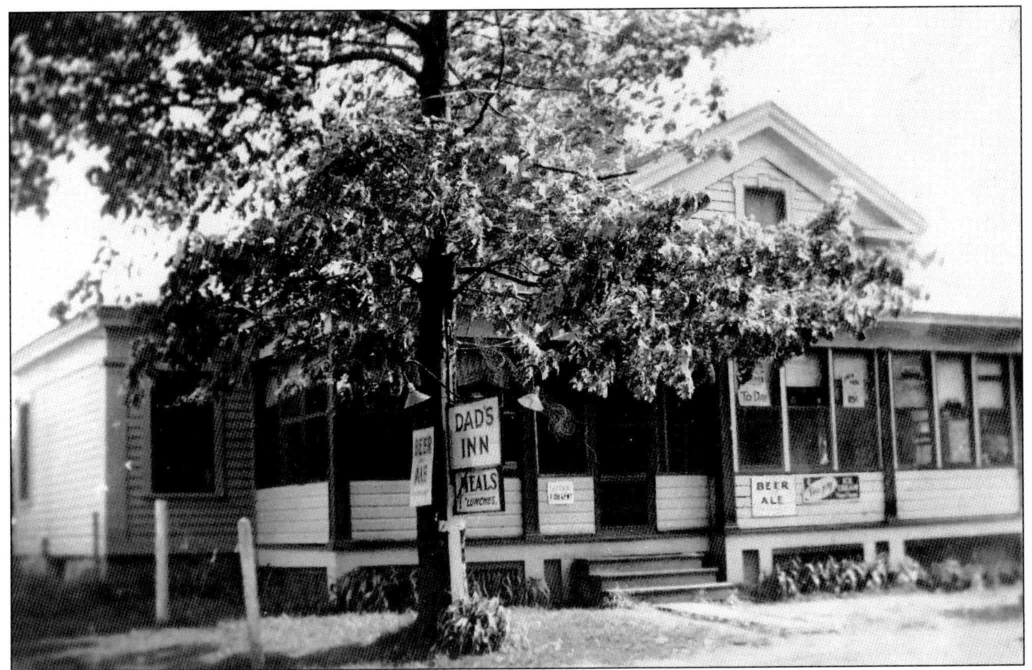

DAD'S INN. Dad Parmallee ran this store, where people could buy groceries, get a fishing license, or just eat lunch. It was located east of the Black North Inn and is now a private residence. (Courtesy of Shirley Bennett Belson.)

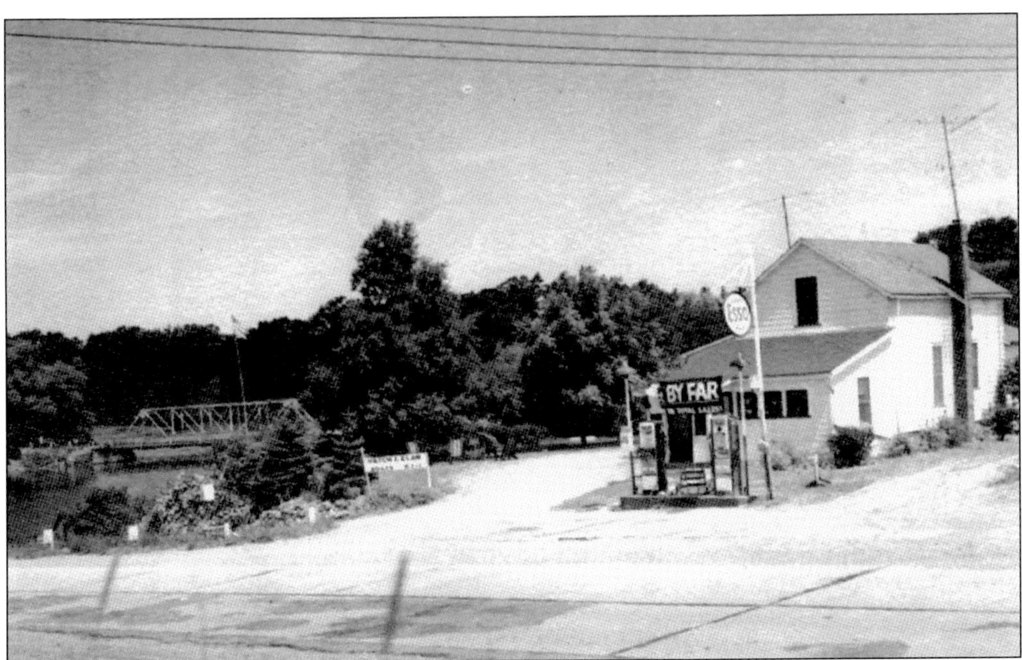

BRIDGES STORE. This was a country store at Twin Bridges around 1936. Mom-and-pop stores were located in each little hamlet and were important stops in rural Carlton. (Courtesy of Mike and Chris Elam.)

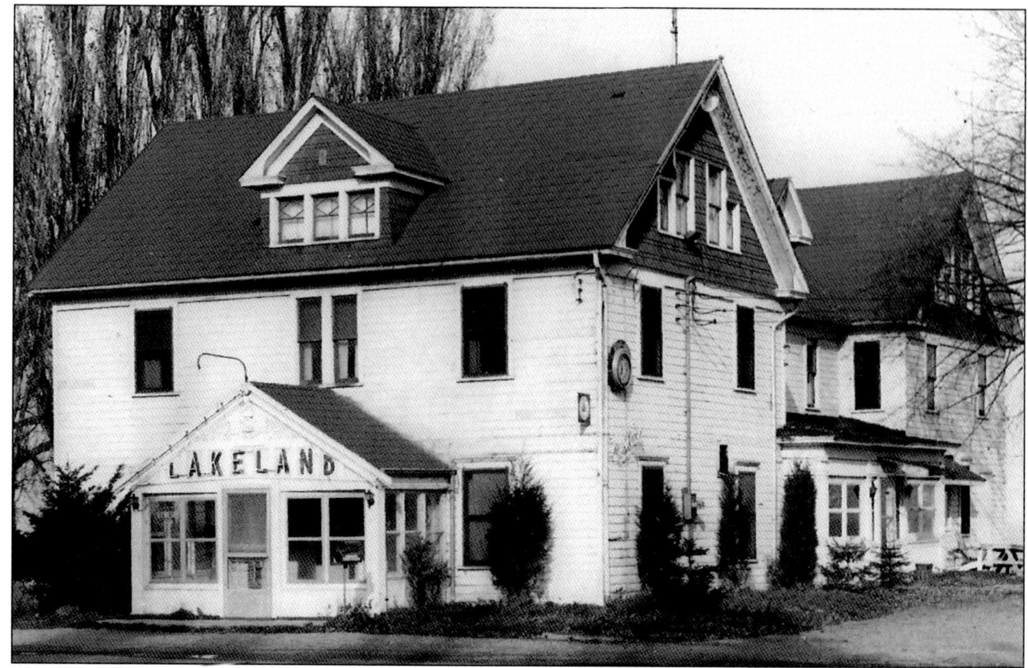

LAKELAND DANCE HALL. During the 1950s and 1960s, people came from all around to dance and listen to live music at the dance hall at Point Breeze. It was a focal point in the area for over 100 years, changing every few decades. (Courtesy of Orleans County Department of History.)

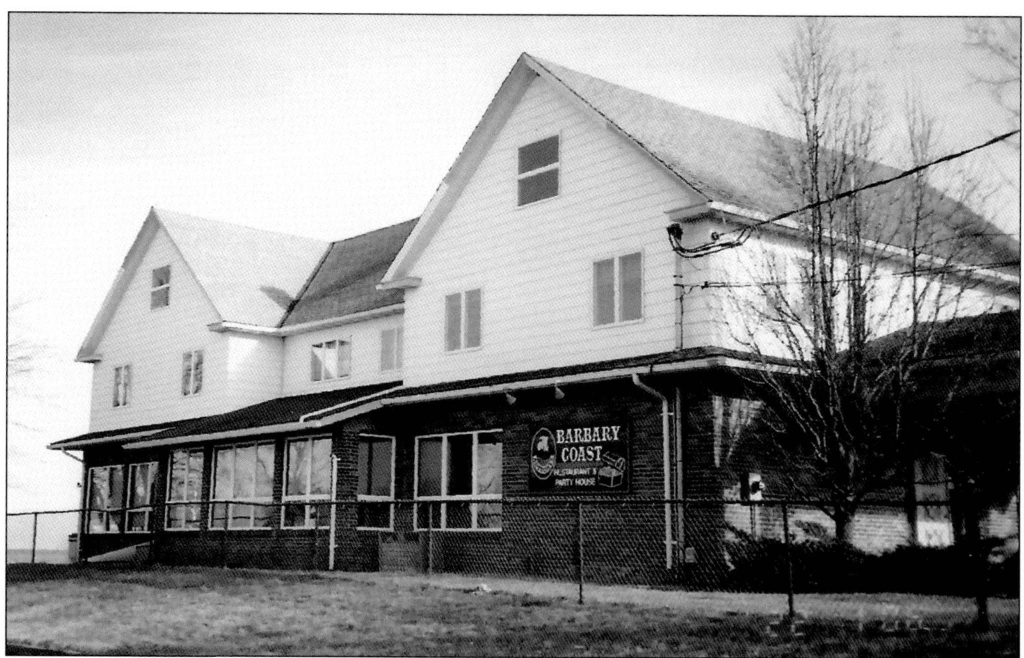

LAKELAND TODAY. The dance hall today is called the Barbary Coast restaurant, but it is currently shut down, with new owners anticipating making it into a bed-and-breakfast. One can see the lake to the left of the building, with the main facade facing the harbor. Each set of windows offers a view of the water, so it will be a lovely place to stay. (Courtesy of Avis A. Townsend.)

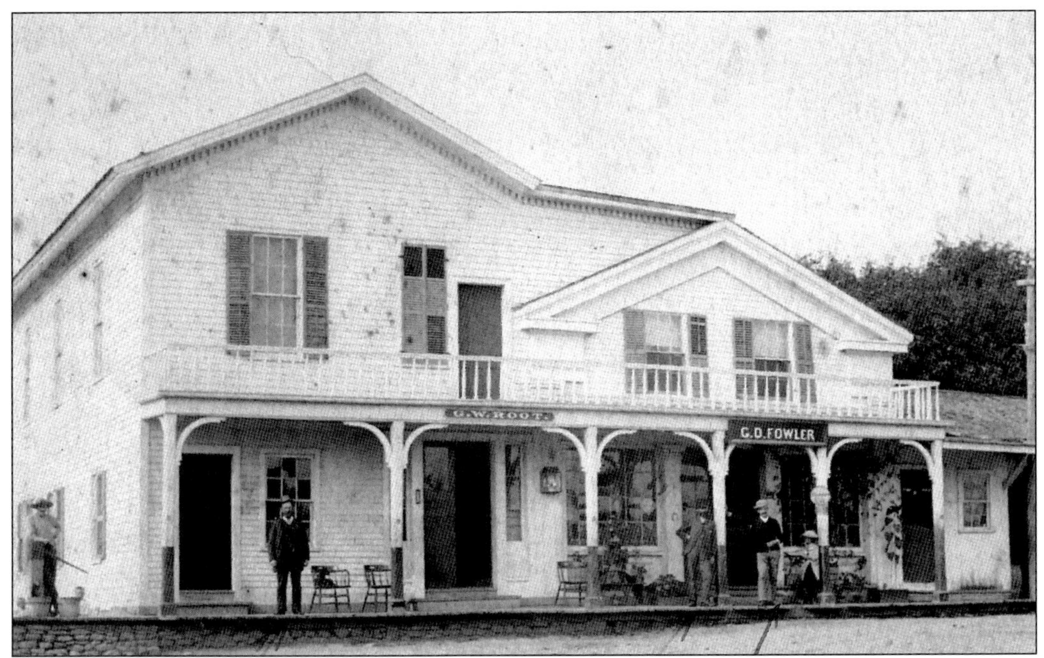

TWO BRIDGES HOTEL. This building is still standing and has been Narby's Superette, a grocery store, since 1968. This photograph was snapped in September 1887, when it was a hotel at Two Bridges. Later it became Ben Bamber's store, then Ward Bamber's store, then Floyd Burns's store. (Courtesy of Orleans County Department of History.)

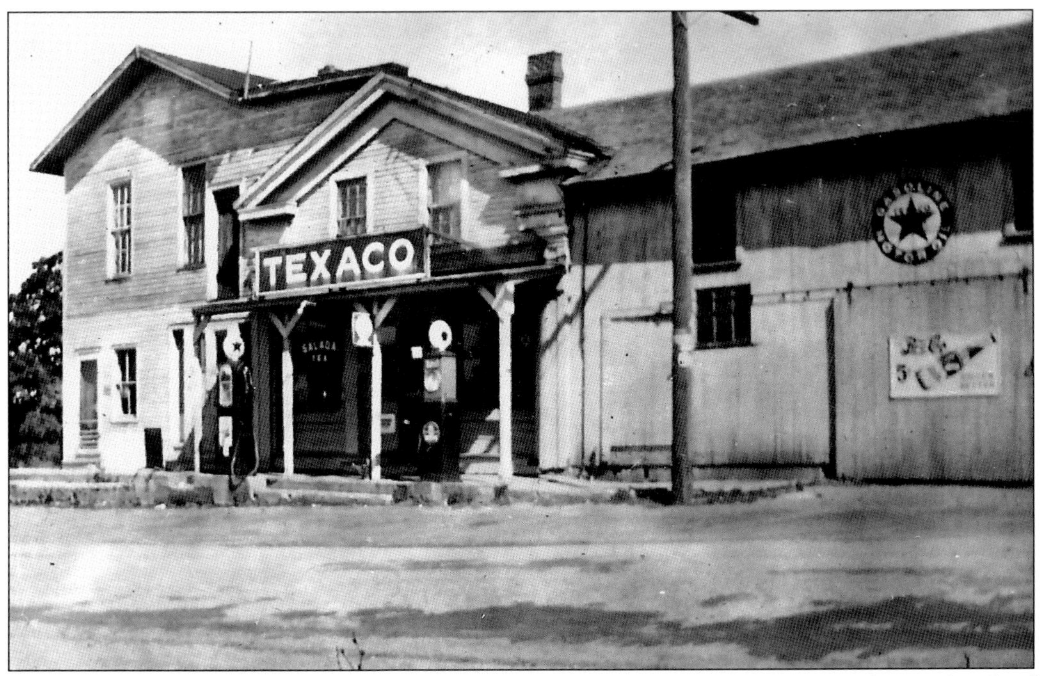

BEN BAMBER'S STORE, 1935. The facade looks the same, but an open garage at the south side of the building was converted into a garage when Bamber's took it over, and gas pumps were added. (Courtesy of Orleans County Department of History.)

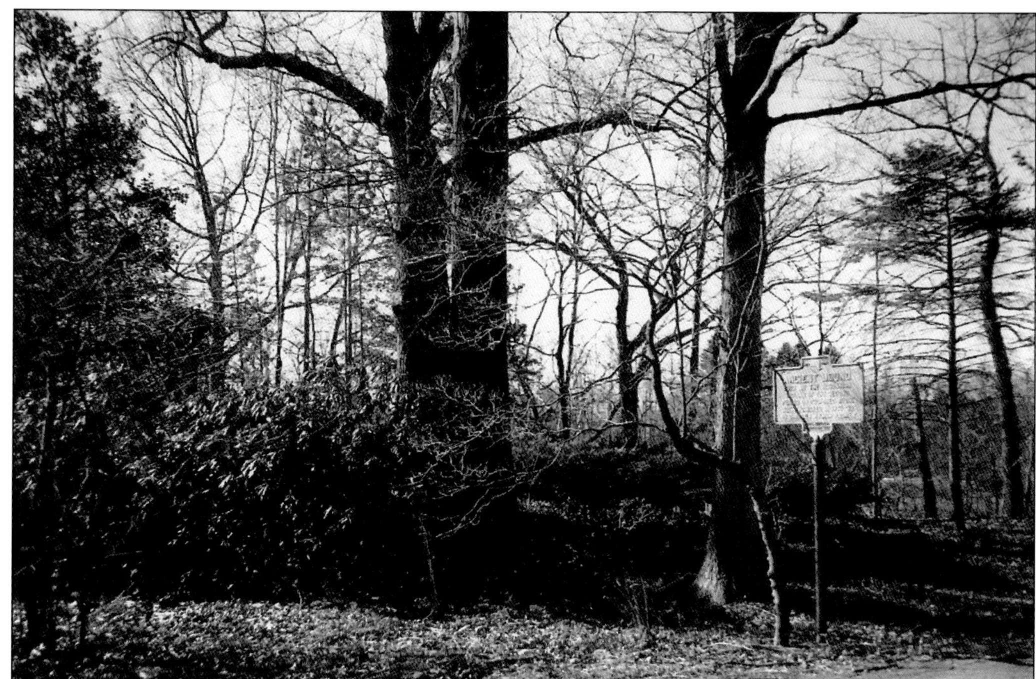

ANCIENT MOUND. Two miles east of Waterport, on Oak Orchard River Road, a historical marker signifies the last of the American Indian mounds. The mound was built by Algonquin Indians around AD 1400 and unearthed in the 1930s. Many artifacts, including dishes and crude farming implements, were discovered. (Courtesy of Bud Canham.)

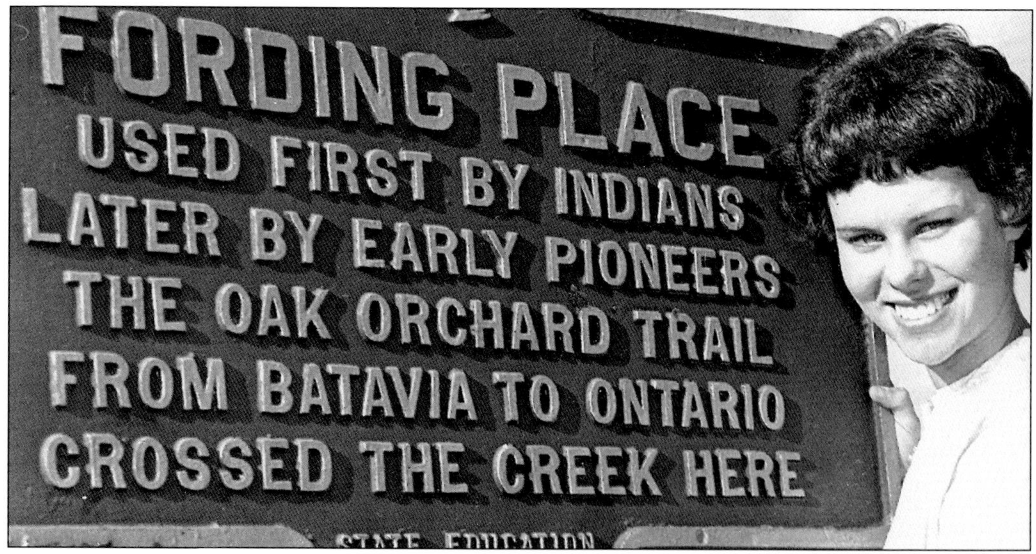

FORDING PLACE. On Oak Orchard Creek, this sign marks a location first used by the American Indians, and then by the pioneers, to cross the creek on Oak Orchard Trail. This is on Oak Orchard River Road near the Bridges. Dow Fenton is the girl in the photograph. (Courtesy of Orleans County Department of History.)

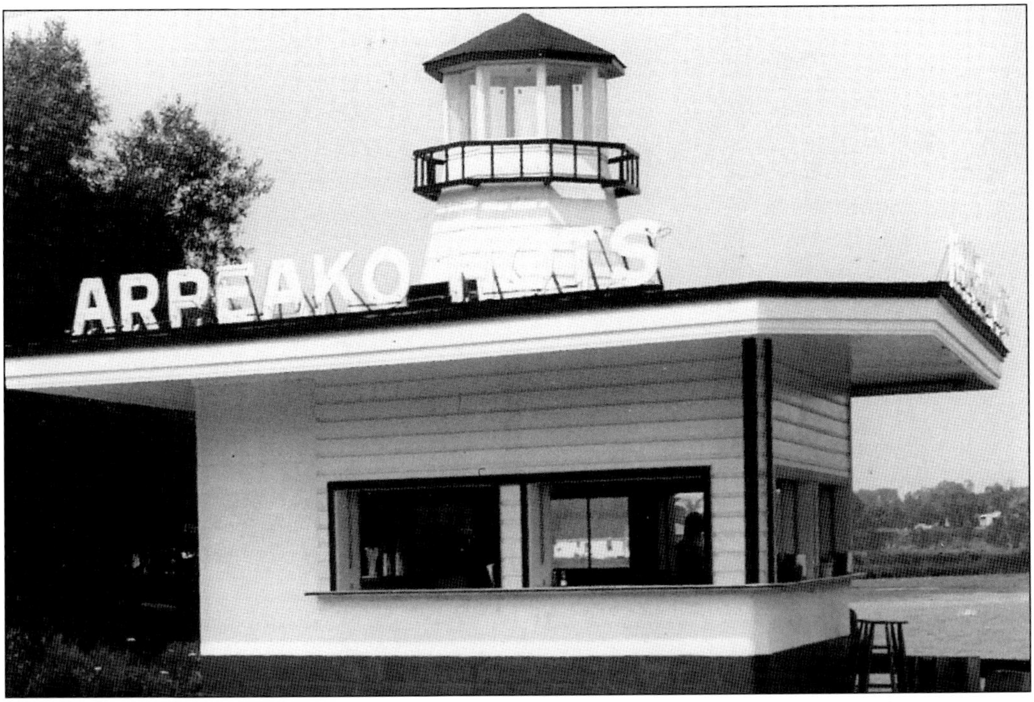

ARPEAKO HOTS. The Zagata family owned and operated this hot dog stand at the Waterport Bridge. Arpeako hots were a popular brand of frankfurter in the 1950s and 1960s. (Courtesy of the Robert Brown family.)

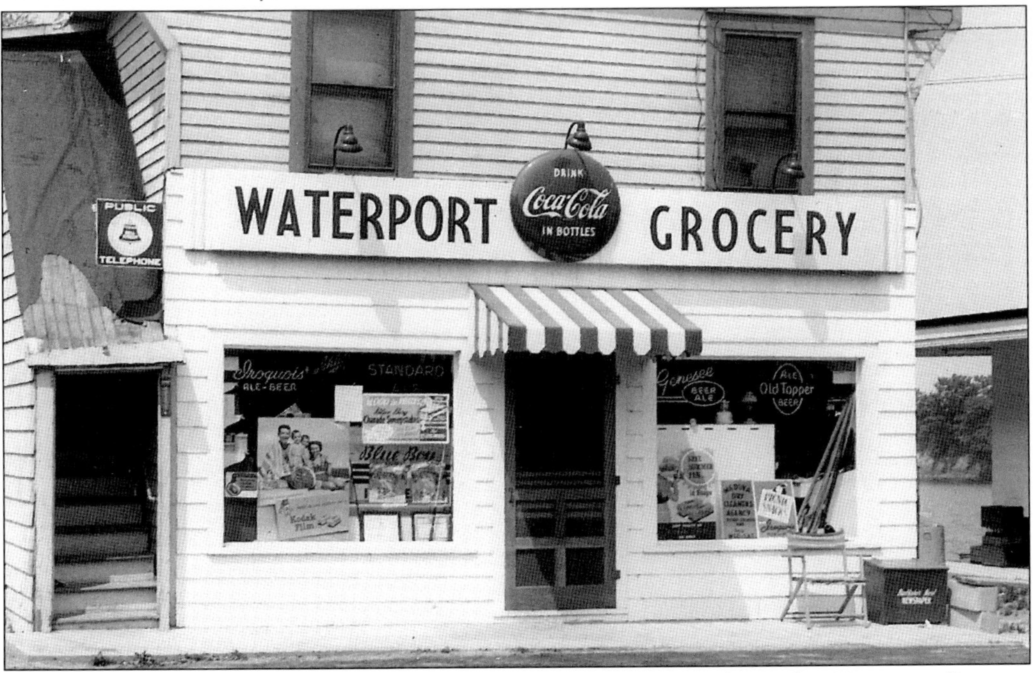

WATERPORT GROCERY. Next door to the Lighthouse hot dog stand was the Waterport Grocery formerly owned by Al and Marie Carlston, who sold it to the Zagatas. Marie wrote one of the dedications on page 4. (Courtesy of the Robert Brown family.)

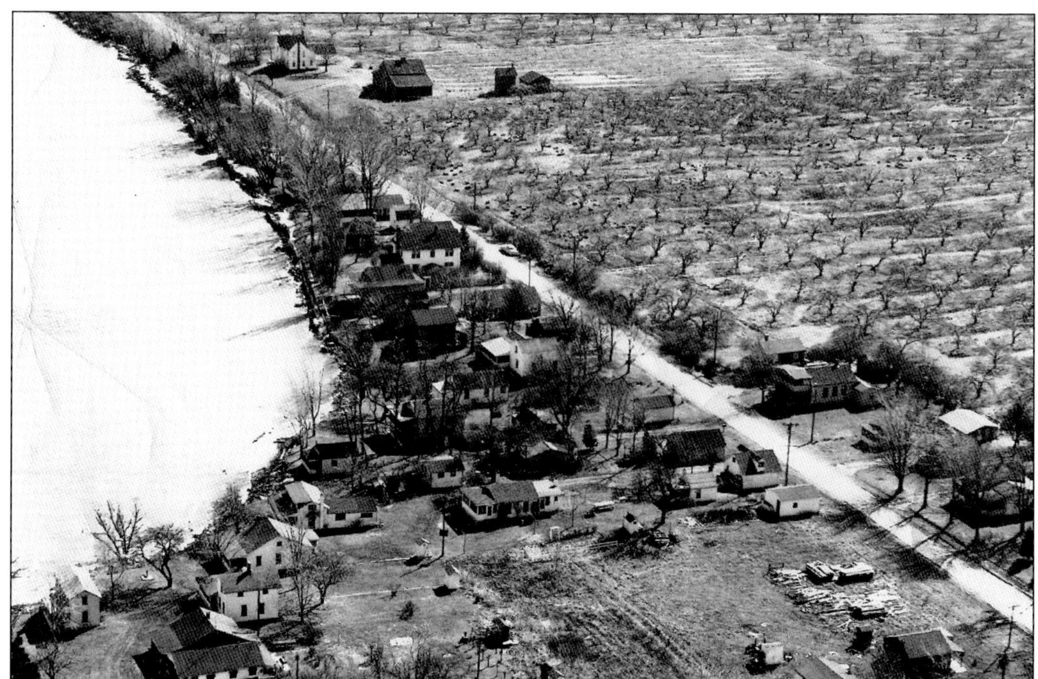

Point Breeze Cottages. This is an aerial view of the shoreline of Lake Ontario around 1940. Note the outhouses behind each cottage. It apparently was a pre–septic tank era. The street is Lake Shore Road. (Courtesy of Garland Miller.)

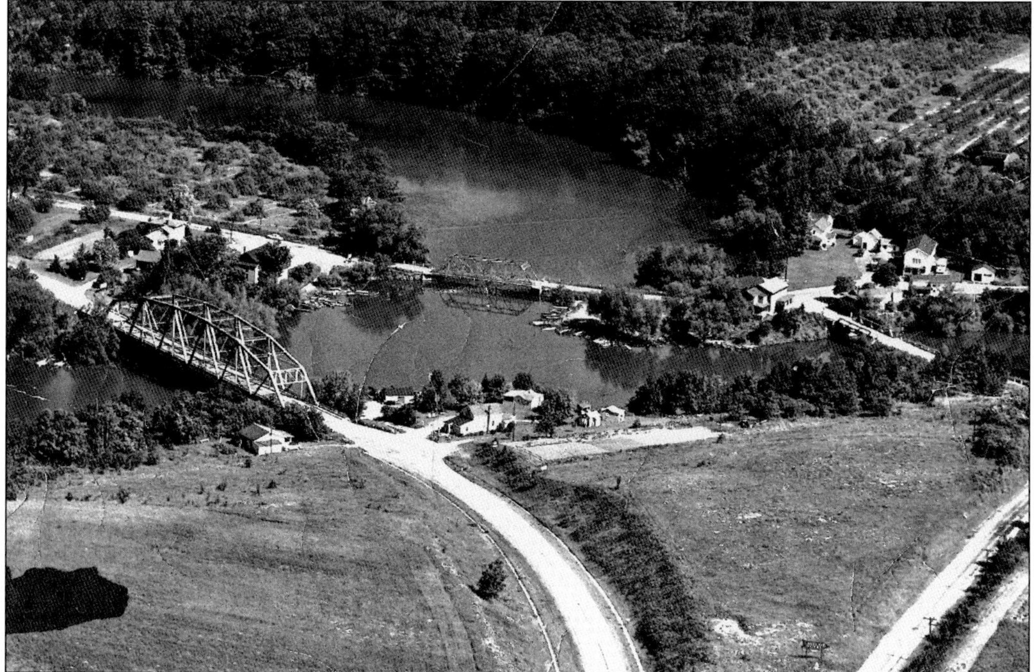

Three Bridges. This is an excellent shot of the three bridges at the Bridges. This area has been called Two Bridges, Twin Bridges, Three Bridges, and is now simply the Bridges. (Courtesy of Garland Miller.)

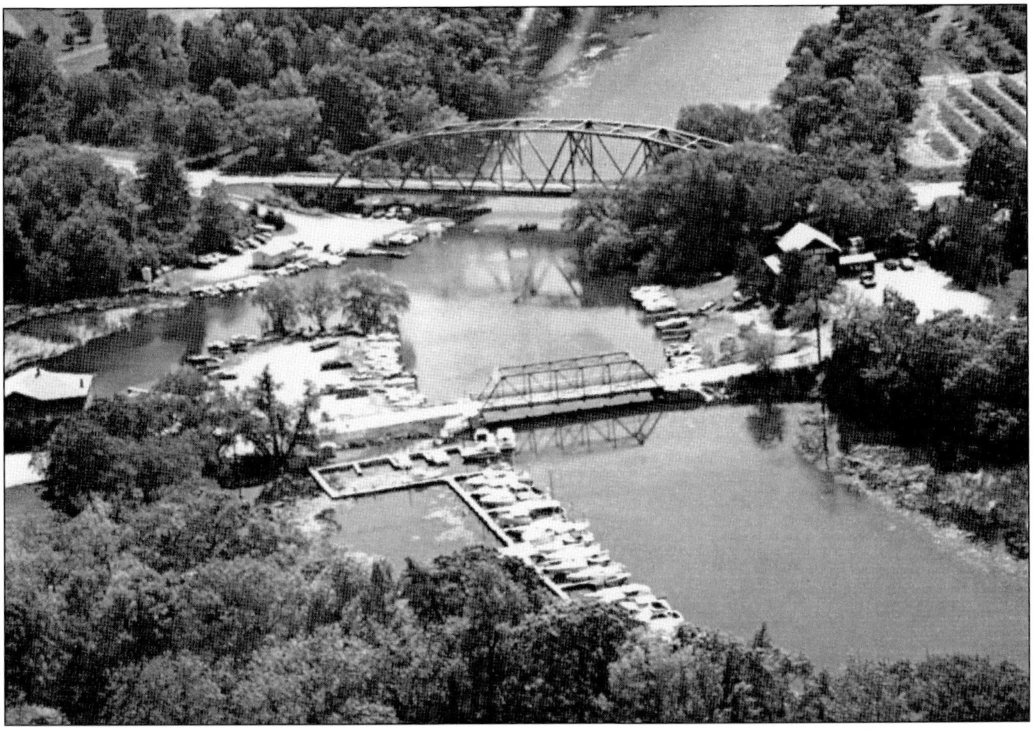

TWO BRIDGES. This is a different aerial view of the Bridges, with only two bridges showing up in this one. (Courtesy of Garland Miller.)

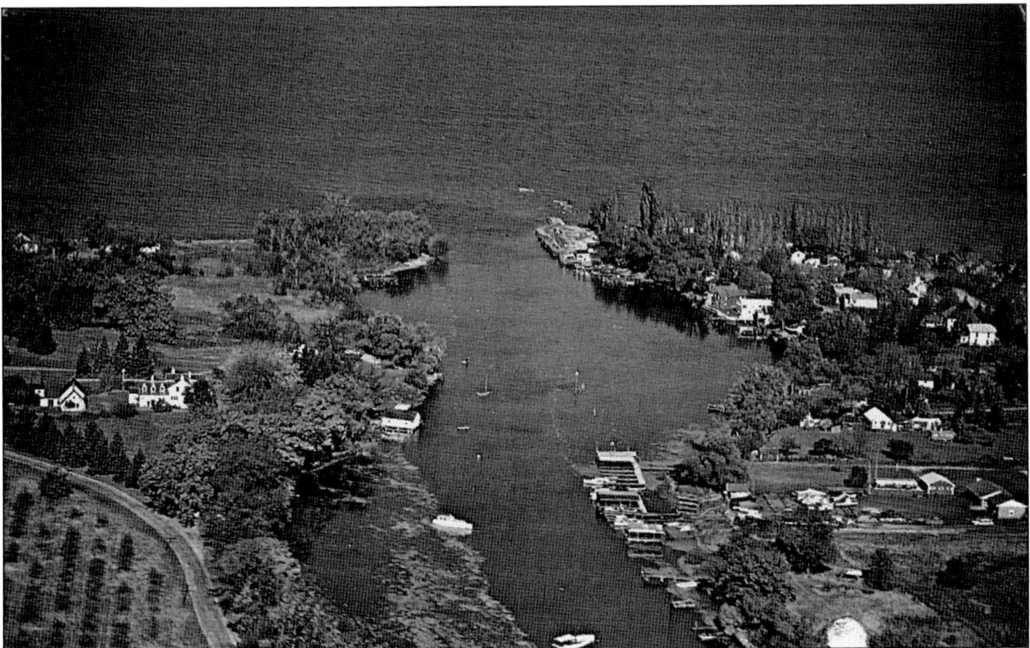

THE HARBOR, 1955. This aerial view of the harbor shows the Archbald Estate at the left. Note the absence of piers in the harbor. (Courtesy of Ashley Ward.)

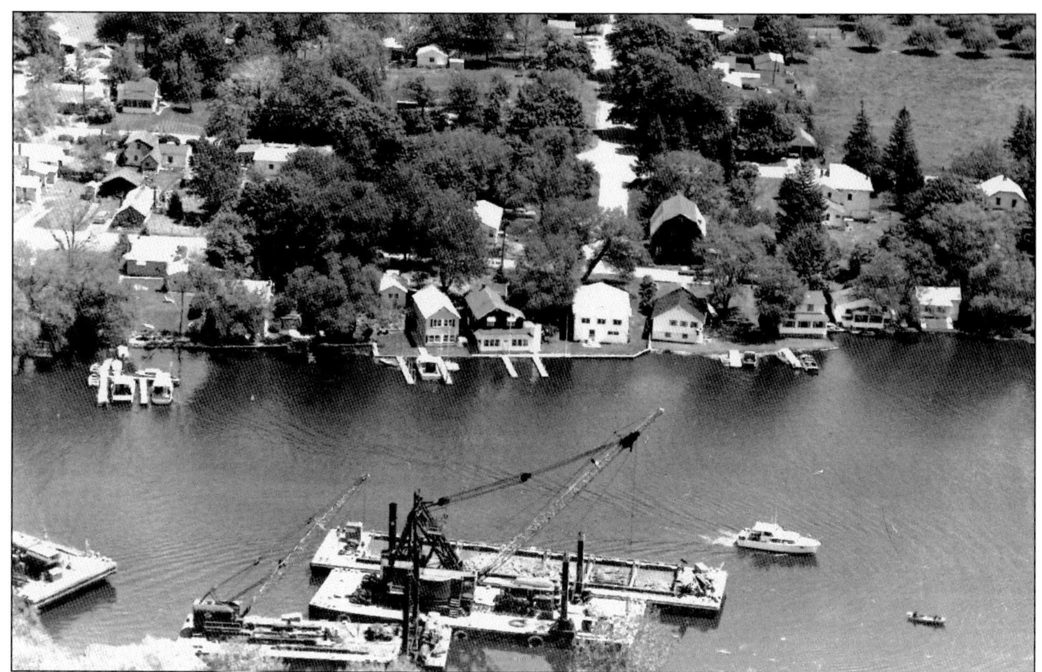

DREDGING THE HARBOR, C. 1975. A dredge rests in Oak Orchard Harbor. The harbor needs to be dredged out of silt and debris now and then so boats with longer hulls can travel through to the lake without injuring their bottom sides. (Courtesy of Shirley Bennett Belson.)

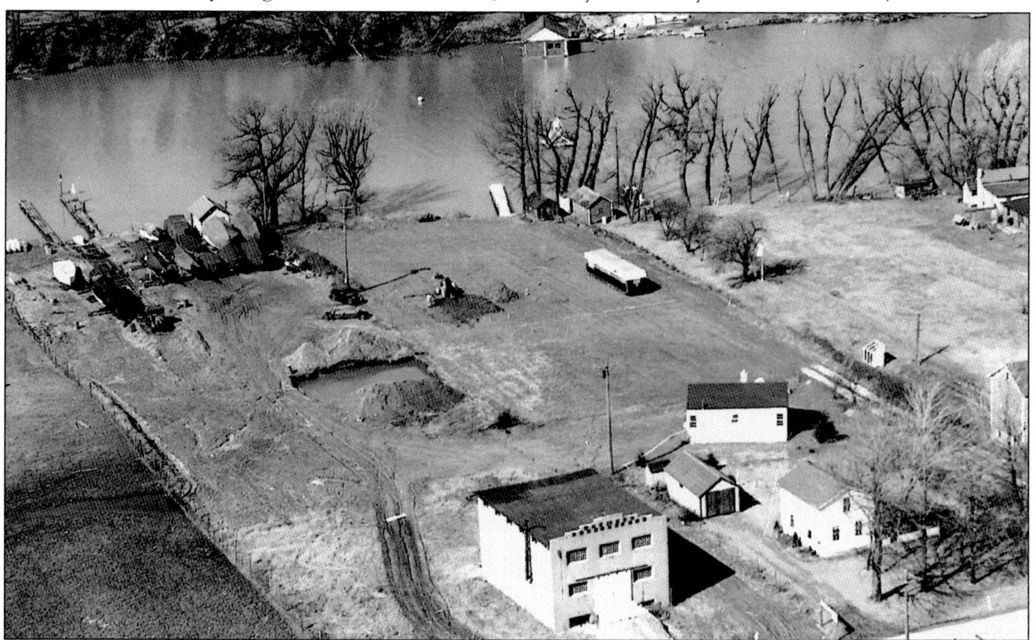

BROWN'S BOATYARD, 1956. The marina area was home to the Oak Orchard Yacht Club. In 1936, the club consisted of five or six men who had boats moored in the middle of the channel and wanted to start a boating organization. The first meetings were held in the back room of the Black North Inn, and the group was charted as the Old Orchard Yacht Club. (Courtesy of Pauline Holly Brown.)

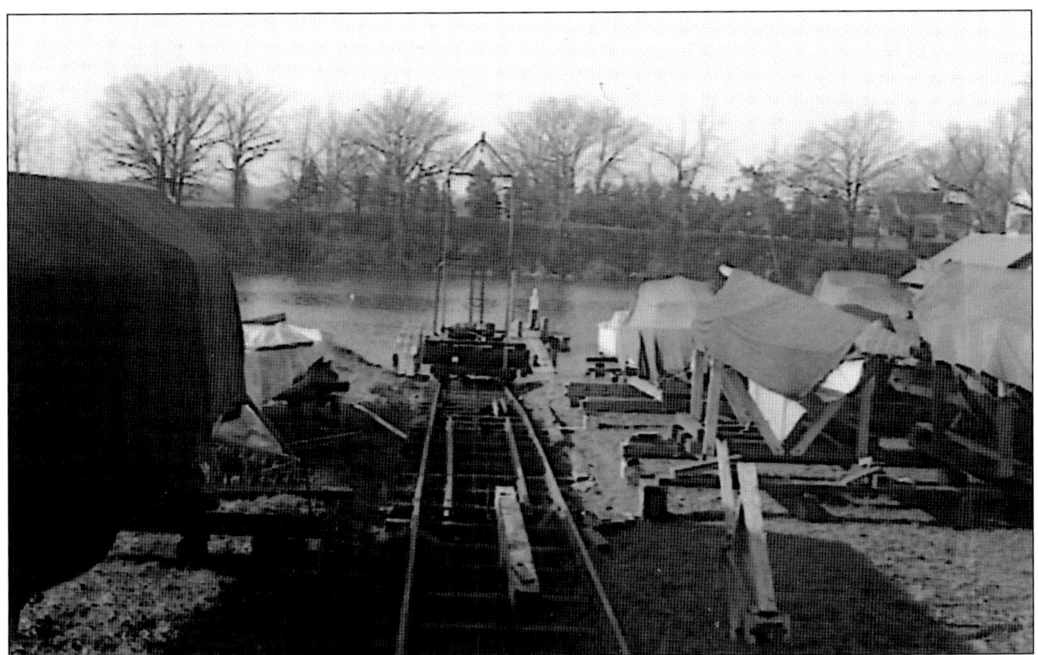

NOW A MARINA. In 1953, Leo and Pauline Brown started the first boatyard at Point Breeze. Brown's Boatyard is now known as 4 C's Marina. The first year, they hauled out eight boats for winter storage using the loading car, rail, and crane method. At first they handled only powerboats but eventually graduated to sailboats. (Courtesy of Pauline Holly Brown.)

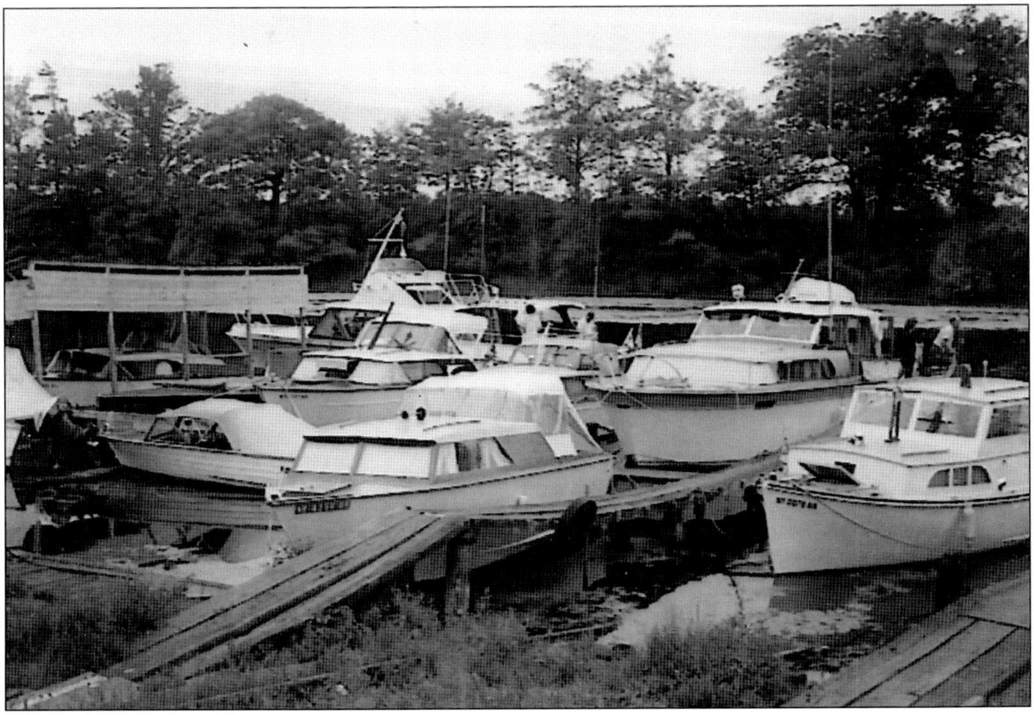

LOTS OF BOATS. Boats were packed in like sardines at Brown's Boatyard during the 1950s. The Browns always called it the boatyard and never a marina. (Courtesy of Pauline Holly Brown.)

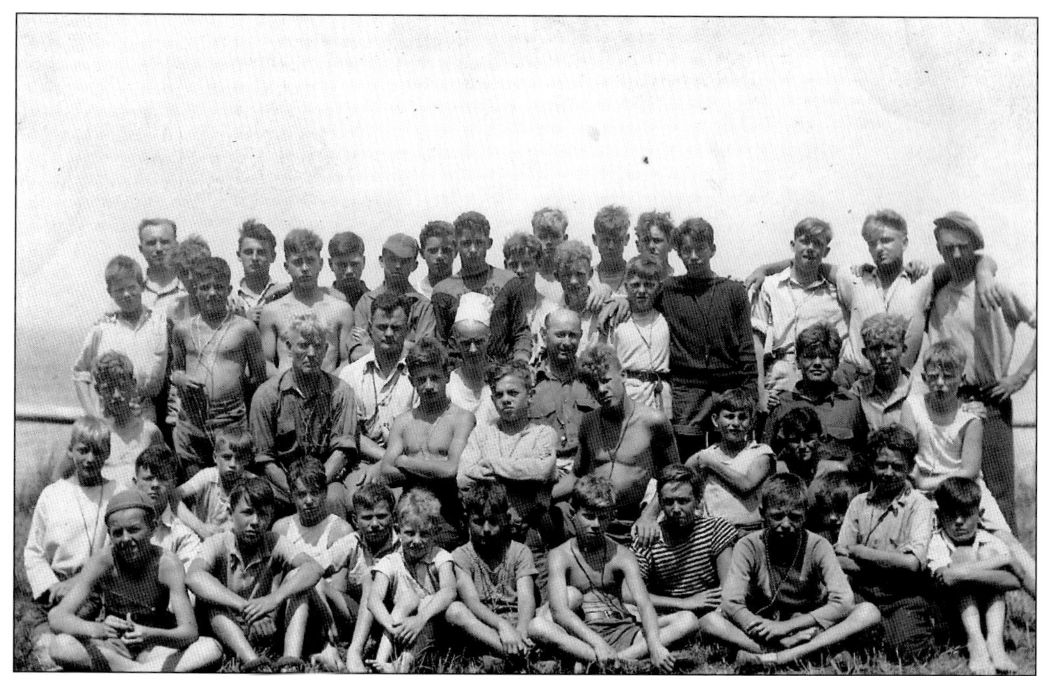

SCOUTING FUN, C. 1955. Clyde Lovewell was the scoutmaster for this troop, which poses for pictures on the Archbald property on the west side of the harbor. (Courtesy of Amelia Hoot Lovewell.)

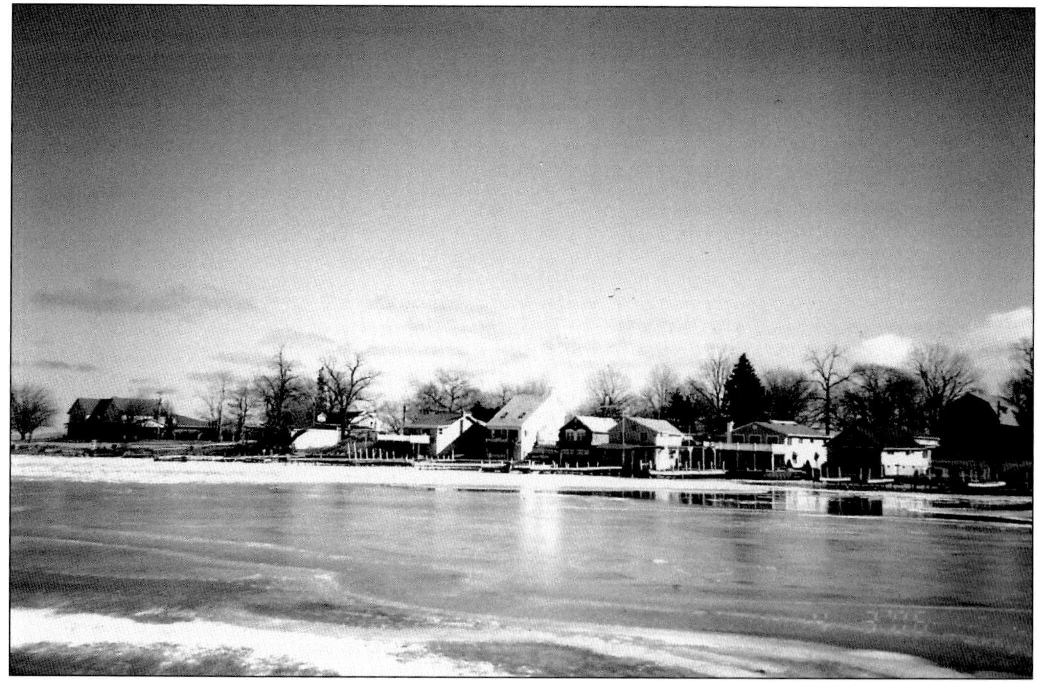

THE HARBOR IN WINTER. This is how the harbor at Point Breeze looks in the winter. The photograph was taken from the west side looking east. Ice covers the harbor. The building at the extreme left is the former Lakeland Hotel, now the Barbary Coast. (Courtesy of Bud Canham.)

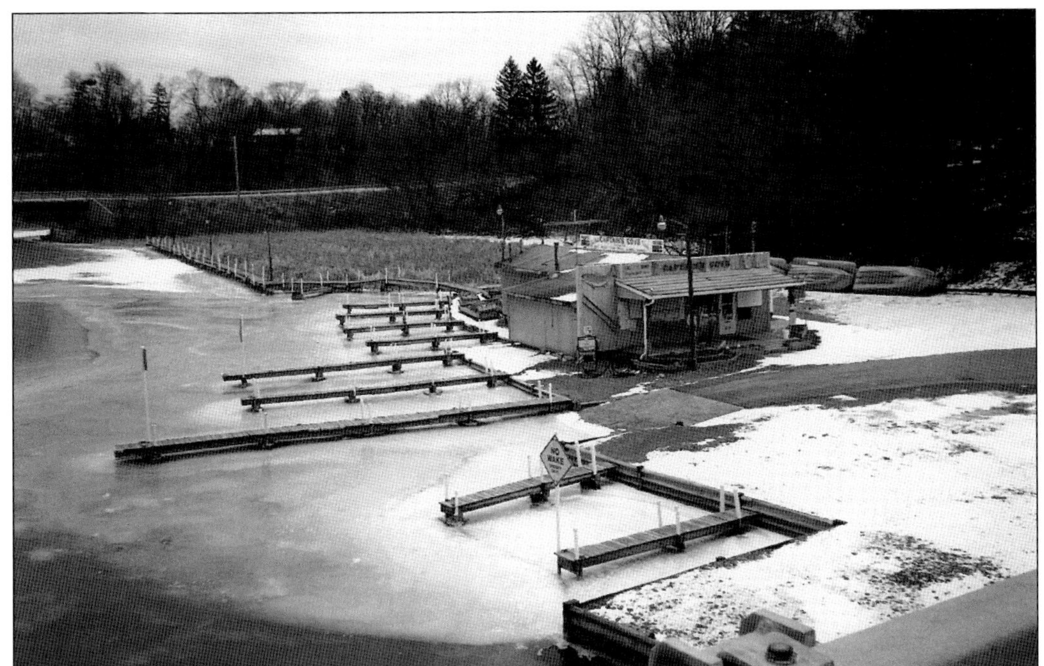

EMPTY DOCKS. Winter is a lonely time at Oak Orchard Harbor, with just a few brave ducks and geese floating in the water, the boats in dry dock and covered with shrink wrap. (Courtesy of Bud Canham.)

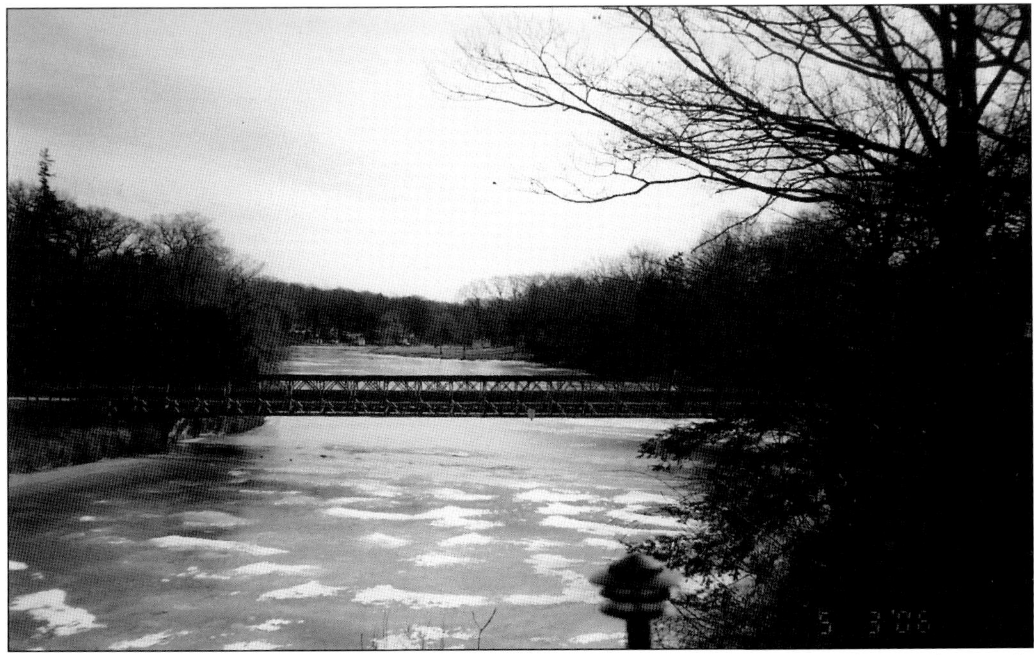

LAKESIDE BRIDGE OVER JOHNSON'S CREEK. Gone is the wooden structure that made people and horses tremble when crossing. Instead, there is a new low structure that can still cause hearts to flutter during the spring, when ice has melted and the creek is high. (Courtesy of Bud Canham.)

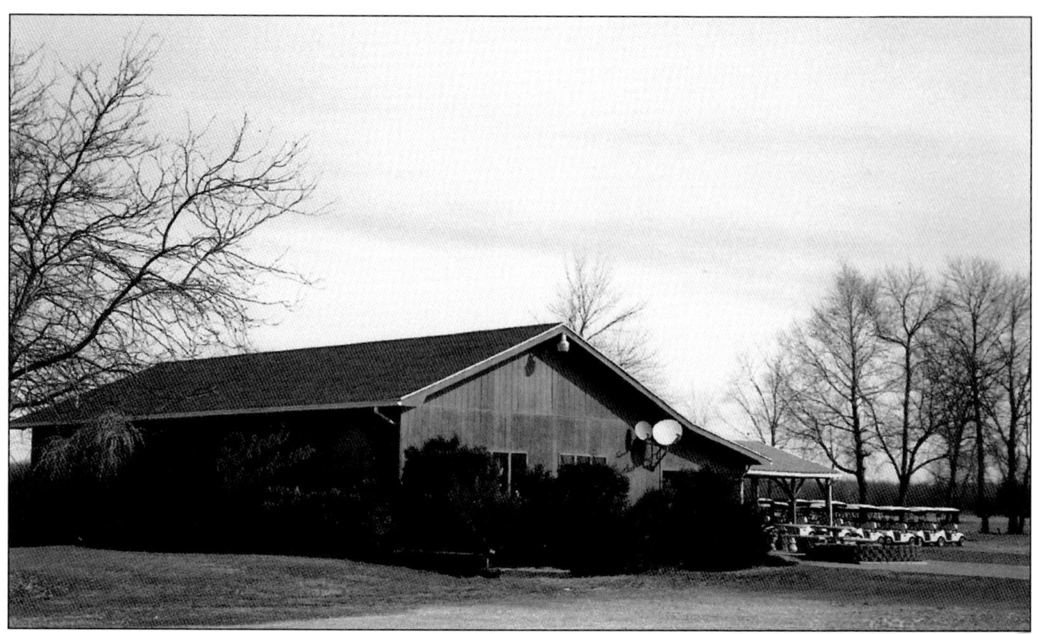

RICCI MEADOWS. Carts sit outside Ricci Meadows Golf Course, one of two courses on Oak Orchard Road. Luther Burroughs built the course in the 1960s. At first it had only six holes. Peter Ricci extended the course to become an 18-hole United States Golf Association course, making it the oldest continuous-running course in Orleans County. It is currently owned and operated by Peter's son Dan and his family. (Courtesy of Bud Canham.)

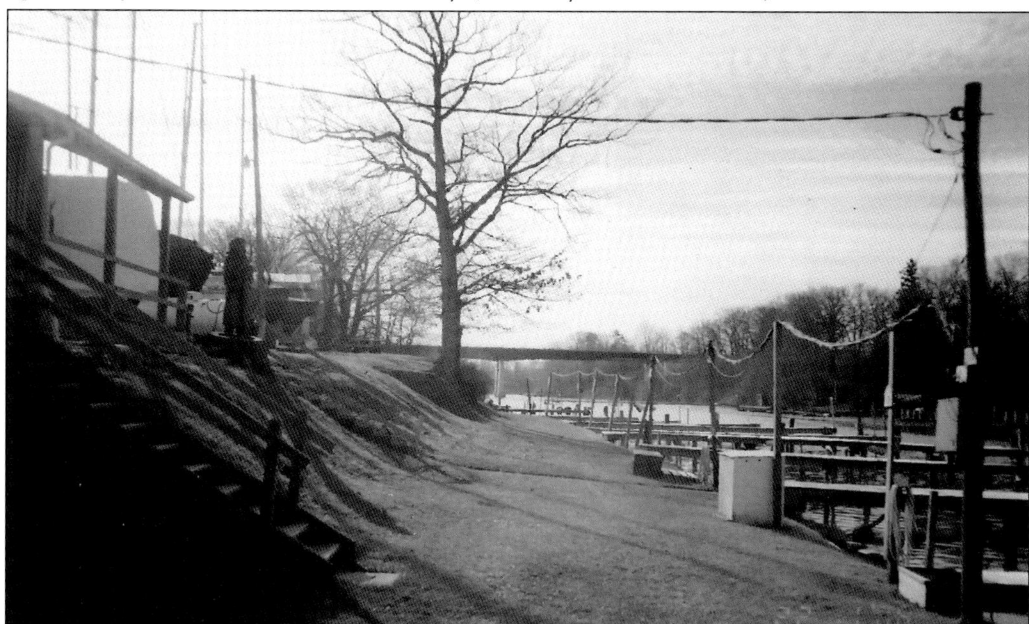

TALL BRIDGE. This photograph, taken from the east side harbor at Lake Breeze Marina, shows the tall bridge in the distance. The view faces south. The bridge runs east-west. Lake Ontario is behind the photographer's back. As it was taken in winter, there are no boats moored to the docks. In summer, there would be no way to see the tall bridge from this vantage point as there would be too many charter boats in the way. (Courtesy of Avis A. Townsend.)

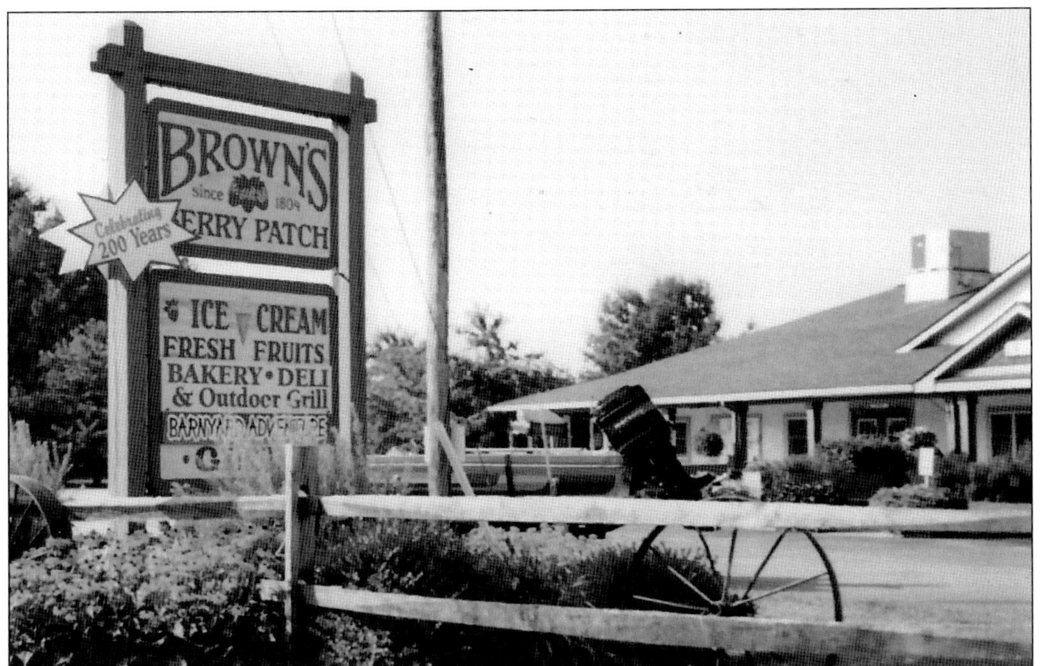

BROWN'S FARM MARKET. Also known as Brown's Berry Patch and Orchard Dale Fruit Farms, the business is on land that was obtained by Bathshua Sheffield Brown, widow of Elijah Brown, who died on ship when the couple was traveling to what is now Carlton. Elijah was the first person buried in Orleans County, and his widow began a legacy that would last for seven generations. (Courtesy of Robert Brown.)

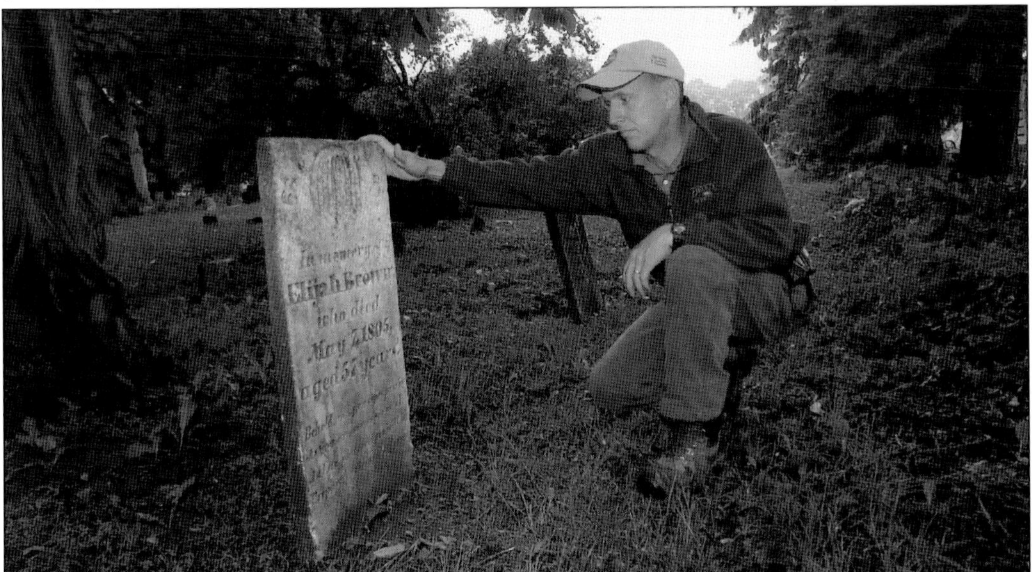

ELIJAH BROWN'S GRAVE. When Elijah Brown first visited the Carlton area, he built a log cabin and then returned home to move his family to this new lush countryside. Although he died aboard the ship before it docked, his family remained to continue his legacy. Here descendant Robert (Bobby) Brown pays his respects to Elijah Brown at the private family cemetery behind the Browns' home. (Courtesy of Robert Brown.)

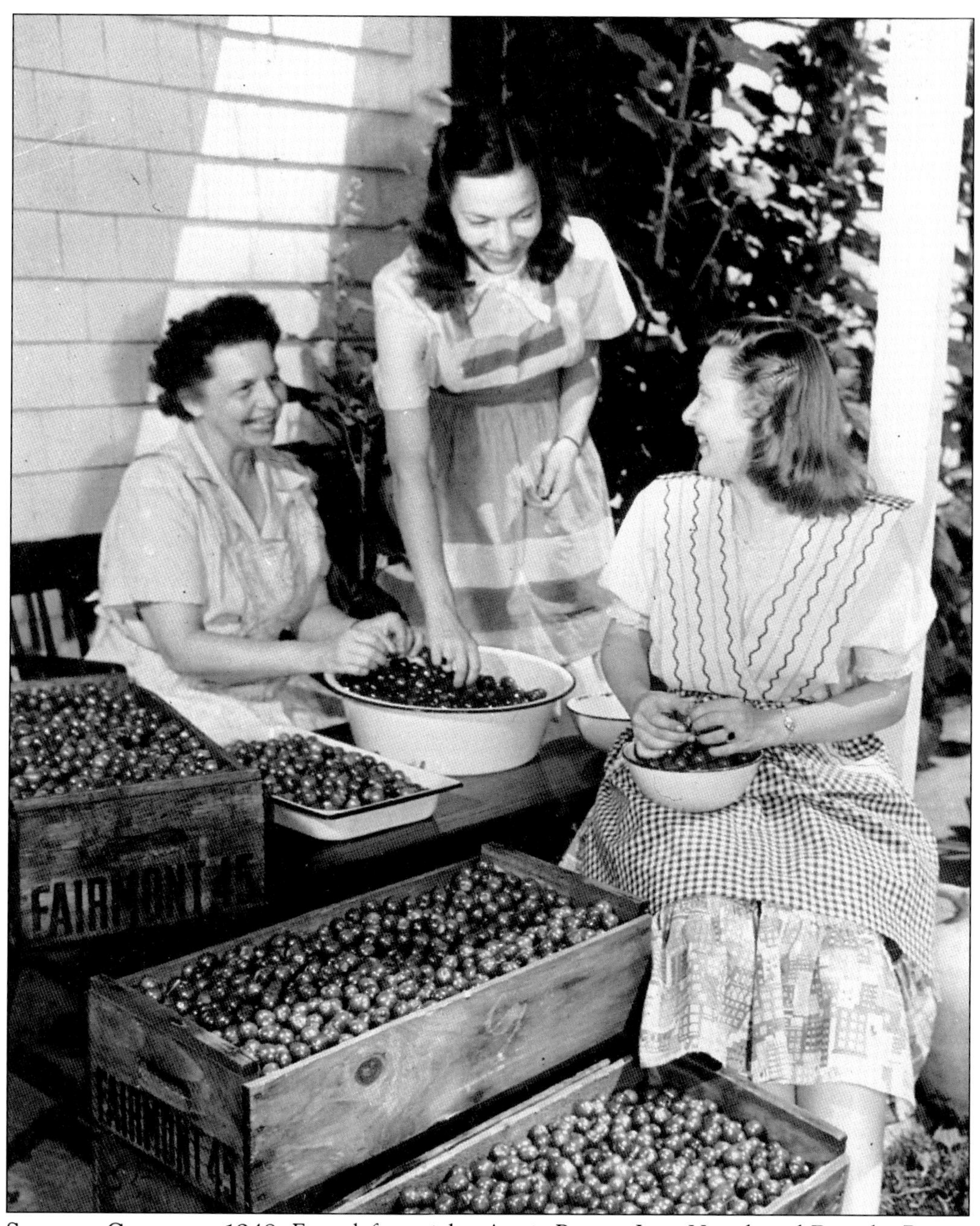

SORTING CHERRIES, 1948. From left to right, Angie Brown, Jean Heard, and Dorothy Brown sort sweet cherries to be sold at market. (Courtesy of Robert Brown.)

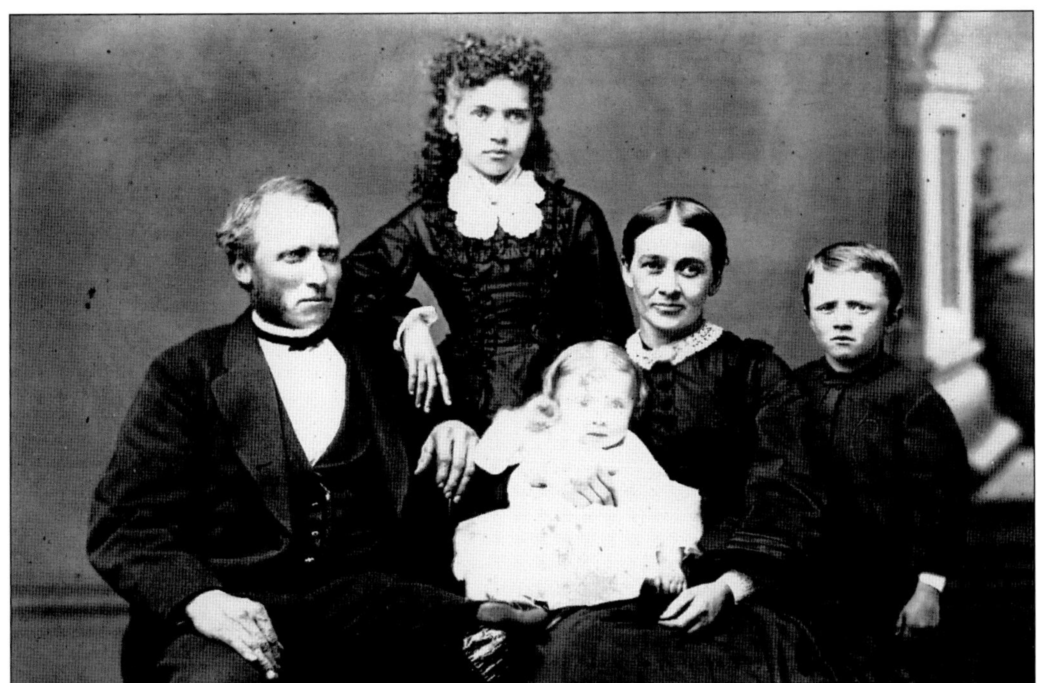

Second-Generation Browns, 1872. From left to right, Robert Ralph Sheffield Brown and Sarah Jane Brown pose with their daughters baby Clara Jane and Anna West, and their son, Harry. (Courtesy of Robert Brown.)

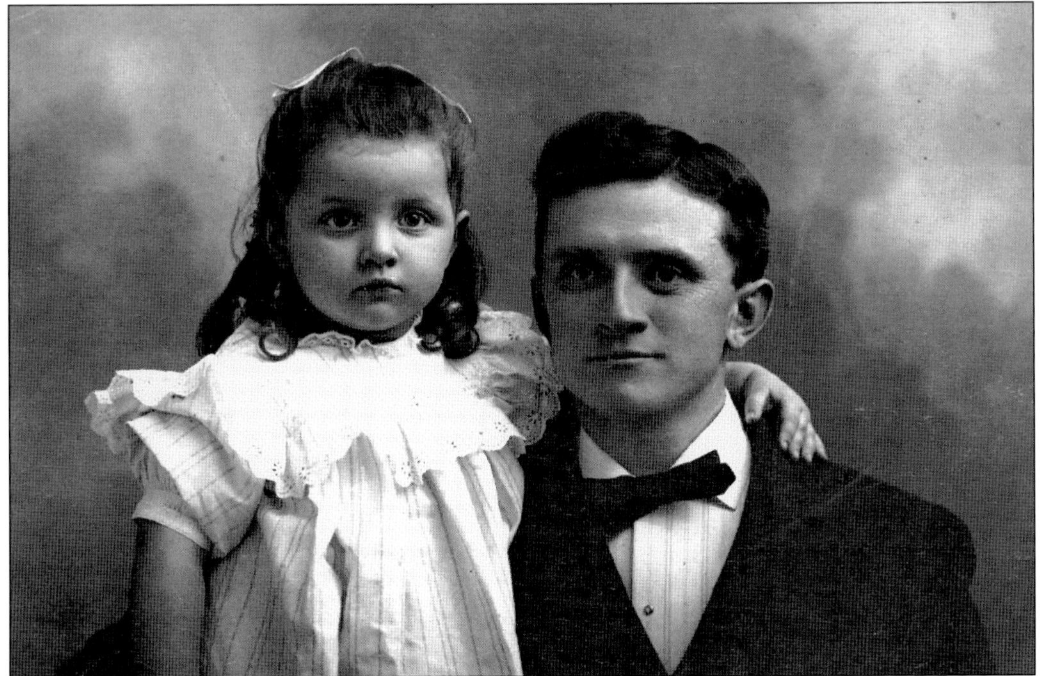

Father and Daughter. Harry L. Brown, seen in the photograph above as a young man, is a young father in this photograph. He poses with his daughter Pauline, who later married Clayton Anderson of Albion. (Courtesy of Robert Brown.)

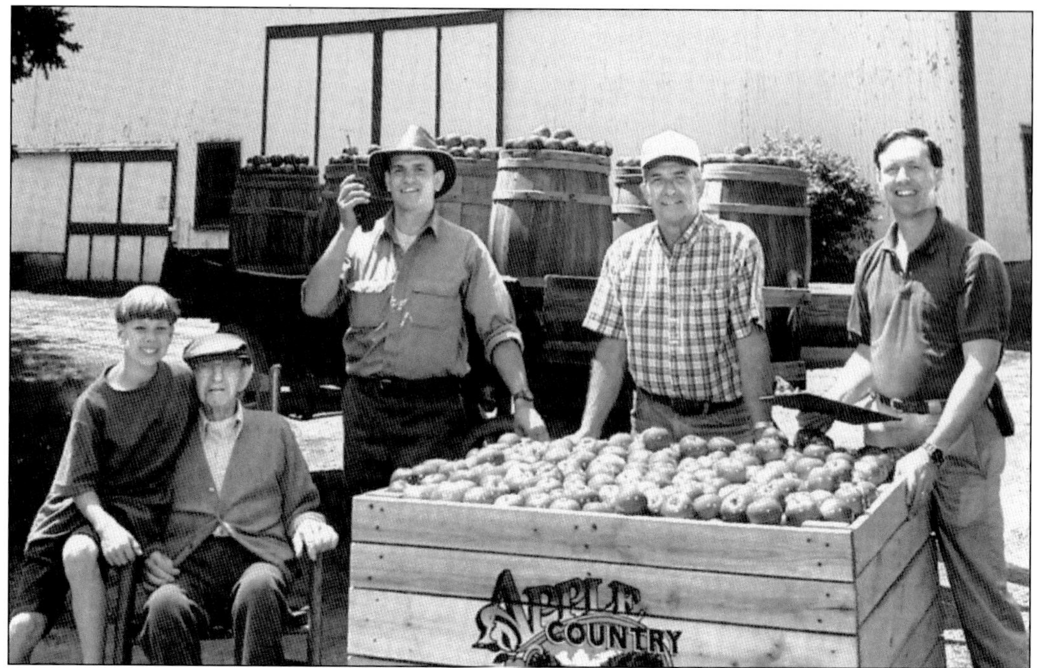

FOUR GENERATIONS. This photograph, taken in 1996, features four generations of the descendents of Elijah Brown. From left to right are great-grandson Robert III, great-grandfather Robert Brown, grandson Eric, son Ralph, and grandson Robert II. (Courtesy of Robert Brown.)

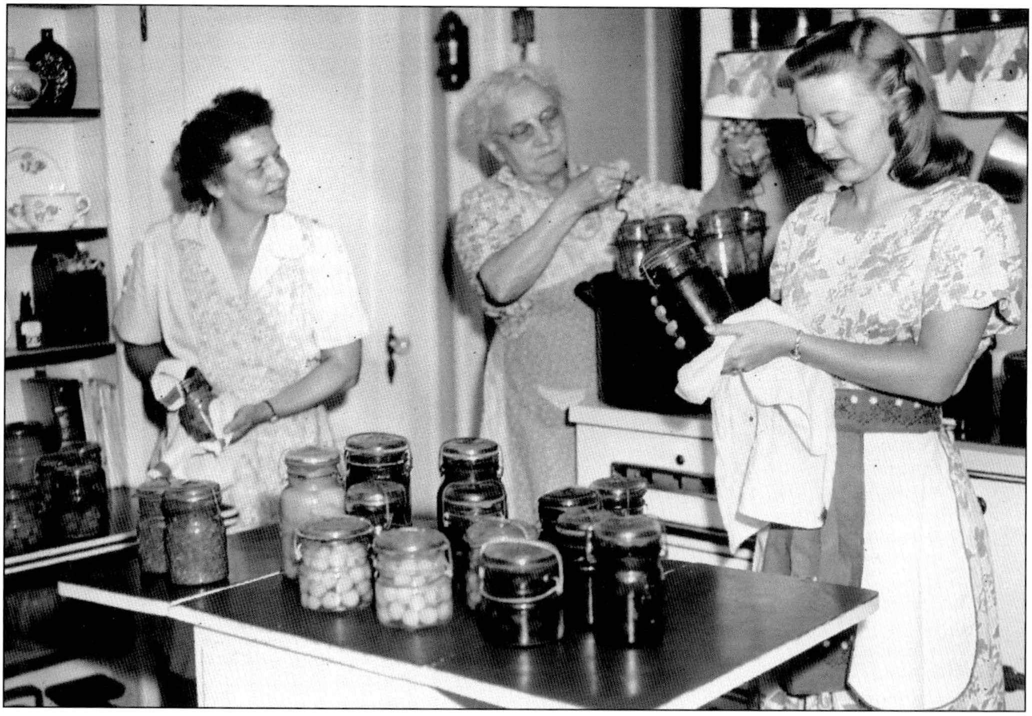

CANNING. From left to right, daughter-in-law Angie, mother-in-law Pearl, and granddaughter Dorothy Brown preserve some fruits grown on the farm around 1948. (Courtesy of Robert Brown.)

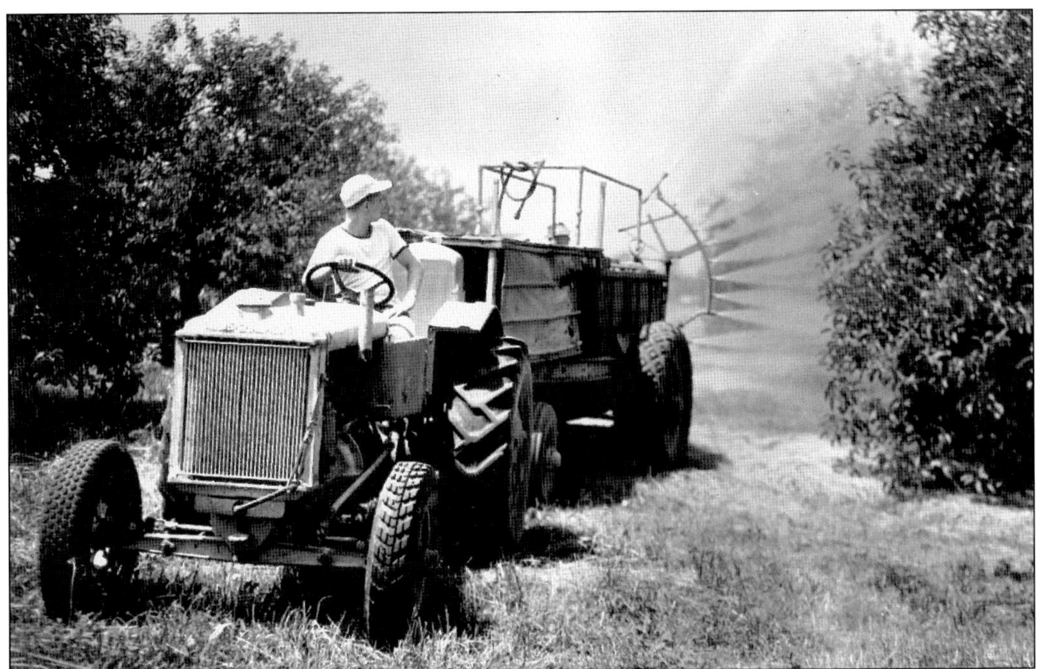

SPRAYING. Ralph R. Brown looks over his shoulder to see how well the spray is covering his crop. Brown's farm began in 1804 and is still going strong today, with the seventh generation of heirs to Elijah Brown working to make the farm successful. (Courtesy of Robert Brown.)

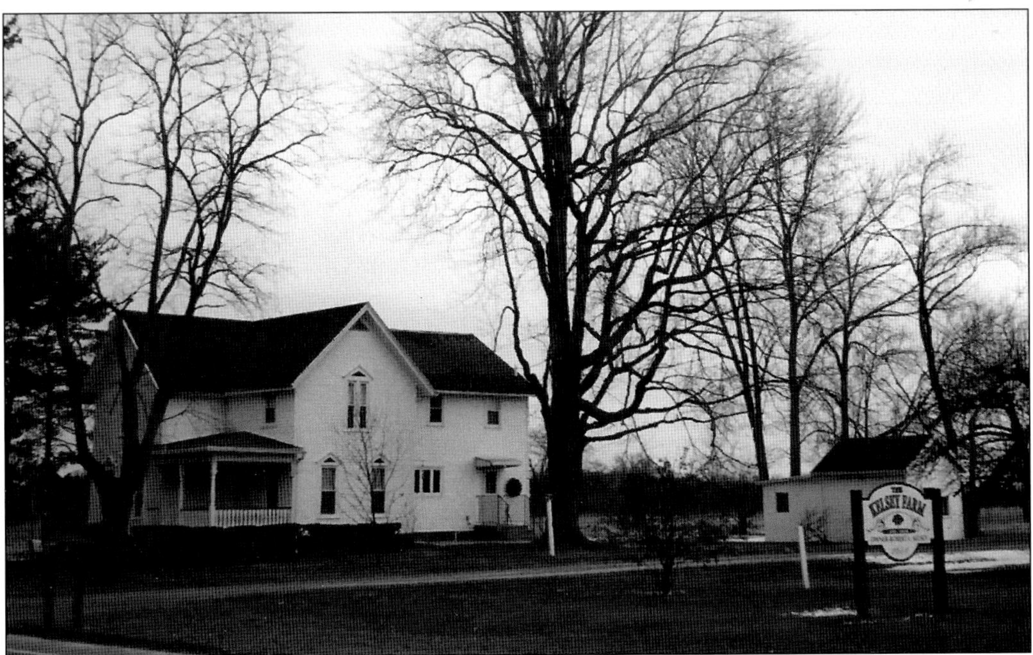

KELSEY FARM. Another longtime farm is the Robert Kelsey farm, located on Oak Orchard Road in Carlton Station. Robert Kelsey's words, remembering life as he knew it, are quoted in the introduction to this photographic journey. The farm began in 1831 and is still in operation today, celebrating its 175th year in farming. (Courtesy of Bud Canham.)

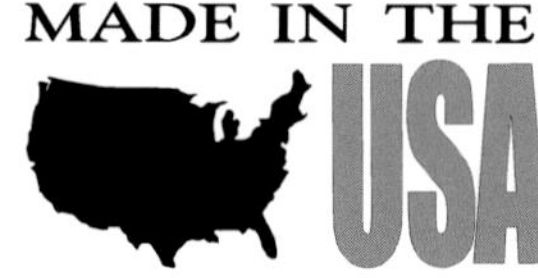
MADE IN THE
USA